Endorsements of

Resilient Nations

Bob Dees well knows that we are a nation at war, in every way. This war threatens the very soul of America. *Resilient Nations* provides an alarming assessment of our crumbling spiritual foundations, and the resulting impacts across all sectors of American life. Gratefully, he also points citizens and statesmen towards a national spiritual rearmament which is our only hope for future generations. Read this book, and join the fight.

Lieutenant General William "Jerry" Boykin
United States Army, Retired
Executive Vice President, Family Research Council

*****

Our nation's founders, led by Almighty God, crafted a model America which became a beacon of hope around the globe. As America increasingly departs from this divine intent, her beacon flickers ever lower, self-absorbed in pursuit of special interests and mired in debt, immorality, and historical revisionism. In *Resilient Nations*, General Bob Dees provides unique national security insights into the challenges we face, and the solutions America desperately needs. Now "We the People" and "We the Statesmen" of this United States must respond to this clarion call on behalf of future generations.

David Barton
Founder and President of Wallbuilders
Prolific Author, Speaker, and "America's Historian"

*****

General Bob Dees has lived National Security for the last four decades. *Resilient Nations* provides a unique perspective on Spiritual Infrastructure as an Element of National Power, highlighting existential threats to America which require decisive action by citizens and statesmen alike. A must read for those who want to shape a positive future for future generations of Americans.

Mathew D. Staver
Founder and Chairman, Liberty Counsel
Dean, Liberty University School of Law

*****

Resilience is a fundamental part of the American story. In the nation's first two centuries, the American people overcame tyranny, civil war, economic depression, and two world wars only to grow stronger, freer, and more prosperous. In *Resilient Nations*, General Bob Dees contributes a powerful verse to

America's next chapter. *Resilient Nations* calls for a renewal of America's spiritual infrastructure, alerts the American people to the greatest set of challenges ever to have faced the nation, and provides a foundational understanding of what it will take to overcome them. This important book is essential reading for the American people.

Shawn D. Akers
Dean, Helms School of Government
Liberty University

*****

The United States is in an existential struggle for its very soul. Like never before, America needs warriors to fight for their families, to fight for their neighbors and communities, to fight for the principles upon which God and our Founders established this great nation. In *Resilient Nations,* General Bob Dees, a warrior himself, gives us a "must read," a road map for rearming America. Now "We the People," "We the Church," and "We the Statesmen" need to get out of our foxholes and march to the sound of the guns. Our very future as a nation depends on it."

Jeff D. Reeter, Managing Partner
The Texas Financial Group, LP

Resilient Nations

The Resilience Trilogy

Major General Bob Dees

US Army, Retired

www.ResilienceTrilogy.com

Creative Team Publishing
San Diego

SCRIPTURE REFERENCES:
All scripture quotations, unless otherwise indicated, are taken from the New American Standard Bible, Copyright © 1960, 1962, 1963, 1968, 1971, 1972, 1973, 1975, 1977, 1995 by The Lockman Foundation. Used by permission. (http://www.Lockman.org)
Scripture quotations marked (NKJV) are taken from the New King James Version. NKJV™ Copyright © 1982 by Thomas Nelson, Inc. Used by permission. All rights reserved.
Scripture quotations marked (NIV) are taken from the Holy Bible, New International Version® NIV® Copyright © 1973, 1978, 1984, 2011 by Biblica, Inc.® Used by permission. All rights reserved worldwide.
Scripture quotations marked (NLT) are taken from the Holy Bible, New Living Translation, copyright © 1996, 2004, 2007. Used by permission of Tyndale House Publishers, Inc., Carol Stream, Illinois 60188. All rights reserved.

DISCLAIMER:
During the process of constructing this book, due diligence has been undertaken to obtain all proper copyright permissions. If it comes to our attention that any citations are missing, they will be readily provided at http://www.ResilienceTrilogy.com.

See Permissions and Credits.

ISBN: 978-0-9897975-6-6
PUBLISHED BY CREATIVE TEAM PUBLISHING
www.CreativeTeamPublishing.com
San Diego
Printed in the United States of America

Resilient Nations

The Resilience Trilogy

Major General Bob Dees
US Army, Retired

www.ResilienceTrilogy.com

Table of Contents

Foreword by Franklin Graham
23

Dedication: This Book Is Dedicated to Future Generations
25

Introduction: America—A Resilient Nation?
27

1   Spiritual Infrastructure: The True Strength and
        Identity of a Nation
        35

        A Lesson Learned
        36

        A Project Earned
        37

        Spiritual Infrastructure as an Element of National Power
        39

                Spiritual Infrastructure Definition
                42

                Measuring Spiritual Infrastructure
                46

                Chart 1: *A Resilient Beginning 1740 - 1960*
                48

Gaining Altitude: America as a Resilient Nation
49

Resilient Nations Takeaways
54

For Further Consideration
55

Additional References
55

2   Global Historical Context: The Rise and Fall of Nations
57

The Life Cycle of Nations
58

            Chart 2: *Resilience Life Cycle* ©
            59

When Nations "Fail"
63

The Turning Radius of Nations
66

Common Denominators of National Decline:
Learning from Rome
68

Common Denominators of National Resilience:
Learning from Israel
71

Gaining Altitude: America through the Lens of Other Nations
82

Resilient Nations Takeaways
87

For Further Consideration
89

Additional References
90

3   God's Design for Nations
91

God's Purpose for Nations and Government
96

Chart 3: *Model Nation*
103

The Founder's "Model Nation"
104

Overview
104

The Founder's Model
105

God's Natural and Revealed Law
105

Man's International and Municipal Law
109

International Law
109

Municipal Law
112

Government
113

The Unalienable Rights: Life, Liberty, and the
Pursuit of Happiness
116

Life
117

Liberty
118

The Pursuit of Happiness
119

Serving the Sovereign: "We the People"
122

Gaining Altitude: "A City on a Hill"
126

Resilient Nations Takeaways
128

For Further Consideration
131

Additional References
132

4   National Historical Context: The Rise and Fall of America
133

        The Decline Becomes Apparent: 1960 - 2001
        136

        Chart 4: *Decline Sets In 1960 - 2001*
        137

        The Decline Accelerates: 2001 - 2014
        147

        Chart 5: *Decline Accelerates 2001 - 2014*
        148

        The Bush Years
        149

        The Obama Years
        151

        Chart 6: *Macro Trendlines 1740 - 2014*
        161

   Government "Gone Wild"
   162

        Chart 7: *Government "Gone Wild"*
        163

   Two Roads: A National Inflection Point
   164

        Chart 8: *The Road Not Taken*
        165

Gaining Altitude: America at a Crossroads
166

Resilient Nations Takeaways
171

For Further Consideration
173

Additional References
173

5   Respecting LIFE
175

Chart 9: *Unalienable Rights*
177

A Culture of Violence and Death
178

Respecting the Unborn
180

Biblical Precepts Respecting LIFE of the Unborn
185

Actions and Policies "Respecting the Unborn"
187

Respecting the Elderly
189

Biblical Precepts Respecting LIFE of the Elderly
193

Actions and Policies "Respecting the Elderly"
196

Respecting the Traditional Family
197

Biblical Precepts Respecting LIFE of the
Traditional Family
207

Actions and Policies "Respecting LIFE of the
Traditional Family"
210

Other Threats to LIFE
211

Gaining Altitude: Returning to a Culture of LIFE in America
215

Resilient Nations Takeaways
218

For Further Consideration
220

Additional References
221

6   Securing LIBERTY
223

A Growing Culture of Appeasement
224

Securing Freedom from External and Internal Threats
227

External Threats
228

Internal Threats
233

Terrorists Operating within the U.S.
233

Racial Discord
235

Lawless Disrespect for Others
239

Apathy
242

Biblical Precepts for "Freedom from Threats"
245

Actions and Policies Securing "Freedom from Threats"
245

Securing Freedom from Government
246

Actions and Policies Securing "Freedom from Government"
252

Securing Religious Freedom
252

Chart 10: *Devolution of Religion in America*
254

Threats to Religious Freedom
255

Devolution of Religion in America
255

Separation of Church and State Mythology
257

        Governmental Obstruction
        258

        Anti-Religion Special Interests
        259

        Rise of "Nones"
        261

Benefits of Religion in America
263

Actions and Policies to Secure Religious Freedom
265

Gaining Altitude: Securing LIBERTY for ALL Americans
266

Resilient Nations Takeaways
269

For Further Consideration
271

Additional References
272

7   Pursuing HAPPINESS
         275

         A Culture of Dependency
         279

         Pursuit of a Better Future: Education
         282

                  Constitutional Guidelines Concerning Education
                  283

                  Religious Freedoms within Education
                  285

                  Biblical Precepts for Pursuing a Better Future:
                  Education
                  289

                  Actions and Policies Pursuing a Better
                  Future through Education
                  290

         Pursuit of a Prosperous Future: The Economy and Work
         291

                  The American Economy
                  292

                  The American Worker
                  294

                  Biblical Precepts for Pursuing a Prosperous Future:
                  The Economy and Work
                  299

Actions and Policies for Pursuing a Prosperous Future
300

Pursuit of a Healthier Future: Health Care Reform
301

Biblical Precepts for Pursuing a Healthier Future
305

Actions and Policies for Pursuing a Healthier Future
307

Gaining Altitude: Noble Self-Sufficiency
307

Chart 11: *Unalienable Rights*
310

Resilient Nations Takeaways
311

For Further Consideration
315

Additional References
315

8   Mandates
317

What Can the Righteous Do?
320

Mandate for "We the People"
321

Personal Spiritual Renewal
321

Strong Traditional Families
323

Civic Responsibility
325

Culture Change Agents
326

Prayer Warriors and Merchants of Hope
327

Mandate for "We the Church"
329

What the Church Should Not Do
330

What the Church Should Do
332

Mandate for "We the Statesmen"
xx

Selfless Public Servants
333

Guardians of Truth
336

Principled Collaborators for Change
339

Chart 12: *Mandates*
344

Gaining Altitude: KEEP UP THE FIRE, AMERICA!
345

Resilient Nations Takeaways
349

For Further Consideration
351

Additional References
352

9   Uncle Sam Needs YOU!
353

        Chart 13: *The Road Not Taken*
        355

Indignation
356

Fear
357

Call to Action
359

An America without God
363

Gaining Altitude: A Hopeful America with God
365

        God Has Not Forgotten America
        367

        You Are Not Alone
        368

A New Birth of Freedom
372

Resilient Nations Takeaways
373

For Further Consideration
375

Additional References
375

Appendix 1: Listing of Charts
377

Appendix 2: Products and Services
379

Acknowledgements
381

About the Author
385

Permissions and Credits
389

Bibliography
411

Index
437

Foreword
Franklin Graham
President & CEO
Samaritan's Purse
Billy Graham Evangelistic Association

I salute General Robert Dees—a great man who has demonstrated the Biblical meaning of Christian leader. I am honored to call this Christian General my friend. In his new book, *Resilient Nations,* he shines a light on the "State of the Union" when it comes to the condition of America and asks compelling questions: "Where is the 'point of no return' for a nation in decline;" and "if the foundations are destroyed, what can the righteous do?" I agree with his response: "Without a course reversal, America is likely in her twilight years."

The General writes about the spiritual foundation of our country and brings Biblical clarity to what he terms "Spiritual Infrastructure," and the importance of God-given pillars making it possible for families, governments, and societies to flourish with His blessing.

General Dees calls our nation to repentance, underscoring that unless "we the people" lay aside our "blurred national vision" and turn to the One true God, we have no hope to see America stirred once again to live according to the truth upon which our country was founded. God is calling us to obey His Word.

In our 200 years, we have overcome enemies, but the greatest enemy among us is the hatred of God. May we as a nation read this book with repentant hearts that will lead to righteousness. May "we the people" resolve to see America triumph over evil oppression and once again become a *resilient nation*.

This Book Is Dedicated to Future Generations

Beginning with our beloved Grandchildren
Austen, Brennan, Isabel, Mitch, Kate, Jandi, Mya

"United States of America
Looks like another silent night
As we're sung to sleep by philosophies
That save the trees and kill the children

"And while we're lying in the dark
There's a shout heard 'cross the eastern sky
For the Bridegroom has returned
And has carried His bride away in the night

"America, what will we miss while we are sleeping
Will Jesus come again
And leave us slumbering where we lay

Bob Dees

"America, will we go down in history
As a nation with no room for its King
Will we be sleeping
Will we be sleeping"

From *While You Were Sleeping*
Casting Crowns

Introduction
America: A Resilient Nation?

"The people don't have a will to work."
Bulgarian President Georgi Parvanov
July 4, 2007

"The people don't have a will to work" stated the Bulgarian President after I queried, "What is your biggest problem?" In eight brief words, President Parvanov summarized the most profound impact of decades of domination by the Soviet Empire: a subjugation and total dependence upon the State which largely stripped the Bulgarian people of their work ethic, their striving for self-improvement, and their very passion to live. While the President could have identified the need for tangible resources (money, natural resources, trading partners, industrial production, and others), he instead identified a very intangible, internal attribute he termed "will to work." Where does that come from? How does a nation lose such essential qualities? How do they get them back?

The reality is that nations have many different "elements of national power" which are critical to their survival and success as a nation-state. Some of these elements may immediately come to mind in tangible form: banking, politics, military power, domestic stability, energy, commerce, and others. In National Security terms, our national security establishment uses the taxonomy of "elements of national power" as a critical concept in strategic thinking to analyze varied forms of influence to achieve national objectives. While these elements are being constantly updated to best conform to the latest geopolitical landscape, one of the most familiar paradigms used in our National Defense University in Washington, DC, is the acronym "PMESII" (Political, Military, Economic, Social, Infrastructure, and Information Systems).

While all of these are obviously very important, the element of "infrastructure" by its very definition (*infra* meaning "beneath" is the structure, the foundation and the interior supports, that undergirds and facilitates the more direct forms of national power. Examples of infrastructure would be transportation, communication, work force, medical, and yes, spiritual. This spiritual infrastructure (SI) includes critical arenas such as the strength of our families, the ethics of our boardrooms, the civility of our discourse, adherence to the rule of law, respect for lives of the unborn and the elderly, regard for the security of future generations, the education of our youth, the relevance of our faith communities, the adherence to national values and accurate historical roots, and the resilience and enterprise of our citizens—including their "will to work." All of these intangible elements of SI (and others) are essential to a nation's identity and survival as an entity which is truly a benefit to its citizens and the world community.

In today's American secular culture, many would be more comfortable with the use of the term "moral infrastructure" versus "spiritual infrastructure," but this finesses the heart of the issue. Moral choices are the acting out of our underlying spiritual values, the lens through which we view every aspect of public and private endeavor, essentially our "worldview." Hence, morality, or lack thereof, is a consequence of our spiritual worldview, both as individuals and as a nation. If we have a strong "Spiritual Infrastructure" (SI) as a nation, then basic morality, and the many other subcomponents of SI, will likewise be strong and healthy. Given that it best describes our concept, we will use the term *Spiritual Infrastructure* in *Resilient Nations*, despite inevitable push back from some who feel use of the term "spiritual" is inherently offensive or exclusive.

> Moral choices are the acting out of our underlying spiritual values, the lens through which we view every aspect of public and private endeavor, essentially our "worldview."

Resilient Nations will explore the relevance of Spiritual Infrastructure, first in a generic sense from a historic and conceptual perspective then very specifically applied to the United States of America. What is our current "State of the

Union?"   What is the status of our SI in our second decade of the 21st Century?   Is our SI solid and stable, or is it sadly weakened, on the brink of collapse and irreversible consequence?   Are life, liberty, and the pursuit of happiness still relevant and reachable? Will our SI, which provided a bedrock foundation from the first days of this Republic (and through subsequent wars, depressions, and national calamities) allow for the continuation of our "American way of life?" Or is that a thing of the past?

Resilient Nations is the last component of *The Resilience Trilogy.* In *Resilient Warriors* we addressed individual resilience, recognizing that we are all warriors on the playing fields of every marketplace and endeavor. How high do we bounce when we are body-slammed to the hard concrete of life? How do we build such bounce ahead of time? How do we weather the storm? After trials and tribulations, how do we bounce back without getting stuck in toxic emotions of guilt, false guilt, anger, bitterness? Then how do we "learn & adapt" for the inevitable next life challenge? We cited many role models of resilience, most particularly the Ultimate Resilient Warrior, Jesus.

In *Resilient Leaders*, we applied these same concepts to the leader level. How do leaders prepare themselves, their organizations, and those they lead to also be resilient? How does a leader "selflessly serve over time from a platform of character and competence?"   We looked at key attributes such as selflessness, integrity, courage, and wisdom.   Then we applied the Resilience Life Cycle© directly to leadership: how does a leader "set the conditions" (before) for the success of his organization and his followers? What does an "in extremis leader" (during) look like, helping others navigate crisis? How does a leader then move others into a new and hopeful future, cultivating a learning organization which "talks to itself?" In like manner, we also considered many leader role models and related numerous personal stories, recognizing again that Jesus is the Ultimate Resilient Leader and the Bible is the world's greatest leadership manual. We can do no better than to "lead like Jesus."

Now we consider resilience applied to Nations. The ultimate question: can the United States of America strengthen its Spiritual Infrastructure in the 21st Century, bouncing back from decades of moral erosion, spiritual skepticism, and alarming trendlines which counter the proposition that we are "the greatest nation on Earth?" Can we weather the current storms of national survival? Can we bounce back to our former greatness, America? Are we still a Resilient Nation?

Numerous observations related to United States' Spiritual Infrastructure, as well as the other elements of national power (Political, Military, Economic, Social, Infrastructure other than Spiritual, and Information Systems) suggest that America is at or even beyond a "national tipping point." One poignant example is education. Aristotle said

> "All who have meditated on the art of governing mankind are convinced that the fate of empires depends upon the education of youth."

Viewed through the lens of education alone, the fate of the American empire is dire: "Nearly 30 people have been killed in school shootings within almost 14 months of the massacre in

Newtown, Conn. At least 44 shootings have occurred at elementary, middle, and high schools, as well as on college campuses, in 24 states across the country since Dec. 14, 2012," alarming mental health trends within our nation's youth population that range from teen suicide because of bullying to homicidal tendencies resulting from media immersion and de-sensitization to violence and killing, the latest "knock out" game on the streets of America which is the height of "teens gone wild," continual cultural warfare (including the use of Common Core as a cultural Trojan horse) in our schools to steal the hearts and minds of our students from the institutions of family and church, and entrenched teacher unions that prioritize longevity above learning. Portending future economic impotence, the Congressional Research Service addresses American student rankings in the critical category "STEM" (Science, Technology, Engineering, and Math):

> "There is growing concern that the United States is not preparing a sufficient number of students, teachers, and practitioners in the areas of science, technology, engineering, and mathematics (STEM). A large majority of secondary school students fail to reach proficiency in math and science, and many are taught by teachers lacking adequate subject matter knowledge.
>
> When compared to other nations, the math and science achievement of U.S. pupils and the rate of STEM degree attainment appear inconsistent with a nation considered the world leader in

scientific innovation. In a recent international assessment of 15-year-old students, the U.S. ranked 28th in math literacy and 24th in science literacy. Moreover, the U.S. ranks 20th among all nations in the proportion of 24-year-olds who earn degrees in natural science or engineering.

In colloquial terms, one must ask rhetorically, "How is that working for you, America?"

These daunting warning signs from the field of education alone, illustrative of equally deteriorating conditions within other sectors of consideration, all have their origins in a greatly weakened national Spiritual Infrastructure. We will soon learn that at the height of Roman decadence, good became evil and evil became good. One can rightly argue that the United States is frightfully close to a similar fate.

> In colloquial terms, one must ask rhetorically, "How is that working for you, America?"

Prayerfully, it is not too late.

Prayerfully, we can demonstrate the resilience and rightness that have characterized America since its inception in 1776.

Prayerfully, *Resilient Nations*, along with other like-minded harbingers, will help turn the tide.

Prayerfully, the United States will mount a spiritual rearmament that is as transformational as the First and Second Great Awakenings in this nation's history.

Prayerfully, God will not give up on us yet.

Prayerfully, the best for America is yet to come.

Only time will tell.

Only "We the People," "We the Church," and "We the Statesmen" can make the difference.

Let us begin.

1

Spiritual Infrastructure

The True Strength and Identity of a Nation

"Our liberties rest with our people; upon the scope and depth of their understanding of the nation's spiritual, political, military, and economic realities."
~ President Dwight D. Eisenhower
34th President of the United States

"The Armed Forces today have to be versed not alone in war, but in government, politics, the humanities – economics, social, and spiritual."
~ Bernard Baruch
Financier, Philanthropist, Presidential Advisor for World Wars I & II

A Lesson Learned

While a student in the Industrial College of the Armed Forces (ICAF, now known as the Dwight D. Eisenhower School for National Security and Resource Strategy) within the National Defense University structure in Washington, DC, during the winter of 1992, I sat yet once again in the "Blue Bedroom" auditorium for another stimulating lecture on National Security. Most of our curriculum that year dealt with "elements of national power": What are they? How do we assess them? How do we use them, individually and collectively? How do we resource them? While these elements are constantly being updated to best conform to the latest geopolitical landscape, a paradigm the National Defense University uses is the acronym "PMESII" (meaning Political, Military, Economic, Social, Infrastructure, and Information Systems). All of these are critically important considerations for future policy and decision makers for all Departments and Agencies of the US Government.

Waiting for another speaker in the parade of distinguished policy makers who spoke to us that year, I actually began to think. Scanning across the front of the auditorium, I noticed two brass plaques (quotes shown above) on either side of the grand stage and wondered, "If these notable quotations by President Eisenhower and Bernard Baruch are worthy to stand before our nation's future national security leaders on a daily basis, why have we not addressed the full context of their remarks?" Specifically, I wondered why we had not addressed the "spiritual" component of national power which both of these prominent national leaders had placed alongside other primary elements of national power.

We had discussed and debated all the others for weeks and months: economic issues, industrial might, military power, international relations, and other important security topics. Yet "spiritual" was conspicuous in its absence. Nothing in the curriculum or the guest lectures acknowledged the reality or the relevance which spiritual considerations, and their related moral implications, play in the life of a nation and its people.

In light of what I felt to be a significant and serious omission, I pondered further: **might nations, specifically the United States of America, also have a "Spiritual Infrastructure" which is equally relevant to their future security and prosperity? Is such a Spiritual Infrastructure also an element of national power? Can it be measured? Is this a current strength or weakness in our national power calculation? What about the future?**

A Project Earned

A favorite saying of one of my life mentors, Dr. John George from Liberty University, is "a lesson learned is a project earned." This maxim certainly proved true when I went to my ICAF faculty advisor and voiced the same observations and questions above. Implying that he didn't think it was a very relevant or promising path to pursue, he basically responded, "Okay, if you feel so strongly about this, write a paper."

My "lesson learned" about spiritual infrastructure had now turned into a "project earned." Little did I know that this interchange would put me on a path of discovery that continues to this day. I was fortunate to benefit early on from the knowledge and experience of a local lawyer and constitutional foundations expert, Neil Markva, as well as David Barton, the head of Wallbuilders, Inc. After considerable research, I wrote a paper entitled "Spiritual Infrastructure as an Element of National Power." When the paper received a class writing award, my faculty advisor then "upped the ante" by directing, "Now you need to give a noon lecture to the combined audiences of the Industrial College, as well as the National War College." This lecture requirement became another "forcing mechanism" to further investigate the concept of spiritual infrastructure and articulate it to others.

Somewhat naively following the bread crumbs of evidence regarding spiritual infrastructure, I soon learned that discussion of spiritual topics (particularly those revolving around religion and personal faith), even in an academic setting in 1992 was very "risky." A number of faculty and student attendees at the lecture (perhaps the majority) applauded my boldness for addressing such a sensitive issue so forthrightly basically implying "It is about time." Other attendees felt the topic was peripheral and too risky to consider in such a venue. My faculty advisor supported this latter group when he cautioned that I would likely not get promoted to any higher rank (I was an Army Lieutenant Colonel at the time) after such a lecture. Despite this caution regarding potential career risk, I sensed that the topic was of primary importance to the national security of nations around the world.

Since this foundational War College experience, I have been asked to address "Spiritual Infrastructure as an Element of National Power" at the Royal College of Defense Studies in London, to the Romanian General Staff in Bucharest, with the

President of Bulgaria in Sophia, to the Chiefs of Defense in Kenya and Liberia, with the President and Vice President of Honduras, and in many other international and national venues. Through these journeys and interactions, I have clearly seen that real world leaders wrestling with real world problems understand the criticality of spiritual infrastructure as a true element of national power and an important consideration in governance. Spiritual infrastructure is equally critical as we discuss the resilience of nations.

Spiritual Infrastructure as an Element of National Power

In his State of the Union address on January 28, 1992, President George Bush optimistically noted that America is still the "freest, kindest, and strongest nation on earth." I wholeheartedly and optimistically agree. Yet he also noted a "rise of ugliness in our country" and talked candidly about the great political, economic, social, and spiritual problems our country faces today. Since these words were spoken in the wake of the 9/11 Twin Towers attack in New York City, the challenges to which President Bush alluded have become even greater. Our nation's strength at home and abroad, including our spiritual infrastructure, has seemingly deteriorated at an alarming rate. Some of these impacts are caused by unwitting players in "the system" to include "We the People" who have not voted enough, lived righteously enough, or stood our ground enough (more about that in Chapters 8 and 9). Equally causal are witting players in the secular culture, including the liberal media which is permeated by a vocal minority of secular progressive interest groups, and even government officials who have taken it as their mandate to strip spiritual considerations, God, and most certainly Jesus out of American public and private life, from boardroom to bedroom and everywhere in between. This truly is a pernicious battle for the very soul of our nation—A Culture War.

Let us for a moment consider the current state of our union—the spiritual state of our union, the United States of America. Consider with me the recessionary economy plagued by a burgeoning deficit and drawn episodically into scandal after white-collar scandal. Reflect with me upon our nation's schools: the plummeting Scholastic Aptitude Test (SAT) scores, the lack of classroom discipline, the perpetuation of mediocre teachers and techniques. Or how can one not observe the blatant evidence of immorality which fills our newspapers, dominates political campaigns, and electronically invades our homes night after night? Or the blight of drugs among our nation's youth? Or the incessant drive toward violence in the media, and in real life? Or the spiraling violence in our schools, where it has become a rare month in which there is not a tragic act of school violence? And, despite the politically driven global warming agenda, we cannot ignore our lack of environmental stewardship, which threatens species, water sources, and geography across our land. Perhaps most serious of all is the lack of confidence in government integrity and effectiveness highlighted by ongoing scandals related to Benghazi, the Internal Revenue Service, the Department of Veterans Affairs, and whatever comes next.

These are realities in our country, the United States of America, the "land of the free and the home of the brave." And each of these realities is rooted in the absence of a strong Spiritual Infrastructure.

So, what is the point? Our thesis is summarized below:

- Our nation possesses a <u>spiritual infrastructure</u> which, like other types of national infrastructure, <u>is an essential element of national power</u>.
- The bedrock tenets of our nation's spiritual infrastructure, embodied in our founding documents, are <u>reverence for God and respect for man</u>.
- Responsible citizenship and statesmanship mandate a <u>critical assessment of spiritual infrastructure</u> at this pivotal time in our country's history.
- A critical assessment reveals that <u>America's spiritual infrastructure is nearing bankruptcy</u>. This constitutes <u>a national security crisis</u>.
- There is <u>hope for America IF</u> "We the People" and "We the Church" wake up now, and "We the Statesmen" lead us with character and competence.
- <u>National Spiritual Rearmament</u> is essential and must include:
  o <u>Personal and Family Renewal</u> by "We the People"
  o <u>Marketplace relevance</u> by "We the People" across every Mountain of Culture
  o <u>Obedience by "We the Church"</u> to humble ourselves, pray, seek God's face, and turn from our wicked ways; followed by compassionate outreach
  o <u>Moral and Wise Leadership</u> by "We the Statesmen" (Public and Private Servant Leaders)

- ○ <u>Reform of Politics and Policy</u> in accord with Founding Principles to restore Life, Liberty, and the Pursuit of Happiness.

The remainder of *Resilient Nations* will expand upon this thesis. We begin by defining spiritual infrastructure.

Spiritual Infrastructure Definition

"Infra-" refers to *beneath* or *below*, such as infracostal (below the ribs) and *infradignatatum* (below one's dignity). In this same vein, infrastructure refers to "elements of national identity which undergird and facilitate more direct forms of national power." Infrastructure examples include transportation (bridges, railroads, highways), communication (phone systems, satellite relays, computer networks), workforce (populace with skills applied to productive purposes), medical (hospitals, trained health care professionals, medical research capabilities), and spiritual.

Spiritual infrastructure is less tangible than the other infrastructures mentioned, but equally real and important. Napoleon, recognizing the large influence of intangible human factors, once said, "The moral is to the physical as three is to one." President John F. Kennedy espoused a similar truth when he stated, "This country cannot afford to be materially rich and spiritually poor." President Dwight D. Eisenhower made the same point: "The spirit of man is more important than mere physical strength, and the spiritual fiber of a nation than its wealth."

Spiritual infrastructure includes the following defining subcomponents:

1. <u>Adherence to Constitutional Foundations</u> (Life, Liberty, Pursuit of Happiness), further discussed in Chapter 3
   - *Contrasted with political operatives, special interest groups, and activist judges for whom the Constitution is not sacrosanct, for whom the ends often justify the means, for whom separation of powers, checks and balances, and other principles of American government are only observed when supportive of partisan agendas*
2. <u>Respect for the Rule of Law</u>, further discussed in Chapters 3 and 6
   - *Contrasted with Executive Branch leadership and an activist judiciary, respectively, who flank established law by executive orders or non-compliance, or who seek to establish law without due process in Congress*
3. <u>Retention of National History and Traditions</u>, further discussed in Chapter 4
   - *Contrasted with historical revisionism which changes facts to meet a desired narrative*
4. <u>Basic Morality in Respect of God and Man</u>, further discussed in Chapters 5 and 6
   - *Contrasted with devaluation of human life, a growing culture of violence, and emergence of special interest groups that twist the Golden Rule into "Do to others before they do it to you;" despite the testimony of God's natural law (the testimony*

of Creation around us) and revealed law (such as the Ten Commandments), a selfish fixation on "if it feels good, do it..."

5. <u>Healthy, Traditional Families as the Primary Building Blocks of Society</u>, further discussed in Chapter 5

   - *Contrasted with single parent, dysfunctional, or destructive families which do not provide safety, stability, security, desirable values, gender modeling, and a loving atmosphere in which children thrive and society benefits; complicated by government policies that do not incentivize traditional families; further complicated by same-sex interest groups which not only seek their own recognition and rights, but also seek to destroy the credibility and foundational importance of traditional families, God's fundamental building blocks of society*

6. <u>Free Exercise and Relevance of Religion in Public and Private Venues</u>, further discussed in Chapter 6

   - *Contrasted with efforts to restrict the "Freedom of Religion" wording of the Constitution to mean "freedom of worship," isolating religion to a private matter not to be discussed or applied in the public square; complicated by witting and unwitting non-Constitutional interpretations of "Separation of Church and State" which conveniently serve humanist agendas*

7. <u>Unity, Diversity, and Civility</u>, further discussed in Chapter 6
   - *Contrasted with racial divisiveness, lack of appreciation and respect for different backgrounds, and a coarseness in discourse and manners which lacks consideration of fellow citizens, fomenting even greater polarization and divisiveness*

8. <u>Moral and Practical Education of our Youth</u>, further discussed in Chapter 7
   - *Contrasted with parental absenteeism and dysfunction which allows a violent and immoral culture to become the primary role models of values, beliefs, and behavior, and a public school system rife with special interest agendas, teacher unions which ensure longevity of substandard teachers, and a culture which denies the relevance of faith communities in the maturation and education of youth*

9. <u>Industrious, Resilient, and Engaged Citizenry</u>, further discussed in Chapter 7
   - *Contrasted with an increasingly apathetic and dependent citizenry that attempts to "game the system" (honestly or dishonestly) to gain maximum government benefits at the expense of others; lack of these traits resulting in voters who opt for government largesse over sound policy, and a workforce which lacks industriousness and "the will to work" to improve their position in life*

10. <u>Spirit of Philanthropy and Volunteerism</u>, further discussed in Chapter 7

- *Contrasted with narcissistic fulfillment of personal needs without regard for the needs of less fortunate members of society; lack of philanthropy and volunteerism robbing our nation of tremendous helping resources that can be applied compassionately to the benefit of giver and receiver alike*

Spiritual infrastructure is less tangible than the other infrastructures mentioned, but equally real and important.

Measuring Spiritual Infrastructure

The health of the national spiritual infrastructure can be gauged by looking at the relative strengths of its defining subsystems. Although quantitative assessments similar to GNP statistics are not frequently available, qualitative assessments are definitely possible through analysis of national behavior, policy, and demonstrated priorities. Our best tool will be anecdotal, historical timelines to note national events related to spiritual infrastructure, and assess downstream consequences. We will do this for different segments of American history: 1740 to 1960, 1960 to present, and "the future." These charts will be introduced at appropriate times as we walk through *Resilient Nations*.

Beginning this historical mapping, Chart 1, *A Resilient Beginning 1740-1960* illustrates a spiritual infrastructure timeline. Certain "defining moments" are noted along the timeline. Although this anecdotal "graph" is generally self-explanatory, several comments are in order. First of all, note that the normal condition over our nation's history is a robust spiritual infrastructure, accounting for our nation's ability in the past to endure and conquer great challenges such as lengthy wars, natural disasters, and economic depression. Secondly, each key event has a positive or negative impact on the overall Spiritual Infrastructure. While not covering each event listed on the chart, let me give some topline observations:

Note that the two Great Awakenings preceded the American Revolution and the Civil War, seemingly preparing the nation for times of great trial. America's wars, and even the Great Depression, resulted in a resurgence of Spiritual Infrastructure, the result of growth through adversity. This trend was broken with the Vietnam War which fomented the growing national divisiveness over a number of cultural issues.

While not apparent until the 1960s, forces of secular humanism and moral relativism began eating away at the inner core of America in the early 1900s. The tumultuous 1960s represented a "perfect storm" of racial divisiveness, war protest, brinksmanship with Communist nation states, and promiscuity driven by the sexual

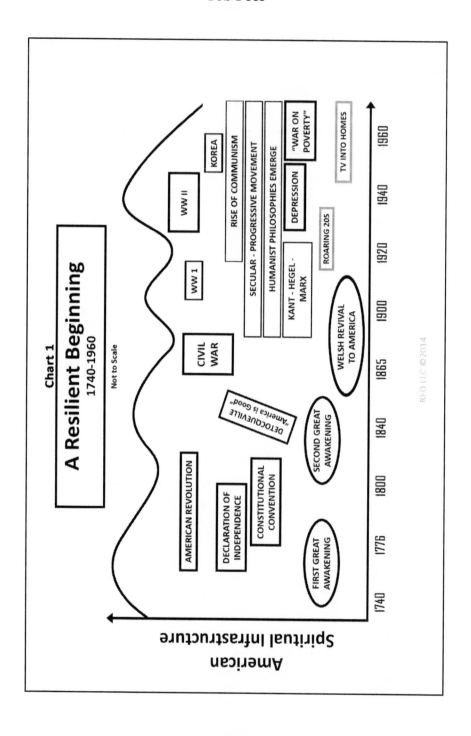

Chart 1
A Resilient Beginning
1740-1960

Not to Scale

American Spiritual Infrastructure

RFD LLC ©2014

revolution. The decline in American Spiritual Infrastructure became serious and readily apparent.

Technology became an enabler, but also accelerated negative influences, beginning with the TV into American homes.

Gaining Altitude: America as a Resilient Nation

America has been a resilient nation for most of its history, amply illustrated by recovery from many catastrophic external and internal events. As well, it has demonstrated a deep and strong Spiritual Infrastructure that has positively impacted every area of endeavor in the American experiment, illustrated by unified effort during war, prosperity during peace, and ascendency to "The Greatest Nation on Earth."

It is impossible not to credit a supernatural influence in the founding and formative years of the United States, manifested in the external affairs of the nation and the internal affairs of its citizens. Most Americans, even today, would clearly recognize this as the benevolent hand of God. Yet, somewhere along the way we began to turn our back on God-given principles of life and governance, and consequently began to lose our way as a people and as a nation. Although we could debate exactly when and how this erosion started, the daunting trends and daily departures from what was once good, right, and pure are shocking and saddening.

America is unquestionably in decline, a point which we will easily substantiate in the remainder of *Resilient Nations*. The question to Americans who have not reached a state of apathy or humanistic blindness is how we recover our goodness in order to reassert our greatness, referring to Alexis de Tocqueville's oft-quoted analysis of 19th Century America that "America is great because America is good. When America ceases being good, then she will also cease being great." In short, how do we regain our heart and our soul as a nation, and how does that impact future policy and practice, as well as future generations in this country and beyond?

Seeking an intentional and proactive strategy to this greatest of national challenges, I restate the thesis of this *Resilient Nations* effort:

- Our nation possesses a <u>spiritual infrastructure</u> which, like other types of national infrastructure, <u>is an essential element of national power</u>.
- The bedrock tenets of our nation's spiritual infrastructure, embodied in our founding documents, are <u>reverence for God and respect for man</u>.
- Responsible citizenship and statesmanship mandate a <u>critical assessment of spiritual infrastructure</u> at this pivotal time in our country's history.
- A critical assessment reveals that <u>America's spiritual infrastructure is nearing bankruptcy</u>. This constitutes <u>a national security crisis</u>.

- There is <u>hope for America IF</u> "We the People" and "We the Church" wake up now, and "We the Statesmen" lead us with character and competence.
- <u>National Spiritual Rearmament</u> is essential and must include:
  - <u>Personal and Family Renewal</u> by "We the People"
  - <u>Marketplace relevance</u> by "We the People" across every Mountain of Culture
  - <u>Obedience by "We the Church"</u> to humble ourselves, pray, seek God's face, and turn from our wicked ways; followed by compassionate outreach
  - <u>Moral and Wise Leadership</u> by "We the Statesmen" (Public and Private Servant Leaders)
  - <u>Reform of Politics and Policy</u> in accord with Founding Principles to restore Life, Liberty, and the Pursuit of Happiness.

For a moment as we end this first chapter, let us return to a former day in America. We were engaged in a global struggle against forces which were powerful and evil, who sought our destruction, who cared not about the means to secure their demented ends. WWII. Nazi Germany and Imperialistic Japan. The United States had been in a life and death struggle for two and a half years. The continent of Europe lay in the iron hand of Adolf Hitler. America had been routed in its first battles in Northern Africa. The sons and daughters of America had shed blood and been taken captive across the limitless Pacific Theatre. It was truly a dark hour in America, one of the darkest.

Here is the account of a young college girl, one of those patriotic Americans on the home front, doing what she could do in support of the cataclysmic struggle between good and evil, light and dark:

"I was in college at Southwestern Louisiana Institute as it was called at that time, at Lafayette, Louisiana. You have the date in mind better than I do. We girls lived in a dormitory, in rooms in which we had to 'double and triple up' because we had Navy V-12 and other Navy men to house on campus .

"We were having to go through in three years in order to 'hasten' everything up for the war effort. I was about 17 or 18 years old, already a junior.

"As you well know, we as a nation were not ready for what we were facing and everyone and everything going on was hurry, hurry, and worry, worry, too. We were hearing every day of someone else being killed in action, or missing. Someone was always crying, with people gathered around weeping as well, helpless to do anything.

"We kept up with the news as best we could, though there was very little to have. Everybody made sure they went to the campus Post Office every day, hoping we would have a letter from our sweethearts, brothers, friends, Dads... Any loved

one... Any news. We stayed glued to our little radios as much as time allowed.

"It had been announced that a mighty invasion of Europe would have to happen, no matter what it cost, in order to turn back the forces of evil that were overrunning the world, and inflicting such horrible atrocities upon human kind.

"We were told that the invasion would be extremely hard, and secret, and that we would know when it had begun when all the church bells began to ring, fire sirens blew, and anything else that could make sound would give the signal to hurry to the churches and places of worship, to drop to our knees to pray for our forces as they were engaging in the invasion of Europe.

"So, around midnight one evening as we all lay sleeping (just as the sun was rising over the beaches of Normandy on June 6, 1944 – D-DAY), we were awakened by the bells, fire sirens, horns honking, excited screaming and calls from others to hurry... hurry to pray! We threw on anything and ran in crowds to the Catholic Chapel which was there on the campus near us, and we fell to our knees praying and crying. I really don't remember all the details, but I do remember the heartfelt earnest pleas and prayers that rose up from that little chapel that night!"

~ Recollections from a lifelong American Patriot,
Bobbie Sue Robinson, my dear Mother-in-Law

This is what Spiritual Infrastructure looks like—national will, moral purity, everyone sacrificing what they can, all gave some and some gave all, one for all and all for one, courage in the darkest hours, strength and solace from a deep faith in God and Country, "heartfelt earnest pleas" to the Providential God of this nation. In many ways, one could remove the dates and places to describe America's response to 9/11, yet what about the next day, and the next month? What about now? Our dependence upon God has waned rapidly, particularly as activist forces seek to strip us of His Presence at the very moment when we as a nation need Him the most.

When will we next have to grasp deeply into our "Well of Courage," America?

Will we come up empty-handed?

Resilient Nations Takeaways

RN 1A – Spiritual Infrastructure is a key element of national power, less tangible than the other infrastructures mentioned, but equally real and important.

RN 1B – Spiritual Infrastructure includes the ten defining subcomponents: Adherence to Constitutional Foundations, Respect for the Rule of Law, Retention of National History and Traditions, Basic Morality in Respect of God and Man; Healthy, Traditional Families as the Primary Building Blocks of Society; Free Exercise and Relevance of Religion in Public and Private Venues;

Unity, Diversity, and Civility; Moral and Practical Education of our Youth; Industrious, Resilient, and Engaged Citizenry; and Spirit of Philanthropy and Volunteerism.

RN 1C – For the major portion of its history (at least until the 1960s), America has been a resilient nation with a robust Spiritual Infrastructure, accounting for our nation's ability in the past to endure and conquer great challenges such as lengthy wars, natural disasters, and economic depression.

RN 1D -- Our dependence upon God has waned rapidly, particularly as activist forces seek to strip us of His Presence at the very moment when we as a nation need Him the most.

For Further Consideration

1. Reflect on the concept of "Spiritual Infrastructure (SI) as an Element of National Power." Would you add any other categories to the subcomponents highlighted in this chapter? What categories are the most significant to you? How have you seen the impacts of SI in your personal life and sphere of influence?
2. Expand your analysis by diving deeper, qualitatively and quantitatively, into some of the anecdotal events and outcomes noted on the Spiritual Resilience graph in this Chapter.

Additional References

1. Johnson, Jim. *Fracture Zone 2015*. Charleston, SC: 2013.
2. Wallbuilders: www.Wallbuilders.com.

2

Global Historical Context:

The Rise and Fall of Nations

"The decline of Rome was the natural and inevitable effect of immoderate greatness. Prosperity ripened the principle of decay; the causes of destruction multiplied with the extent of conquest; and as soon as time or accident had removed the artificial supports, the stupendous fabric yielded to the pressure of its own weight."
~ Gibbon, *Decline and Fall of the Roman Empire*

As we begin this journey regarding "How Nations Bounce Back" (and most specifically, "How does the USA Bounce Back?"), we will benefit from a broad overview of the global historical context of the rise and fall of nations. Remembering from our earlier resilience writings that "with height comes perspective," we will "gain altitude" by looking at the historic life cycle of nations before we dive into the temporal realities of the American Experiment which thus far reaches into four centuries.

Each chapter of *Resilient Nations* provides structure and catalyst to dive deeper into the myriad of details and perspectives upon which our topline observations are founded. This chapter is no exception. While not attempting to replicate the depth of Gibbons' *Decline and Fall of the Roman Empire*, the entire *Old Testament* reflecting God's shaping of Israel as a people and a nation before the appearance of the Messiah, Martin Gilbert's extensive history of modern *Israel*, or other equally extensive studies of particular eras or civilizations; we will establish sufficient historical perspective to begin the validation of our concern for America's future, and to inform our subsequent recommendations pertaining to policy and practice in 21st Century America.

The Life Cycle of Nations

Intuitively, we all know that nations rise, nations fall, and <u>some</u> nations rise again. They are resilient. They bounce back. Conversely, many nations do not bounce back, condemned forever to the "trash bin of history." Each nation has a life cycle which represents the ebb and flow of its' internal health and external influence. The Resilience Life Cycle© model (shown below) which we applied to individuals and leaders in *Resilient Warriors* and *Resilient Leaders*, respectively, is also relevant to the life of nations.

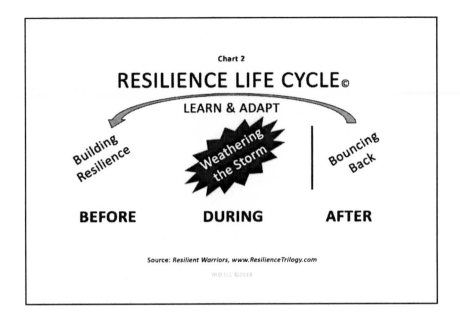

Chart 2

RESILIENCE LIFE CYCLE©

LEARN & ADAPT

Building Resilience

Weathering the Storm

Bouncing Back

BEFORE   **DURING**   **AFTER**

Source: *Resilient Warriors, www.ResilienceTrilogy.com*

Analogous to individuals and leaders, nations must sustain security and prosperity (in the broadest sense of the term) in the PRESENT, build strength for the FUTURE, and ensure readiness for inevitable "national body slams" due to internal and/or external causes. We have come to know this as the "BEFORE" phase of the Resilience Life Cycle©. This is the "ounce of prevention worth the pound of cure." This is "setting the conditions" ahead of time to ensure continuity and resilience when the "storm" hits.

Similarly, all nations experience periodic storms, serious crises, which can become an existential fight for survival if not addressed early or properly. This is the DURING phase of the Resilience Life Cycle©. This takes many forms on the national level: the rise of a totalitarian government which threatens you or others, a monumental natural disaster which overwhelms local governmental response capabilities, a crisis of confidence or corruption exhibited by influential national leaders, a costly war in which the means and ends becoming increasingly blurred, economic conditions which jeopardize individual and collective prosperity and hope, internal strife and instability which threaten cohesion of government and society, and so many other scenarios. These are all storms, the national equivalent of Jesus' assurance "in the world you <u>will</u> have tribulation." (John 16:33, NKJV, underline added)

Following such a national crisis, the challenge is to regain "vital optimism" (discussed in Chapter 8, *Resilient Warriors,* in concert with British recovery from the devastating losses in the Battle of the Somme in World War I) and to return to essential function as a nation and as a people. This represents the AFTER phase of the Resilience Life Cycle©, the hardest part of the journey where a nation must avoid getting stuck in malaise, unproductive partisan recriminations, blurred national vision and purpose, or weakened world stature due to the perception or reality of decreased national power and influence. For example, following its most recent national crisis (the attacks of September 11, 2001 and the ensuing aftermath of second and third order effects) the United States is still navigating this AFTER phase. Whether America can resiliently reassert its former positive and pervasive influence on the world stage and in the hearts of a united populace at home remains to be seen.

Finally, the Resilience Life Cycle© contains a "LEARN and ADAPT" feedback loop that implies a nation's ability to learn the lessons of history and be even more adept, agile, and prepared for future national challenges. We are well familiar with philosopher George Santayana's maxim:

"Those who fail to learn the lessons of history
are destined to repeat them."

In *Resilient Leaders* I used the phrase "good outfits talk to themselves." So it is with nations. How does a nation "talk to itself," learning from the past in order to create a less perilous (and ideally more prosperous) future? Together we will wrestle with such questions, particularly as they pertain to current American challenges.

While one would hope that a nation could navigate the ups and downs of the Resilience Life Cycle© for centuries and even millennia, the reality is that nations rise and nations fall, some never to return to the stage of history. There are many historical observers who have attempted to describe and explain this rise and fall of nations. One respected thesis which has stood the test of time is often attributed to Alexander Tytler, a Scottish history professor at the University of Edinburgh, who in 1887 observed about the fall of the Athenian Republic some 2,000 years prior:

"A democracy is always temporary in nature; it simply cannot exist as a permanent form of government. A democracy will continue to exist up until the time that voters discover that they can vote themselves generous gifts from the public treasury. From that moment on, the majority always votes for the candidates who promise the most benefits from the public treasury, with the result that every democracy <u>will finally   collapse</u> <u>over loose fiscal policy,</u> (which is) always followed by a dictatorship." (underlines added)

This thesis certainly rings true in light of centuries of observation, and is often linked with the following summary of the longevity and progression of decline in failing nations:

"The average age of the world's greatest
civilizations from the beginning of history,
has been about 200 years.
During those 200 years,
these nations always progressed
through the following sequence:

From bondage to <u>spiritual faith</u>;
From spiritual faith to <u>great courage</u>;
From courage to <u>liberty</u>;
From liberty to <u>abundance</u>;
From abundance to <u>complacency</u>;
From complacency to <u>apathy</u>;
From apathy to <u>dependence</u>;
From dependence back into <u>bondage</u>."
(underlines and italics added)

It is perhaps intuitively obvious that the United States is in the final stages of this progression to bondage, with ample evidence of national complacency, apathy, and welfare dependency. Having introduced our primary thesis of "Spiritual Infrastructure as an Element of National Power" in Chapter 1, we will provide global historical context in this Chapter 2. Then, Chapter 3 will complete our stage setting as we examine "God's Design for Nations" before diving microscopically into our assessment of current American Spiritual Infrastructure in Chapters 4 - 7. Chapters 8 and 9 conclude our journey with mandates for "We the People" and "We the Statesmen" as a means and a hope for spiritual rearmament and national renewal.

When Nations "Fail"

Lest we view this end state of "bondage" in overly sterile terms, it is important to emphasize that such "national collapse" is not orderly or pleasant. It is characterized by unfathomable human suffering, chaos, and increasing hopelessness which accompanies spiritual and eventually physical death of the nation. Sometimes the decline and fall of a nation occurs over decades or even centuries (such as with Rome, Greece, or the British Empire). Conversely, sometimes the fall is unexpected, instantaneous, and conclusive (such as the fall of the Iron Curtain and the rapid dissolution of the Soviet Union). Whether it is a hard crash or a soft landing, a common denominator is default by the government to provide for the protection and welfare of the populace. The result is inevitably human suffering, dashed dreams, and tragic loss of human and national potential.

As a graphic example of such suffering in a "nation gone awry", consider the Roman persecution of early Christians recounted in the book of Hebrews:

> "They were stoned, they were sawn in two, they were tempted, they were put to death with the sword; they went about in sheepskins, in goatskins,

being destitute, afflicted, ill-treated (men of whom the world was not worthy), wandering in deserts and mountains and cave and holes in the ground." (Hebrews 11:37, 38)

Although one might hope or assume that modern society has progressed beyond such barbarism, also consider more recent examples: the fate of Soviet dissenters exported to the Gulags of Siberia, or six million Jews exterminated by the Nazi regime, or "child soldiers" pressed into combat by Charles Taylor in Liberia and beyond, or Pol Pot's "Killing Fields" of Cambodia, or Idi Amin's rape of Uganda, or the daily maiming of Christians and burning of churches along the Christian-Muslim fault line in Nigeria, or the beheading of Daniel Pearl by Muslim extremists in Pakistan in 2002, or the daily tragedies of human trafficking, or the atrocities visited upon the people of South Sudan as these words are being written. Consider these excerpts from a letter sent by a Sudanese chaplain in the region (name withheld):

"May I take this opportunity to highlight what happened in our country, on December 15, 2013. South Sudan has broken into war again which has led to loss of many lives in the Capital Juba. This was a true attempted military coup which displaced as well as affected all residents of Juba as if it were a civil war. This reminded South Sudanese of the past civil war of 1983 – 2005 ... The affected states are Upper Nile (Malakal), Jonglei (Bor) and Unity (Bentiu). Children, women, elderly people, the mad, the blind, the deaf are being killed mercilessly by

the rebels... Please pray for South Sudan to escape that darkness of her people killing each other. Our hearts as pastors and believers of Jesus long for peace and forgiveness to prevail.

"Many people are scattered and others got lost, wounded or killed during the incidence. Our people have fled to the neighboring countries while others sought refuge in the bushes and along River Nile bank (waters). People are still suffering from hunger, thirst, diseases e.g. severe diarrhea, cholera, UTIs among others; mosquito bites, cold, harm from wild animals; even others drowned in water when crossing the rivers on foot or by boats. The list of suffering is endless in South Sudan."

This Sudanese chaplain understandably continues with an appeal for prayer on behalf of his nation. While to American readers such accounts may sound far away, abstract, unrelated to life in the United States or other nations, such tragedies must be more than theoretical. Consider if these are your parents, your children or grandchildren, your beloved country. Instances such as this are all around us, and they serve as cautionary tales. Over time, poor governance, misguided economic policy, brutal oppression, or rampant immorality in a nation-state result in serious consequences and tragic outcomes. These conditions often lead to default of the nation-state in its basic responsibilities to its people, characterized by unfathomable human suffering, chaos, and increasing hopelessness which presages spiritual and eventually physical death of the nation. We should not be so naive to think that such national tragedies only happen "over there."

This was certainly true in the classic example of the Roman Empire, once the grandest, the most powerful, the most prosperous, the most advanced, the most secure, and the eventually the most decadent nation on earth at that time.

> We should not be so naive to think that such national tragedies only happen "over there."

The Turning Radius of Nations

Given the disastrous outcomes associated with a failed nation-state, we must do everything possible to avoid such a fate, and we must take action before it is too late. Hence, an important consideration in the rise and fall of nations is timing. Assuming the requisite national will and commitment to do an "about face," what is the "turning radius" of such a nation? Having watched many a captain of huge barges (over a football field in length) navigate the tight turns of the Hudson River near West Point, I was always amazed at the lead time required to initiate a turn that would successfully avoid grounding or collision with other vessels. Just as a river barge or a Navy Aircraft Carrier has a much larger turning radius than a small ski boat (and hence a need to initiate a turn much sooner), so a small organization or private enterprise can turn more rapidly that a large nation-state, particularly if that nation is afflicted by the ills of a deeply seated bureaucracy. As well, if the rudder (decision and steering mechanism) of the nation-state is not functional and the thrust of the propeller (conversion of resources to power, including people power) is lacking, then the turn will take much longer, if at all.

In the case of many nations in decline or collapse, the "form" of government lasts long after the effective "function" of the government on behalf of the nation. As one historical example, in ancient Babylon, King Nebuchadnezzar (during the time he was having Daniel interpret his dreams) was carrying on with the ceremonial affairs of state (form) even while Darius of Persia was diverting the waters of the Euphrates River to bring about the eventual doom of Babylon in the arid Middle East (function). The die was cast long before King Nebuchadnezzar realized his nation's eventual fate. You can no doubt think of many other historical examples where an inevitable outcome became visible to the inattentive or apathetic leader or populace long after they should have applied corrective action. They simply failed to see or heed the warning signs before it was too late.

One must ask, "Where is the 'point of no return' for nations in decline?" No doubt this is different for each nation. Prayerfully it is not too late for America to initiate a sharp turn towards morality, as well as towards smaller government and greater influence by "We the People." We must begin the turn NOW, for the shoals of destruction and the headwaters of irreversible calamity are in clear view on our national horizon.

Resilient Nations will substantiate this assertion in subsequent chapters.

Common Denominators of National Decline: Learning from Rome

Before we begin to dissect the "American experiment," let us seek more historical perspective from Rome, perhaps the foremost example of a nation who "had it all" yet declined and fell victim to its own excess. While Gibbon's *Decline and Fall of the Roman Empire* is generally considered the most comprehensive work on this topic, there are a multitude of ancient and contemporary researchers who have plumbed the depths of this question. After significant literature review of this oft-studied topic, I have found a variety of opinions which cover all points of the compass, ranging from singular causal factors to multi-variable rationale to theories that Rome simply transformed (instead of "fell"). There are also many views about when the decline of Rome actually began or when it culminated. For a deeper dive into the specific instance of Rome, Greece, and other historical examples of national decline, you may refer to "Additional References" at the end of this chapter for a listing of useful resources.

For our purposes here, I will identify certain common denominators which are transferable to our later analysis of the United States. My synthesis of these "Common Denominators of National Decline" includes the following:

- <u>Failed economic policies</u> which discouraged trade and minimized exports, along with inflation resulting from currency devaluation (making more money as a short lived expedient for economic duress).

- <u>Increasingly oppressive taxation</u> of middle class to pay for the excesses of the ruling class, the loyalty and readiness of the military, and use of "the dole" to ensure ever increasing dependency of the lower class.
- <u>Crumbling infrastructure</u> (particularly Roman road and aqueduct systems) which deterred Rome's ability to project military and economic power.
- <u>Degradation of military readiness</u> and <u>increasing military overreach</u> into foreign territories, resulting in vulnerability and eventual defeat of Roman military forces.
- <u>Moral degradation</u> which led to lack of civility in culture, extreme violence as entertainment, sexual promiscuity and perversity which undercut public health and community values, and corrupt business and political practices.
- <u>Self-serving and inept leadership</u> which generally lacked character and competence, resulting in failed systems of governance and inability to provide basic protections for the populace and the nation.
- <u>Apathetic populace</u> which became puppets and eventually overly dependent victims of the state.

Gibbon's profound top level conclusion, reiterated below, is certainly relevant to our upcoming assessment of America's "State of the Union":

> "The decline of Rome was the natural and inevitable effect of <u>immoderate greatness</u>. <u>Prosperity ripened the principle of decay</u>; the causes of destruction multiplied with the extent of

conquest; <u>and as soon as time or accident had removed the artificial supports</u>, the stupendous fabric yielded to the <u>pressure of its own weight</u>..."
(underlines added)

One of the most respected conservative commentators and authors in the world today, Charles Krauthammer, provides his own observation of Rome's decline. Describing his transformation from a social-democratic world view to a philosophy of restrained, free-market governance, he pens the following in correlating the fate of Rome with the current descent of the United States:

> "I'm open to empirical evidence. The results of the Great Society experiments started coming in and began showing that, for all its good intentions, <u>the War on Poverty was causing irreparable damage to the very communities it was designed to help</u>. Charles Murray's *Losing Ground* was one turning point.
>
> "Another, more theoretical but equally powerful, was Mancur Olson's *The Rise and Decline of Nations*, which opened my eyes to <u>the inexorable "institutional sclerosis" that corrodes and corrupts the ever-enlarging welfare state</u>."
> Charles Krauthammer, *Things that Matter*
> (underlines added)

Dr. Krauthammer's implication is clear: the United States likewise possesses an "inexorable 'institutional sclerosis'" that is corroding and corrupting our ever-enlarging welfare state. Let us look at Israeli history for some ways to escape such a fate.

Common Denominators of National Resilience
Learning from Israel

Just as there are "common denominators of national decline," there are also "common denominators of national resilience." Although certainly not the case with ancient Hellenic or Roman empires (and many other examples) that declined into oblivion, we observe that some nations are able to "bounce back," to be resilient. In this vein, our only point of departure from Professor Tytler's seemingly deterministic sequence of national demise would be to highlight inflection points along the way that allow opportunity for a nation to reverse its course and improve its future. In particular, the last four transitions which he describes (*abundance to complacency, to apathy, to dependence, to bondage*) are junctures where a nation can possibly escape such a downward spiral. Specifically, **how does a nation reverse complacency and apathy towards internal and external threats, or reduce overdependence on state largesse, or escape bondage to internal governmental oppression or external occupation by a foreign power? As well, how does a nation recognize the symptoms early and muster the will to "self-correct" before moving beyond a tipping point?**

We will investigate Israel as a foremost example of national resilience.

Israel has "fallen" many times in its history, yet in God's Providence has redemptively risen as they returned to God's plan

71

for them as His chosen people. Consistent with Tytler's sequence of national deterioration (referenced above),

- Israel as an emerging nation went from a position of <u>bondage</u> (such as captivity in Egypt) to a position of <u>spiritual and moral strength</u> (consistently the result of God rescuing the nation, often miraculously, in their time of need, such as the Exodus).
- From there Israel demonstrated <u>courage</u> under the leadership of Moses and Joshua (such as battling the Amalekites in their first external security challenge after escaping from Egypt) which resulted in <u>liberty</u> from the tyranny of external threats and internal dissent.
- Yet, after enjoying the <u>abundance</u> of God's provision (security, water, manna) in their wilderness journey, Israel quickly became <u>complacent</u> and <u>apathetic</u> towards God. In their apathy, they would be enticed by idol worship, leading to <u>dependence</u> on false gods and ultimately <u>bondage</u> to their own sinfulness and depraved actions.

Yet, contrary to the deterministic final collapse suggested by Professor Tytler's thesis, the nation of Israel proved resilient time and again through God's redemptive provision and a return to their one true God. Over its national history, Israel has repeatedly bounced back from calamity or near-calamity to once again find liberty, abundance, and moral rightness as a nation.

These cycles of Israeli resilience were certainly evident in the period of the Judges (Book of Judges). In *Explore the Book*, J. Sidlow Baxter describes the process in more direct theological terms, moving from SIN to SUFFERING to SUPPLICATION to

SALVATION. He recounts six episodes which begin with "*And the children of Israel did evil (again,* added in some of the verses) *in the sight of the Lord...*" (Judges 3:7, 3:12, 4:1, 6:1, 10:6, and 13:1). Each of these episodes ended with deliverance (salvation) through rediscovery of national values and priorities and the influence of a God-ordained resilient leader, in this case ranging respectively from Othniel, to Ehud, to Deborah, to Gideon, to Jephthah, to Samson.

We see a similar dynamic during the period of the Kings. Note the rediscovery of the Holy Scriptures in II Kings 22 and 23 (NKJV) where King Josiah sent word through Shaphan to the High Priest Hilkiah regarding rebuilding the house of the Lord. The dramatic moments are reflected below:

- (REDISCOVERY OF VALUES) "*Then Hilkiah the High Priest said to Shaphan the scribe, 'I have found the Book of the Law in the house of the LORD.'*" (v. 22:8, underline added)
- (CONVICTION OF FLAWED POLICY AND PRACTICE) "*Then Shaphan the scribe showed the king. And Shaphan read it before the King.*" "*Now it happened, when the king heard the words of the Book of the Law, that he tore his clothes...*" (v. 22:10,11)
- (DIRECTION BY A GOD-HONORING RESILIENT LEADER) "*...and directed* "*Go, inquire of the lord for me, for the people and for all Judah, concerning the words of this book that has been found, for great is the wrath of the LORD that is aroused against us, because our fathers have not obeyed the words of this book, to do according to all that is written concerning us.*" (v. 22:12,13, underlines added)

- (NATIONAL RESPONSE AND REVERSAL) *"Now the king sent them to gather all the elders of Judah and Jerusalem to him (v. 23: 1) ... And <u>he read in their hearing all the words of the Book of the Covenant</u> which had been found in the house of the LORD (v. 23:2b) ... Then <u>the king stood by a pillar and made a covenant before the LORD,</u> to follow the LORD and to keep His commandments and His testimonies and His statutes, with all his heart and all his soul, <u>to perform the words of this covenant</u> that were written in this book. <u>And all the people took a stand for the covenant.</u>"* (v. 23:3, underlines added)

Clearly King Josiah's influence as a resilient leader was pivotal in this process. After descriptions of how King Josiah eliminated idols from among the people, chastised corrupt leadership, and restored God honoring traditions throughout the nation, this chapter of Scripture concludes regarding King Josiah's leadership and heart for God:

"Now before him there was <u>no king like him</u>, who turned to the LORD with all his heart, with all his soul, and with all his might..." (II Kings 23:25a, underline added)

While not totally sufficient (because of other determinant factors), such leaders of principle and conviction are absolutely essential to the resilience of a nation.

To expand further on this point, a courageous national renewal requires determined, charismatic, and <u>resilient leaders</u> ("a selfless servant over time who leads from a platform of character and competence," as defined in *Resilient Leaders*). In

Israel's history, the fifteen "judges" of Israel (Book of Judges) or rulers such as King Josiah were examples of such resilient leaders whose courage and morality turned the course of a nation. Esther was also an unsuspecting resilient leader who courageously spoke truth to power "for such a time as this." (Esther 4:14)

Even the example of King David (often remembered for his moral free fall begun with an illicit relationship with Bathsheba) is instructive. As the Prophet Samuel was admonishing King Saul and portending the selection of King David as the right resilient leader for the nation, he said the following:

> "[13]Samuel said to Saul: 'You have acted foolishly; you have not kept the commandment of the LORD your God, which He commanded you, for now the LORD would have established your kingdom over Israel forever. [14]But now your kingdom shall not endure. <u>The LORD has sought out for Himself a man after His own heart</u>, and the LORD has <u>appointed him as ruler over His people, because you have not kept what the LORD commanded you</u>.'" (I Samuel 13:13, 14, underline added)

Resilient Leadership is critical to National Resilience, a theme we will see in the life of every resilient nation.

To fast forward in Israel's history, we also recognize that the second Israeli exodus (returning from the Babylonian captivity which began in 586 B.C.) back to the destroyed capital Jerusalem was yet another Resilience Life Cycle© iteration to illustrate the

BEFORE-DURING-AFTER-LEARN & ADAPT sequence, as well as the role of the resilient leaders Ezra and Nehemiah.

In *Resilient Leaders* (Chapter 6), I related the circumstances of assuming command of the Second Infantry Division in Korea in the middle of physical and moral crisis. You may recall my application of a Biblical parallel from the life of Nehemiah, who also "assumed command" of a very difficult situation when he returned to Jerusalem to "rebuild the wall" (reestablishing not only infrastructure, but also governance, leadership, and will of the people). Nehemiah became a role model for me as I navigated a similarly complex and challenging leadership scenario in Korea.

The roots of this Israeli rebound under the leadership of Nehemiah actually began much earlier. The scribe and priest Ezra was an equally important resilient leader who "set the conditions" for Nehemiah's return to Jerusalem as part of the nation's resilient recovery from debilitating immorality and foreign captivity.

To provide broad context, recall that Jeremiah the prophet had cried out faithfully for twenty-three years, warning the nation of Israel of impending doom because of their growing indifference and decadence before God. Jeremiah (as with many modern day American prophets who since the 1960's have been shouting their warnings) alerts Israel to pending judgment, yet the nation and its leaders do not receive his message. Jeremiah Chapter 25 describes the woeful consequences that God will bring though King Nebuchadnezzar of Babylon. This prophecy was realized in the Babylonian Captivity of 586 BC when Jerusalem was sacked, and surviving Israelites were taken to captivity in Babylon.

For greater specifics and appreciation regarding the return of the people of Israel to Jerusalem and Judah, I recommend a full reading of the books of Ezra and Nehemiah.   In short, in his first year of reign, King Cyrus of Persia proclaimed that the God of Heaven had appointed him "to build Him a house in Jerusalem, which is in Judah." (Ezra 1:2) The resulting expedition of many Jews to rebuild the temple met with initial success, but later encountered opposition by "people of the land" and eventually a royal edict that the work be discontinued. Subsequently (after a period of many years and a succession of leaders), the mandate to rebuild the temple in Jerusalem was revalidated and the temple was completed:

> "...And they finished building according to the command of the God of Israel and the decree of Cyrus, Darius, and Artaxerxes king of Persia. This temple was completed on the third day of the month Adar; it was the sixth year of the reign of King Darius." (Ezra 6:14b, 15)

Signifying completion of the temple and an obedient return to their worship of their God, the faithful remnant in Jerusalem celebrated a very significant Passover which brought joy to the partakers and "turned the heart of the King of Assyria toward them, to strengthen their hands in the work of the house of God, the God of Israel." (Ezra 6:23)

This is when the work really began for the scribe and priest Ezra, as a leader who was granted favor by God and by man:

> "[6]This Ezra went up from Babylon, and he was a scribe skilled in the law of Moses, which the LORD God of Israel had given; and the king (Artaxerxes of Persia) granted him all he requested because the hand of the LORD his God was upon him... [13]I have issued a decree that any of the people of Israel and their priests and the Levites in my kingdom who are willing to go to Jerusalem, may go with you. (Ezra 7: 6, 13, parentheses and underlines added)

Thenceforth (Ezra 7 and forward), Ezra used the law of Moses to lay a solid legal and moral foundation for the resurgent nation Israel, addressing taxation, civil law, fundamental governance, means of enforcement, and political leadership. In the process, he always modeled a penitent and humble dependence upon God, fueled by deep knowledge and adherence to the law of the Lord: "For Ezra had set his heart to study the law of the LORD and to practice it, and to teach His statutes and ordinances in Israel. (Ezra 7:10) In essence, Ezra followed the resilient model of his ancestors as he went through the same cycle to move from bondage to eventual national vitality: Rediscovery of Values – Conviction of Flawed Policy and Practice – Direction by a God-honoring Resilient Leader – National Response and Reversal. This national "about face" certainly impacted all Israeli "elements of national power," but was rooted in spiritual transformation and obedience to their deepest values as a Jewish nation. The defining moment occurs in Chapter 10 of Ezra:

"[7]They made a proclamation throughout Judah and Jerusalem to all the exiles, that they should assemble at Jerusalem. … [10]Then Ezra the priest stood up and said to them, '<u>You have been unfaithful</u> and have married foreign wives adding to the guilt of Israel. [11]Now therefore, <u>make confession to the LORD God</u> of your fathers and do His will; and <u>separate yourselves from the peoples of the land and from the foreign wives</u>.' [12]Then all the assembly replied with a loud voice, '<u>That's right! As you have said, so it is our duty to do.</u>'… [14]'<u>Let our leaders represent the whole assembly </u>and let all those in our cities who have married foreign wives come at appointed times, together with the elders and judges of each city, <u>until the fierce anger of our God on account of this matter is turned away from us</u>.' …[19]<u>They pledged</u> to put away their wives, and <u>being guilty, they offered a ram of the flock for their offense</u>.
(Ezra 10:7, 10-12, 14, 19, underlines added)

The account above is remarkable. Here we have a nation who had ignored God and paid the price of subjugation to another national power and culture. Their means of personal and national salvation was a path of rediscovery, repentance, restitution, and renewal. The remarkable aspect is that they actually did it. They actually heard and obeyed. They actually admitted they were headed the wrong way, and turned in the right direction. They actually resisted their base human instincts to find the hope and future which God had waiting for His obedient children. This was a true "spiritual act of worship" akin to the battle cry often heard by many American revivalists:

> "(If) My people who are called by My name <u>humble themselves</u> and <u>pray and seek My face</u> and <u>turn from their wicked ways</u>, then I will <u>hear from heaven</u>, will <u>forgive their sin</u> and will <u>heal their land</u>."
> (2 Chronicles 7:14, underlines and parentheses added)

Moving from Biblical history to the present day, the contemporary history of Israel also demonstrates considerable resilience as a nation. Following declaration of independence as a nation on May 15, 1948, Israel was attacked the next day by surrounding Arab nations. Inexplicable apart from the hand of God, Israel survived overwhelming odds and began its rapid growth economically, militarily, and culturally. Major conflicts with Arab neighbors in 1967 and 1973 resulted in the same general outcome, despite surprise attacks by overwhelming numbers against them. Although Egypt and Jordan have provided reasonably secure flanks since 1973, Hezbollah (Shia) in Lebanon and Hamas (Sunni) in Gaza have been the frequent source of attacks against the Israeli homeland, necessitating periodic Israeli contingency operations which have experienced mixed success. Most recently, Arab Spring events around the region and specifically in Egypt and Syria have generated even greater potential for spontaneous combustion in the Middle East. As well, an Iranian regime determined to achieve status as a nuclear power, and who publicly denies the right of Israel to exist, are the latest of threats to Israeli survival as a nation and as a people. This Israeli security equation is further complicated by the real and perceived decline of America's international prestige, influence, and support to Israel on the world stage.

Given this history and their lack of strategic depth and warning time, military readiness is an imperative for the Israelis. While this readiness in part depends upon tangible technology and training, the real distinctives of Israeli readiness are intangible factors such as will, commitment, cohesion, and courage which draw from a spiritual well. **Just as with Israel of antiquity, the Jewish people and the modern day Israeli nation continue to demonstrate remarkable resilience, fueled by all facets of their national power, but most significantly undergirded by a strong spiritual infrastructure and the obvious hand of God.**

In summary, despite the many existential threats to the nation of Israel from Abraham to present day, Israel has demonstrated remarkable resilience as a nation. While the Israelis have often shown themselves to be a proud and obstinate people, they are also "God's chosen people" and have survived insurmountable odds again and again to bounce back as a nation. Israel has experienced many "body slams" as a nation (often because of their own immorality and rebellion), yet have been able to follow the lead of God honoring resilient leaders, have repented from their self-destructive path, and have repeatedly experienced national renewal and prosperity as a people and as a nation. **Israel's historic view as an exceptional nation under God's protective umbrella, a strong national cohesion forged through shared hardship, a distinctive national pride**

achieved through difficult victories, a laser focus upon national readiness to face external threats, and other elements of a strong "Spiritual Infrastructure" (as defined in Chapter 1) have been the fundamental building blocks of Israel as a resilient nation.

The same has been true of America—at least until the 1960's and beyond. The future is less certain.

Gaining Altitude: America through the Lens of Other Nations

Some of you may have seen the movie *The Book of Eli* starring Denzel Washington which describes the United States as a "failed state" after a nuclear holocaust. *The Book of Eli* plot line is parallel to cycles of resilience in the history of Israel, America, and others.

One review of this movie by Tara Bennett, Fandango Film Commentator, summarizes this searing foreshadow:

"In *The Book of Eli*, Washington dips his boot into the current post-apocalyptic trend playing a character traversing the ruins of our nation 30 years after a nuclear holocaust. Humans are almost feral, creature comforts are to be treasured like gold and books, especially Eli's last copy of the *King James Bible*, are just about extinct. It's in a vision from God that Eli is charged with protecting the tome, taking it west where it may become the saving grace of humanity. Along the way, cannibals, a corrupt power lord and all manner of thugs try to end Eli's mission from God." (underlines added)

In *The Book of Eli*, we see that the path to national restoration was the rediscovery and protection of the fundamental values that were instrumental in founding the nation (the *King James Bible* in this case). As well, we see that it took a courageous visionary leader, Denzel Washington's character Eli, to stand up against the forces of evil and instill courage, direction, and hope. These principles repeat in the lives of nations large and small, and across the span of history from antiquity to this future scenario in the mid-21st Century.

Clearly one would hope for national turnaround and a resilient response long before nuclear holocaust, or widespread civil unrest, or total moral meltdown, but the pattern and sequence of national resilience has certain irreducible minimums (common denominators) which we will investigate throughout *Resilient Nations*. The common denominators of national resilience which we have surfaced thus far are:

- Rediscovery of Values
- Conviction of Flawed Policy and Practice
- Direction by a God-honoring Resilient Leader
- National Response and Reversal

America has demonstrated such resilient actions in many earlier cycles in its own history, such as surviving and prospering after the American Revolution (notably preceded by the First Great Awakening), bouncing back after a bitterly fought Civil War (notably preceded by the Second Great Awakening), growing into a world power that defended free peoples and became a beacon of hope in the two World Wars, recovery from the Great Depression, and some might add the recent rebound from the attacks on the Twin Towers on September 11, 2001.

One must question, however, whether America has been on the same resilient path for the latter half of the 20th Century, particularly with the apparent cultural, political, and spiritual erosion from the 1960s forward. Of recent vintage: did the "exogenous shock" of 9/11 and subsequent events graphically illustrate a longer term lessening of national will, a failing economic trajectory (with a debt bubble which has grown geometrically over the past decade), the ills of a rapidly expanding welfare state (accentuated by recent Affordable Care Act, aka Obamacare, experimentation with an even greater dependency structure), and an accelerating moral degradation and culture of violence? Is it even more alarming to know that a growing majority of Americans don't even care about such trends? In short, has America reached a "tipping point? Are we "fiddling while Rome is burning" (referring to the Emperor Nero) as we pass milestones of potential national renewal, recovery, and resilience?

We will examine such questions rigorously as we progress through *Resilient Nations*.

Let us close this chapter with a more graphic illustration regarding one possible outcome for America. For this we return to Edward Gibbon's visceral description of the ruins of Capitol Rome in the 15th Century:

"In the last days of Pope Eugenius the Fourth, two of his servants, the learned Poggius and a friend, ascended the Capitoline hill; reposed themselves among the ruins of columns and temples; and <u>viewed from that commanding spot the wide and various prospect of desolation.</u> The place and object gave ample scope for moralizing on <u>the vicissitudes of fortune</u>, which spares neither man nor the proudest of his works, <u>which buries empires and cities in a common grave</u>; and it was agreed, that in proportion to her former greatness, <u>the fall of Rome was the more awful and deplorable.</u>" (underlines added)

Gibbon continues with an even more detailed description:

"...the temple is overthrown, the gold has been pillaged, <u>the wheel of fortune has accomplished her revolutions, and the sacred ground is again disfigured with thorns and brambles.</u> The hill of the Capitol, on which we sit, was formerly the head of the Roman Empire, the citadel of the earth, the terror of kings; illustrated by the footsteps of so many triumphs, enriched with the spoils and tributes of so many nations. <u>The spectacle of the world, how it is fallen!</u> How changed! How defaced! The path of victory is obliterated by vines, and the benches of the senators are concealed by a dunghill. Cast your eyes on the Palatine hill, and seek among the shapeless and enormous fragments the marble theatre, the obelisks, the colossal statues, the porticos of Nero's palace: survey the other hills of the city, the vacant space is interrupted only by ruins and gardens. <u>The forum of the Roman people where they assembled to enact their laws and elect their magistrates, is now enclosed for the cultivation of pot-herbs, or thrown open for the reception of swine and buffaloes.</u> The <u>public and private edifices, that were founded for eternity, lie prostrate, naked, and broken, like the limbs of a mighty giant</u>; and the ruin is the more visible, from the stupendous relics that have survived the injuries of time and fortune." (underlines added)

With this picture of the Roman Capitol in mind, let us project two or three generations ahead to a similar vantage point overlooking our own nation's capital, Washington, DC. Will it have become a "spectacle to the world" of profligate near-sighted decline, or will it continue to be a beacon of freedom and prosperity? Will foreign powers have toppled the Washington Monument obelisk and pulled Abraham Lincoln from his perch above our institutions of government? Will the "forum of the people where they enacted their laws" (U.S. Congress) still be functional? Will it still be standing, or "thrown open for the reception of swine and buffaloes?" Will the "path of victory" in front of the Capitol be "overgrown by vines?" Will Thomas Jefferson still sit respectfully among the words and ideas upon which this nation was founded? Will the welfare state have imploded, resulting in civil unrest and the U.S. government's inability to resource internal functions and external security? In a less tangible sense, will the nation's culture of violence and growing moral perversions have left the institutions (family, church, and state) "that were founded for eternity, (to) lie prostrate, naked, and broken, like the limbs of a mighty giant?"

In short, what will our nation's grandchildren see and experience in a few short decades?

Some may regard this potential comparison as overly dramatic fear-mongering. I am not of that opinion. Without a course reversal, America is likely in her twilight years.

To restate a quote used from Archbishop Signorelli in *Resilient Leaders*,

"...we fall the way we lean."

As with Rome over a thousand years ago, America is leaning in the wrong direction, for almost a century now. The tipping point is here. The time for private conviction and public mobilization is now... or never.

Resilient Nations Takeaways

RN 2A – Each nation has a life cycle which represents the ebb and flow of its' internal health and external influence. The Resilience Life Cycle© model is equally relevant to the life of nations.

RN 2B – Poor governance, brutal oppression, or rampant immorality in a nation state result in serious consequences and tragic outcomes. These conditions often lead to "national collapse," characterized by unfathomable human suffering, chaos, and increasing hopelessness which accompanies spiritual and eventually physical death of the nation.

RN 2C – "Common Denominators of National Decline" include failed economic policies, increasingly oppressive taxation, crumbling infrastructure, degradation of military readiness and increasing military overreach, moral degradation, self-serving and inept leadership, and an apathetic and dependent populace.

RN 2D – With nations in decline or collapse, the "form" of government lasts long after the effective "function" of government has been mortally dismantled. Barring God's divine intervention, when the "turning radius" exceeds the time required to reverse course; the nation has reached the "tipping point" of no return.

RN 2E – "Common Denominators of National Resilience" include rediscovery of national bedrock values, conviction and correction regarding destructive policies and practice, courageous leadership by resilient leaders, and willing adherence by citizens, families, and communities.

RN 2F – A courageous reversal at one of the potential national "inflection points" (complacency, apathy, dependence, bondage) requires determined, charismatic, <u>resilient leaders</u>; and a <u>willing citizenry</u> who will stand against dictatorial government overreach and cultural decadence which lead to demise and destruction.

RN 2G — As a foremost example of national resilience, Israel has repeatedly bounced back from physical and moral calamities to repeatedly regain liberty, prosperity, and moral rightness. The Jewish people and the modern day Israeli nation continue to demonstrate remarkable resilience, fueled by all facets of their national power, but most significantly undergirded by a strong spiritual infrastructure and the obvious hand of God.

RN 2H — Despite the resilience of the United States in the past, its future is in serious question. The American tipping point is near.

For Further Consideration

1. Given the importance of courageous resilient leaders in enabling restoration or redirection of nations, identify and characterize historical figures who have "made the difference" in their nation's resilient response. For example, consider Esther as a Biblical difference maker, or Joseph as one who ensured Egyptian resilience from debilitating drought, or Nelson Mandela as a 20th Century conscience for South Africa and the world.

2. Dive deeper into Israel as a contemporary example of a Resilient Nation. Identify critical success factors that have allowed the nation to "bounce back," and the risks it faces in the future. Using major episodes in Israeli history since 1948 (most of which revolve around major conflicts and security issues), map the Israeli experience into the Resilience Life Cycle© paradigm (Before-During-After-

Learn & Adapt). What do you project that the next iteration of this cycle will look like?

3. Using the Common Denominators of National Resilience (Rediscovery of Values – Conviction of Flawed Policy and Practice – Direction by a God-honoring Resilient Leader – National Response and Reversal), select an example of a contemporary resilient nation (such as South Korea, Uganda, Estonia) or another of your choice for further analysis. How was each of the common denominators relevant to their capacity for resilience as a nation? How did the various elements of Spiritual Infrastructure identified in Chapter 1 assist their resilient recovery?

Additional References

1. Dees, Robert F. *Resilient Leaders*. San Diego, CA: Creative Team Publishing, 2013.
2. Gilbert, Martin. *Israel*. London: Doubleday, 1998.
3. Gibbon, Edward. *The History of the Decline and Fall of the Roman Empire*, ("The Online Library of Liberty, a project of Liberty Fund, Inc.") Accessed at http://oll.libertyfund.org.
4. Mancur, Olson. *Rise and Decline of Nations*. Yale University Press, 1982.
   http://ancienthistory.about.com/od/fallofromearticles/

3

God's Design for Nations

"Then render to Caesar the things that are Caesar's,
and to God the things that are God's."
~ Jesus (Matthew 22:21)

In Chapter 1 we introduced the concept of "Spiritual Infrastructure as an Element of National Power," discussing the largely intangible qualities that represent the true heart and soul of a nation, essential to national resilience and survival over time. As well, we "water skied" through the first 210 years of United States' history (from 1750 to 1960), illustrating many "significant emotional events" in the life of this nation (wars, depression, internal strife, external threats) and the resilience factors which allowed America to weather existential storms. In later chapters we will continue this survey of U.S. history through the lens of Spiritual Infrastructure, placing a microscope on the 1960s to the present. Maintaining that America is at a "national tipping point," we will assess alternative futures for the United States and identify key areas of policy and practice which will lead us to the desired resilient outcome.

In Chapter 2 we provided "Global Historical Context" as we briefly surveyed the rise and fall of nations. We applied Resilience Life Cycle© concepts used earlier in *Resilient Warriors* and *Resilient Leaders* to the life of nations.   While using Rome's decline and fall, and Israel's cycles of resilience as illustrations, we identified common denominators of national decline and national resilience which will prove useful as we assess our current situation in America. We closed this chapter with an apocalyptic view of a fallen America whose Capitol, government, and way of life are indistinguishable from the ruins of Rome over 500 years ago. With this as a cautionary tale for every American, we now turn our efforts to avoiding such a fate, that we might continue to be the "Land of the Free and the Home of the Brave" for generations to come.

Pressing forward on our *Resilient Nations* journey, we now examine "God's Design for Nations" which began with Creation (Laws of Nature and of Nature's God), continued with the Abrahamic covenant establishing the first nation, bridged across the Great Flood with the Noahic covenant of protection, became even more specific with provision of the "Decalogue" to Moses (Ten Commandments), was illustrated in principle and practice by the teachings of Jesus and his disciples, and gained greater rigor and application through the contributions of many over almost 1,800 years (Justinian Code: consolidating Roman and Byzantine Law), the Book of Dooms (which added the concept of grace), the Magna Carta (which granted rights to the people), *On the Laws and Customs of England* (by Henry of Bratton, who introduced Common Law), the English Bill of Rights, and numerous other milestones in the evolution of law which the serious student of the law may want to investigate further. Then came Sir William Blackstone's seminal work in 1753, *Commentaries on the Laws of England*.

As a brilliant and comprehensive synthesis of prior advancements in jurisprudence and the proper role of government (which was widely read and highly regarded in colonial America), Blackstone's body of legal theory and practice, totally consistent with natural and revealed law of God, was the blueprint upon which America's Founders relied as they sought to establish "a more perfect Union."
We will benefit from Blackstone's words at a
number of points in this chapter.

Having just described the gradual and very deliberate evolution of modern legal theory over hundreds of years, this is an important place to warn against "historical revisionism" in its various forms. While we will address this further in later chapters, historical revisionism is antithetical to "proper retention of national history," earlier identified as an important component of Spiritual Infrastructure.

David Barton's book, *Original Intent* also warns of the pitfalls of revisionism. In the Foreword, he provides important reminders as we begin to discuss the Biblical and historical foundations of our nation:

"Our Constitution operates on <u>long-standing principles</u> which were recognized and incorporated into our government over two hundred years ago; <u>each constitutional provision reflects a specific philosophy implemented to avoid a specific problem</u>.

"For example, when adjudging the permissible in the realm of public religious expressions, courts revert to what they perceive to be the intent of those who, in 1789, drafted the religion clauses of the Constitution. Likewise, the perception of historical intent similarly affects the debates on gun control and the Second Amendment, States' Rights and the Tenth Amendment, abortion and the Ninth and Fourteenth Amendments, flag-burning and the First Amendment, etc.

"Therefore, <u>if our understanding of historical facts and constitutional intent becomes confused or mistaken, the resulting policies may be not only ill-founded but may actually create the very abuses that the Founders originally intended to avoid</u>. (underlines added)

Understanding the philosophical and historical underpinnings of United States' law and government is essential to a proper interpretation of Constitutional and cultural issues and proper implementation of resulting policy. "Historical revisionism" in its simplest terms is the expedient omission or change of historical facts to fit a desired narrative or policy position.

As a first safeguard against such revisionism or inaccurate thinking regarding our nation's Constitutional foundations, I challenge each reader to multiple readings of our nation's founding documents: *The Declaration of Independence*, and *The Constitution of the United States of America*, including Amendments I-XXVII. Understandably, I will refer to these frequently. As well, I refer the reader to *Original Intent*, Chapter 10 (Selective History) and Chapter 16 (Revisionism), for an in-depth analysis of the witting and unwitting ways in which original intent is overtaken by "convenient truths" (actually fallacies) in order to support a particular modern agenda of the courts or various advocacy groups.

With this emphasis upon the importance of proper retention and respect for national history and founding intentions, we now look at God's "Design for Nations," starting with the purpose for nations and government.

God's Purpose for Nations and Government

> Just as God's creation of the earth was an intentional and
> orderly masterpiece over which He granted man dominion,
> His establishment of three primary institutions
> (family, church, and state) to regulate the orderly affairs of
> men and nations was equally intentional.

God's establishment of <u>the family as an institution</u> (begun with Adam and Eve) served to propagate the human race, to be the primary incubator for the physical, mental, spiritual, emotional, and relational maturation of young people into responsible and productive persons, family members, and citizens, and to provide a platform from which to reach out to less fortunate members of society.

Similarly, God established <u>the church as an institution</u> (illustrated by the function of the Levites in early Israel, the role of prophets to provide spiritual discernment to nations, leaders, and peoples, and eventually the early church after the death of Christ) to train and exercise relational health with God and others, to equip believers to be resilient and relevant to the society in which they serve, and to be an arm of compassionate outreach to those in need.

<u>God's third ordained institution is the state (nation)</u>, intended to safeguard the "unalienable rights" which God bestows to each member of His human creation. In *Resilient Nations*, we focus primarily on the role of government (the state), "We the People" (the citizen), and "We the Statesmen" (private and public sector

leaders), although the institutions of family and church are inextricably linked to the roles and practices of citizens, statesmen, and the state.

In King David's Prayer for his son, Solomon, to govern well, we observe some of God's intended results when righteous and effective leadership and governance are in place:

> ^{4}May he <u>vindicate the afflicted</u> of the people,
> <u>Save the children of the needy</u>
> And <u>crush the oppressor</u>...
> ^{7}In his days <u>may the righteous flourish</u>,
> And <u>abundance of peace</u> till the moon is no more...
> ^{14}He will <u>rescue their life from oppression and violence</u>,
> And <u>their blood will be precious in his sight</u>...
> ^{16}May there be <u>abundance of grain</u> in the earth on top of the mountains...
> And may <u>those from the city flourish</u> like vegetation of the earth.
> (Psalm 72:4, 7, 14, 16)

While we will add further specifics from Scripture to more comprehensively define the role of government, David gives us a pretty good list:

- *vindicate the afflicted* (ensure justice)
- *save children of the needy* (extend compassion)
- *crush the oppressor* (provide internal and external security and accountability)

- *safeguard an environment in which the righteous flourish* (set conditions for right living)
  - *abundance of peace*
  - *rescue their life from oppression and violence*
  - *abundance of grain* (stimulate economic prosperity)
  - *those from the city flourish* (promote civility and opportunity)

While we will see that God's Design for Nations was intentional and evident from the very beginning of Creation, the story of Jesus' wise answer ("Render unto Caesar") to the plotting Pharisees well illustrates the respective roles of government and citizen upon which our American system of government has been built. Asking a malicious question regarding whether one should pay taxes to Caesar, the Pharisees sought to lure Jesus into either offending Caesar (with resulting punishment from the government) or blaspheming God (with hoped for loss of credibility amongst Jesus' many followers). In short, Jesus acknowledged the appointed role of government and governing leaders while simultaneously recognizing the existence of "the things that are God's," all in proper balance versus an artificial separation of church and state.

As always, Jesus proved "innocent as a dove and wise as a serpent," displaying the same God-given wisdom as with Solomon when he was confronted with two women, both claiming that each was its mother. Solomon directed, "Get me a sword... Divide the living child in two and give half to the one and half to the other." (I Kings 3:24, 25) He quickly discerned that the true mother was the one who then sacrificed her right to the baby in order to save its life. Word of this incident spread throughout Israel and "they feared the king, for they saw that <u>the wisdom of God</u> was in him <u>to administer justice</u>." (I Kings 3:28, underlines added)

This theme of subjugation to God-appointed government and leaders, as well as leaders and governments
that ensure justice for the people, is replayed many times throughout the Old and New Testaments.

For instance, the Apostle Paul instructs the Romans regarding their role as citizens:

> "Every person is to be in <u>subjection to the governing authorities</u>. For there is <u>no authority except from God</u>, and <u>those which exist are established by God</u>. [2]Therefore whoever resists authority has opposed the ordinance of God; and they who have opposed will receive condemnation upon themselves."
> (Romans 13:1, 2, underlines added)

As one more example, the Apostle Peter writing to Jewish believers in the early Church also clearly defined the key roles of government, and provided fundamental instruction to citizens. This passage is particularly apt to conditions which we see emerging in America today, having been written in a time when

Christians were experiencing ridicule and persecution at the hands of a declining and oppressive Roman government and a delusional Roman Emperor, Nero. Despite harsh treatment and evil practices from government, Peter mirrors Jesus' "Render unto Caesar" instructions by exhorting Christian citizens to:

> "[13a]Submit yourselves for the Lord's sake to every human institution..."
> (I Peter 2:13a, underlines added)

Displaying the entirety of I Peter 2:13, 14 for the broader context, we now see two very definitive roles for government:

> "[13]Submit yourselves for the Lord's sake to every human institution,
> whether to a king as the one in authority,
> [14]or to governors as sent by him
> for the punishment of evildoers and the praise of those who do right.
> (I Peter 2:13, 14, underlines added)

Hence, we see in simplest terms that God's intended role of government is to restrain evil and to promote righteousness while the complementary role of citizen includes submission and right living under the law of God and the law of man.

These Biblical guidelines for government (with which the Founding Fathers were very familiar and supportive) conveyed directly through the subsequent development of law and political theory that led to the United States' Declaration of Independence, its Constitution, and its Bill of Rights.

Thomas Paine's *Common Sense*, published just seven months before the Declaration of Independence was signed, had a profound impact on "We the People" and "We the Statesmen" (the Founders in this case). It truly provided the common sense explanation, fully consistent with the Biblical precepts we have discussed, regarding the purpose of nations and government.

A few excerpts from Thomas Paine's Chapter, "Of the Origin and Design of Government in General... " prove instructive:

> "Society is produced by our wants, and government by our wickedness; the former pro- motes our happiness positively by uniting our affections, the latter negatively by restraining our vices. The one engages intercourse, the other creates distinction. The first is a patron, the last a punisher.
>
> "Society in every state is a blessing, but govern- ment even in its best state is but a necessary evil; in its worst state an intolerable one...
>
> "For were the impulses of conscience clear, uniform, and irresistibly obeyed, man would need no other lawgiver; but that not being the case, he finds it necessary to surrender up a part of his property to furnish means for the protection of the rest; and this he is induced to do by the same

prudence which in every other case advises him <u>out of two evils</u> to choose the least.

"<u>Wherefore, security being the true design and end of government, it unanswerably follows that whatever form thereof appears most likely to ensure it to us, with the least expense and greatest benefit, is preferable to all the others</u>." (underlines added)

In short, Thomas Paine rightly assessed that the nature of humanity requires a degree of external moderation.

> Government serves to restrain human vices,
> often necessitating the punishment of evil doers.
> This function of punishment is a necessary evil that should be
> administered at least to achieve maximum benefit,
> implying a limited nature to government that avoids
> excessive intrusion or overreach into the lives of individuals,
> their communities, or their professional endeavors.

In addition to providing very clear rationale for the existence of nations and government, Biblical precepts and man's subsequent expansion of legal and political thought also led our nation's Founders to a specific construct, one which we will call the "Model Nation."

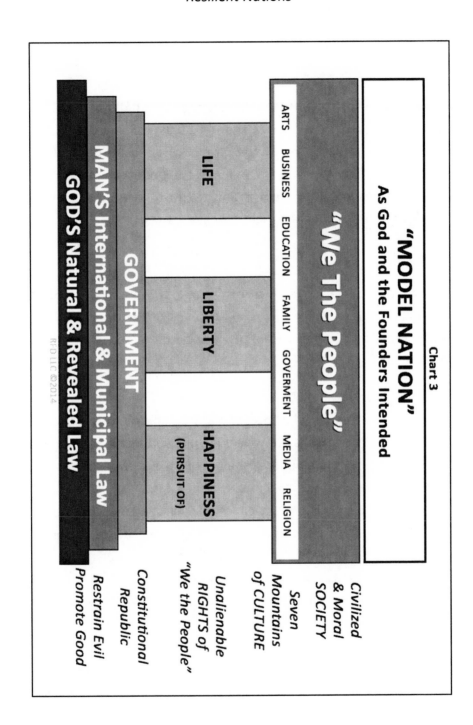

Chart 3

"MODEL NATION"
As God and the Founders Intended

"We The People"

ARTS BUSINESS EDUCATION FAMILY GOVERMENT MEDIA RELIGION

LIFE

LIBERTY

HAPPINESS
(PURSUIT OF)

GOVERNMENT

MAN'S International & Municipal Law

GOD'S Natural & Revealed Law

RFD LLC ©2014

Civilized
& Moral
SOCIETY

Seven
Mountains
of CULTURE

Unalienable
RIGHTS of
"We the People"

Constitutional
Republic

Restrain Evil
Promote Good

The Founder's "Model Nation"

To set the stage for our discussion, Chart 3, *Model Nation* (prior page) illustrates in simple terms the Founder's vision for America derived from their synthesis of Biblical principles, the maturation of law since the time of Christ (particularly Blackstone's *Commentaries*), and their experiences under the hand of a despotic King George and a British government which abridged their "unalienable rights" at every turn.

Overview

We provide an overview of what our nation's Founding Fathers considered to be "what right looks like" before describing each component of model nation in detail.   Working from the bottom up:

- "Natural and Revealed Law of God" (referred to in the *Declaration* as "the Laws of Nature and of Nature's God) is evident in God's Natural Creation and His revelation to man as depicted in the Bible. This divine law provides the genesis and bedrock of our model nation.
- "Man's International and Municipal Law" which governs interactions between nation states (the "law of nations") and "Municipal Law" which governs interactions between individuals ("civil law"). The fundamental intent of these foundational layers is to restrain evil and promote good, as the primary role of government.
- "Government" defines the means by which our government makes, enforces, and interprets laws which derive from the underlying precepts of natural, revealed,

international, and civil law. It also describes the political processes critical to governance.

- "Life, Liberty, and the Pursuit of Happiness" represent the "unalienable rights" referenced in our *Declaration of Independence*. These are the primary governmental responsibilities on behalf of "We the People."

- "We the People" (first three words of the *Constitution*) are the actual "Sovereign" of the United States (as opposed to a Sovereign such as King George of England). Based on "Consent of the Governed" (*Declaration* wording), "We the People" grant authorities to government for the purposes previously stated, specifically "to effect their Safety and Happiness." (*Declaration* wording) They are the benefactors of then rest upon these fundamental liberties in a rich environment of culture, morality, and civilized society.

We now describe each element of "The Founder's Model," beginning with Biblical and Constitutional foundations derived from the "Natural Law of God," and ending with the role of "We the People."

The Founder's Model

God's Natural and Revealed Law

Neil Markva, the Northern Virginia lawyer and constitutional foundations expert identified in Chapter 1, mentored me regarding cultural issues from a Biblical perspective during my year in Washington, D.C. as a National Defense University student. In his *Our Christian Heritage* articles, he provides a useful description of our Biblical and Constitutional Foundations:

> "The men of the First Continental Congress are among those called the Founding Fathers or The Founders. On July 4, 1776, they unanimously published the words:

> *When in the course of human events, it becomes necessary for one people to dissolve the political bands which have connected them with another, and to assume among the powers of the earth, the separate and equal station to which the Laws of Nature and of Nature's God entitle them, a decent respect to the opinions of mankind requires that they should declare the causes which impel them to the separation.* (United States *Declaration of Independence*, underline added)

> "This first sentence of the American Declaration of Independence proclaims the unique embodiment of *The Law* above our nation's written laws. The Founder's appealed to the Laws of Nature and of Nature's God as the ultimate legal authority for doing two things: (1) to dissolve the political bands connecting *the people* of the United States of America with England, and (2) for *the people* of our nation to assume a separate and equal station among all the other powers of the earth.

Markva then quotes Blackstone to link directly to the Declaration's reference to "Laws of Nature and of Nature's God":

"Man, considered as a creature, <u>must necessarily be subject to the laws of his Creator</u>, for he is entirely a dependent being... As man depends absolutely upon his Maker for everything, it is necessary that he should in all points conform to his Maker's will. <u>This will of his Maker is called the law of nature</u>...

"When He created man, and endued him with freewill to conduct himself in all parts of life, He laid down <u>certain immutable laws of human nature</u>, whereby that <u>freewill is in some degree regulated and restrained</u>, and gave him also the <u>faculty of reason to discover the purport of those laws</u>.

"<u>This law of nature</u>, being co-eval with mankind (meaning created at the same time) and dictated by God himself, is of course <u>superior in obligation to any other</u>. It is binding over all the globe, in all countries, and at all times: no human laws are of any validity, if contrary to this; and such of them as are valid derive fall their force, and all their authority, mediately or immediately, from this original."

(Blackstone, Volume I, underlines and parentheses added)

To summarize thus far, we can see clearly that the Founders established "the laws of Nature and of Nature's God" as the ultimate legal authority in our nation. As a prime example of "the laws of Nature's God," consider Exodus, Chapter 20 (with elaborating verses omitted) where God passes *The Law* to the nation of Israel through their appointed leader Moses:

[3] "You shall have no other gods before Me.
[4] "You shall not make for yourself an idol...
[7] "You shall not take the name of the LORD your God in vain...
[8] "Remember the Sabbath day, to keep it holy.
[12] "Honor your father and your mother...
[13] "You shall not murder.
[14] "You shall not commit adultery.
[15] "You shall not steal.
[16] "You shall not bear false witness...
[17] "You shall not covet..."

Man is subject to these and other natural and revealed laws from God, and they are superior in obligation to any laws made by man. When governments or peoples fail to regard or uphold God's Natural or Revealed Law (such as the Ten Commandments above), they subject themselves to the consequences of violating God's established order.

Man's International and Municipal Law

International Law

Blackstone's *Commentaries, Volume I,* describe the rationale for a "Law of Nations" that is essentially what today we would call International Law. He states:

> "However, as it is impossible for the whole race of mankind to be united in one great society, they must <u>necessarily divide into many</u>; and form separate states, commonwealths, and nations; <u>entirely independent of each other and yet liable to a mutual intercourse</u>. Hence arises a third kind of law to regulate this mutual intercourse, called <u>"the law of nations;"</u> which, as none of these states will acknowledge a superiority in the other, cannot be dictated by either; but <u>depends entirely upon the rules of natural law, or upon mutual compacts, treaties, leagues, and agreements between these several communities</u>…" (underlines added)

While the purview of *Resilient Nations* does not allow a deep dive into the complexities of International Law, I offer the following: while there are some important precepts and judicial organizations to help govern relations between nations (for example: Law of War, Law of the Sea, International Criminal Court, United Nations' Tribunal for Rwanda, European Court, et cetera), <u>international law is inherently political</u>. As with national law, international law does not autonomously limit itself to minimum essential laws and regulatory requirements. It is inherently expansive, a dynamic which leads to the necessity for nations such as the United States to determine which international laws to embrace as responsible members of the community of nations and which international "laws" to not abide by because of their highly politicized agendas.

Wikipedia identifies two categories regarding the binding nature of international law (underlines added):

> "Much of international law is <u>consent-based governance</u>. This means that a state member of the international community is not obliged to abide by this type of international law, unless it has expressly consented to a particular course of conduct. This is an issue of state sovereignty. However, other aspects of international law are not consent-based but still are <u>obligatory upon state and non-state actors such as customary international law and peremptory norms (*jus cogens*)</u>."

Regarding these distinctions, the discretionary "consent-based governance" is keyed to <u>voluntary</u> agreements between nations, such as the Kyoto Protocol which addresses global environmental concerns. The latter, non-discretionary "customary international law" is generally rooted in "Natural Law," such as with the "Law of War" example which is based upon Biblical precept.

Over the last century there has been a proliferation of "consent-based" international legal venues and statutes that are often politically motivated. International Law is sometimes used to leverage nations into relegating national interests in order to conform to the desires of other nations. In recent United States' experience, the United Nations has become a vehicle through which lesser nations, peer competitors, and adversaries often unjustifiably "litigate" grievances about U.S. policies or actions. In the extreme case, these represent thinly veiled efforts to generate "wealth transfer" from richer to poorer nations, or to in some way diminish U.S. global power and influence. This is perhaps understandable, but the difficulty arises when U.S. leadership unwittingly sacrifices national sovereignty or resources in order to appease such international bodies. Although some of the goals are appropriate, the *Kyoto Protocol to the United Nations Framework Convention on Climate Change* is an example of such a highly politicized international accord. For example, the emission tariffs levied on industrialized nations which are used for investments in underdeveloped nations appear to be thinly veiled efforts to transfer wealth to the third world. In the unvarnished words of British website, www.answers.com, "This makes the Kyoto Protocol agreement nothing more than political rhetoric and a method of transferring billions to developing countries while allowing unmitigated increases in CO2."

For an example which is more directly related to "Natural Law" and Biblical precept, the customary (*jus cogens*) international "Law of War" is largely based upon work by Saint Augustine and Saint Thomas Aquinas in the 4th and 13th Centuries, respectively. The resulting "Just War Theory," a synthesis of Christian doctrine and political thought from the beginning of warfare, has been an important international legal construct, providing clarity for countries who seek to operate justly on the world stage and deterring countries and leaders who violate such international norms. These "Laws of War" have provided useful rationale for appropriate apprehension, trial, conviction, and punishment of numerous war crimes, genocide, and other crimes against humanity.

The albeit imperfect application of these rules of international conduct, whether of the voluntary "consent-governed" variety or the customary international laws derived directly from "Natural Law," is an essential means of regulating interactions between nations and a reality which must be factored into "model nation."

Municipal Law

Again using Blackstone's *Commentaries* as our basis:

> "...municipal or civil law, that is, <u>the rule by which</u> particular districts, communities, or nations are governed... MUNICIPAL law, thus understood, is properly defined to be 'a rule of civil conduct prescribed by the supreme power in a state commanding what is right and prohibiting what is wrong.'" (underline and all caps added)

> Summarizing Blackstone's lengthy and precise elaboration regarding Municipal Law, such rules to govern interactions between individuals within a community are not transient or specific to a particular person, but permanent, uniform, and universal. As well, such rules are more than mere suggestions and carry the power of law for the willing and unwilling alike.

In the course of *Resilient Nations*, we will discuss the specifics of numerous legislative policies which result in municipal law.

Government

"We the people of the United States, In order to form a more perfect Union, establish justice, insure domestic tranquility, provide for the common defence, promote the general welfare, and secure the blessings of liberty to ourselves and our posterity do ordain and establish this Constitution for the United States of America." *U.S. Constitution* Preamble

We now build upon our earlier discussion regarding the purpose and roles of government. One way in which Merriam-Webster defines "government" is "the continuous <u>exercise of authority over</u> and the performance of functions for a political unit." The act of governing includes the exercise of authority. A nation exercises this authority through the use of power. In Chapter 1, we referred to "elements of national power," one of which is Spiritual Infrastructure.

In the context of the Natural, Biblical, and Constitutional origins discussed earlier in this chapter, governmental power exercised within the constraints of God-granted authority is legitimate and serves God intended purpose of government. This is the type of government the Founders envisioned. Governmental power exercised independent of God-given authority becomes abusive, overreaching, and tyrannical.

Markva elaborates further on this relationship between authority and power:

> "The first principles of the American Constitutional Republic center around authority while raw power controls the operation of an Atheistic Socialist Republic. (Author's note: or a Theistic Totalitarian Republic) Authority centered in Almighty God was at the heart of the Founders' work and must be restored to the people. We must teach the difference between authority and power so that the fundamental principles of the American Constitutional Republic can once again prevail in our society."

"We must teach the difference between authority and power so that the fundamental principles of the American Constitutional Republic can once again prevail in our society."

The most fundamental safeguard against abuse of power by our government is that "We the People" understand the authority which is granted to their government and the limits of power which are prescribed.
It is extremely dangerous when the citizens of a free nation do not possess the knowledge or the interest to understand and perform their civic responsibilities.

Hearkening back to my own public school civics classes in Houston, Texas, in the early 1960s, I still recall some of the basic principles: constitutional republic, rule of law, representative government, limited government, three branches of government, separation of powers, enumerated powers, checks and balances, establishment clause (no law respecting an establishment of religion), free exercise clause (no law prohibiting the free exercise of religion), freedom of speech, right to bear arms, state's rights, along with other rights of "We the People" and other functions of government. As well, I was clearly taught about the Judeo-Christian origins of our government, and gained deep appreciation for our nation's founding documents and the "heroes" who crafted them. Overall, junior high students in those years were given extensive and largely unbiased instruction in civics. Ironically, as we will soon observe, the 1960s was also the decade in which the unraveling of our Spiritual Infrastructure accelerated greatly.

At later points in *Resilient Nations*, we will assess the degree to which our U.S. Government is adhering to their Constitutional authorities and limiting themselves to their enumerated powers.

We will "grade the paper" regarding whether our three branches of government are adhering to Constitutional division of labor. We will ask: "Is our U.S. government performing the roles and achieving the purposes for which it was established? Are our national and local governmental leaders serving selflessly or selfishly being served?"

We will find many points of departure from Constitutional intent, most of which are directly related to a weakened Spiritual Infrastructure.

The Unalienable Rights: Life, Liberty, and the Pursuit of Happiness

Neil Markva notes that the Founders recognized a "principle of creation authority" when they wrote the second sentence of the Declaration,

> "We hold these truths to be self-evident: that all men are created equal; that they are endowed, *by their Creator*, with certain *unalienable rights*; that among these are life, liberty, and the pursuit of happiness—That to secure these Rights, Governments are instituted among Men, deriving their just Powers from the Consent of the Governed." (emphasis added)

In short, the Creator (God) has given the Created (Man) certain unalienable rights. God has (also) given (man) authority or jurisdiction over various responsibilities to the primary governing agencies including the individual, the family, the church, and the state. One significant conclusion, therefore, is that God has given man authority to establish government (the state) in order to protect the unalienable rights which He granted to mankind.

> Therefore, the state exists to serve "We the People,"
> not vice versa. In essence, "We the People" are actually the
> Sovereign of our nation. This has immense implications
> when we consider the proper role of government
> in the lives of its citizens.

We should rightly ask "What does Life, Liberty, and Pursuit of Happiness mean?" Here are some of the fundamentals:

Life

While the Merriam-Webster definition of "life" refers primarily to "the quality that defines a vital and functional being," the connotations of "life" are far broader than this. Looking at human life, which is the primary focus of the declaratory right in our founding documents, life consists of the totality of human experience in the physical, mental, spiritual, emotional, and relational realms, directly corresponding to Christ's Great Commandment in Mark 12: 30, 31 to:

> "LOVE (HONOR, SERVE) THE LORD YOUR GOD WITH ALL YOUR HEART, AND WITH ALL YOUR SOUL, AND WITH ALL YOUR MIND, AND WITH ALL YOUR STRENGTH... [39]YOU SHALL LOVE YOUR NEIGHBOR AS YOURSELF." (capitalization and parenthetical emphasis added)

Christ's holistic reference to every dimension of human existence illustrates the breadth of this unalienable right.

The Declaration and the Constitution further support this broader definition, clearly implying that "life" refers to more than being alive or dead, but also conveys a <u>respect for life</u> which goes beyond mere existence to include minimum essential qualities of life. Hence, *Resilient Nations* will use the concept of respect for life across a variety of applications. Chapter 5, "Respecting LIFE," will include three primary categories: Respect for the Unborn, Respect for the Elderly, and Respect for the Traditional Family.

Liberty

Liberty, according to Merriam-Webster, is simply "the state or condition of people who are able to act and speak freely." Liberty is one of the most prized of human conditions, reminiscent of Patrick Henry's famous declaration, "Give me liberty, or give me death." This thirst for liberty was the driving force for the American revolutionaries who were driven from the arms of colonial England by growing threats to their religious, economic, and political freedoms. It was for this very liberty that the signers of the Declaration pledged their lives, their fortunes, and their sacred honor.

As a short aside, we all have pictures in our minds of similar acts of freedom-loving peoples. Perhaps you think of the young Chinese student in Tiananmen Square, bravely standing in front of the advancing tank. Or your remembrance might be of courageous protesters in Tahir Square in Cairo during the Arab Spring uprisings. Or soon the picture of courage may be for

Christian college students to confront liberal college faculty members regarding religious freedoms.

For me, I cannot help but recall the death-defying attempts to escape from behind the Iron Curtain. During the Cold War years, evening newscasts would often depict action videos of someone dashing towards freedom, risking everything... through the minefields, through the barbed wire, past the snarling dogs, into the very teeth of marksmen and machineguns on the Berlin Wall... all for the prospect of freedom. Many never made it, but their thirst for freedom drove them to try. They also sought Liberty, or Death.

Resilient Nations will use the concept of "freedom from" something, or similarly, "freedom of" something. Chapter 6, "Securing LIBERTY," will address Freedom from External and Internal Threats, Freedom from Government Intrusion, and Freedom of Religion.

The Pursuit of Happiness

The "pursuit of happiness" can be defined as "a fundamental right mentioned in the Declaration of Independence to freely pursue joy and live life in a way that makes you happy, as long as you don't do anything illegal or violate the rights of others."

Your first question might be why "pursuit of happiness" instead of just "happiness?" PURSUIT is an important first qualifier. Pursuit implies a running after, a seeking to obtain, a goal to be achieved, a degree of happiness to be obtained.

Defining this unalienable right as "pursuit of..." means that all Americans have the right to pursue their dreams, to pursue happiness.

PURSUIT also implies a degree of effort, industriousness, and commitment to work towards one's goals. This pursuit brings out the best in people. In a political sense, "pursuit of happiness" is a democratic term connoting "equality of opportunity" whereas "happiness" unqualified would be a socialist term connoting "equality of outcome." Such a guarantee of happiness which does not include personal responsibility brings out the worst in people.

> In a political sense, "pursuit of happiness" is a democratic term connoting "equality of opportunity"
> whereas "happiness" unqualified would be a socialist term connoting "equality of outcome."

The definition above also provides an important second qualifier. While LIFE, LIBERTY, AND PURSUIT OF HAPPINESS are unalienable rights, they are placed in the context of civic life (community). They must be qualified to ensure that the same unalienable rights of others in the community are not violated. In a Biblical sense, this might be described as the "law of love." Paul dealt with this issue when writing to the Galatians regarding their new found freedoms in Christ: "For you were called to freedom, brethren; only <u>do not turn your freedom into an opportunity for the flesh</u>, but <u>through love serve one another</u>." (underlines added)

While we will assess the implications later, I note here that Americans have radically departed from this Constitutional and Biblical principle of freedom exercised within the boundaries of love. Today the opposite is true. Interest groups with exclusionary agendas militantly demand their rights at the expense of all others. It is not sufficient for these groups to obtain the rights which they seek. Such advocacy groups also press to strip others of their unalienable rights. This "zero sum" approach to individual rights results in division among peoples, lack of civil discourse, a counterproductive focus on differences instead of shared goals, and civic toxicity which is unprecedented in America.

While the United States was once referred to as a "melting pot" of immigrants from diverse backgrounds who became the strongest and best nation on earth, we have degraded to a "boiling pot" of self-serving narcissists who insist upon their own rights at the expense of others. This was certainly not what the Founders intended when they emphasized the unalienable rights of "We the People."

While Chapter 5 on LIFE will discuss <u>minimum essential guarantees</u> to respect life, Chapter 7, "Pursuing Happiness," will address <u>maximum possible opportunities</u> to pursue and achieve individual and collective happiness. Specifically, we will address the Pursuit of a Better Future (Education), Pursuit of a Prosperous Future (Economy and Prosperity), and Pursuit of a Healthier Future (Healthcare Reform).

> While the United States was once referred to as a "melting pot" of immigrants from diverse backgrounds who became the strongest and best nation on earth, we have degraded to a "boiling pot" of self-serving narcissists who insist upon their own rights at the expense of others. This was certainly not what the Founders intended when they emphasized the unalienable rights of "We the People."

Serving the Sovereign: "We the People"

Directly establishing the sovereignty of "We the People," the latter part of the second sentence of the *Declaration* states:

> "That to secure these Rights, Governments are instituted among Men, deriving their just Powers <u>from the Consent of the Governed</u>..." (underline added)

Addressing our nation's current departure from this founding precept, Markva asserts:

> "The State has moved from the role of public servant responsive to **we the people** to that of public master feared by we the people. Unknowingly, we have exchanged the truth of God for a lie and now worship and serve the creature (the Humanistic/Atheistic State) rather than the Creator."

Resilient Nations will examine and validate this thesis in later chapters.

More fundamentally, what does "We the People" really mean?

As established earlier, "We the People" are collectively <u>the Sovereign of the United States</u>, referring back to the British King and to the principles of authority which we have discussed. "We the People" are <u>the Governed</u>, from which government derives its "just powers." "We the People" form <u>Society</u>, a community of individuals, which affords protection to all through the submission of all. "We the People" are <u>Patriots</u> who love, serve, and live in our country. Bill Bennett says it well in his introduction to *Our Country's Founders*:

> "Patriotism means love of country. How do we demonstrate our love of country? At the most basic level, we do so by voting with our feet—by remaining here in this country rather than living elsewhere. But there are more active ways to be a patriot. We stand for the national anthem. We obey the laws. We vote, and hold elective offices. We celebrate our national birthday, the Fourth of July, and throughout the year we observe other national holidays... And in times of war, Americans risk their lives to fight for their country and its ideals.
>
> "Another way for us to be patriotic is to learn about the deeds of the Founders. Without

knowledge about the men and women who fought for the establishment of this country and who formed our political institutions, it would be difficult for us to carry on the American experiment in self-government."

While such civics education of "We the People" (regarding the role and working of government, as well as the role of the citizen) is definitely part of our Spiritual Infrastructure and critical to the continuation of our Constitutional Republic, patriotic civic participation has in large measure given way to uninformed apathy. In a February 15, 2014, speech to the Union League Club in Chicago, Supreme Court Justice Antonin Scalia voiced the following concern about civic participation in today's America:

> "You know what I worry most about is... **the decline of the republican spirit**," Scalia said softly during a brief question-and-answer session.

> "It doesn't exist in our people with a vigor that used to exist. That's what **I'm most worried** about, that we're **going to become just another**, I don't know, another **undemocratic, politician-run state. Which our framers would never have supported**. That's why I think **education in democracy, education in republicanism,** is so important." (bolding added)

Clearly, Justice Scalia was not referring to the Republican Party, rather a "republican spirit" which manifests itself in active and informed exercise of civic responsibilities as a member of "We the People."

I add that a key role of "We the People" is the <u>selection of leaders to govern</u>. Although this role is most prominent at the ballot box at every level of government, "We the People" also place trust and confidence in leaders for every sector of society. Regarding this leader selection, Blackstone suggests minimum essential criteria:

> "... <u>in whose hands are the reins of government to be entrusted?</u>... In general, all mankind will agree that government should be reposed in such persons, in who those qualities are most likely to be found, <u>the perfection of which are among the attributes of him who is emphatically stiled the supreme being</u> (inferring that our leaders should possess Godly character); the three grand requisites, I mean, of <u>wisdom</u>, of <u>goodness</u>, and of <u>power</u>: wisdom, to discern the real interest of the community; goodness, to endeavor always to pursue that real interest, and strength, or power, to carry this knowledge and intention into actions. (underlines and parenthetical added)

While we will periodically touch on the critical role of leaders in *Resilient Nations*, I refer the reader to *Resilient Leaders* for an in-depth discussion of leaders who "selflessly serve over time from a platform of character and competence." That is the type of leaders that We the People deserve and desperately need.

Note also that the "model nation" includes a box within "We the People" which relates to CULTURE. The "Seven Mountains of Culture" (Arts, Business, Education, Family, Government, Media, and Religion) are the cultural terrain on which public and private sector activities either empower or impede the everyday lives of "We the People." These are the sectors of influence which represent primary "battlegrounds" on which our nation's Spiritual Infrastructure is most at risk.

Gaining Altitude: "A City on a Hill"

Over the last 150 years, there have been cultural change agents who swam upstream against the prevailing culture to bring about cultural transformation and reform. Some examples which readily come to mind are William Wilberforce (elimination of the slave trade and reform of manners in Britain), Susan B. Anthony (fighting for women's suffrage), Sojourner Truth (mobilizing others to eliminate slavery in America), Dietrich Bonhoeffer (resisting the Nazi regime and the complicity of the German Church), Martin Luther King, Jr. (fighting for racial equality), and a number of "culture warriors" from the 1960s forward who have worked incessantly to reverse the decline of American culture and morality (Bill Bennett, Merrill Oster, Jerry Falwell, Pat Robertson, Gary Bauer, Ralph Reed, David Barton, Mike Huckabee, Bill O'Reilly, Glen Beck, Tony Perkins, Mat Staver, Alan Sears, and others).

As well, a number of organizations have established culture change as a primary objective. Pinnacle Forum traces back to a small number of valiant men who had the vision and courage to develop and carry out a strategy to impact culture. These men were Bill Bright, founder of Campus Crusade for Christ, Loren Cunningham, founder of Youth with a Mission (YWAM), and Dr. Francis Schaeffer, founder of the L'Abri community. Each man independently (and providentially) envisioned seven components (later called mountains) of culture (listed in the previous section). They further postulated that the "pinnacle" of each cultural mountain was "influenced" by a small number of key leaders. Hence, the current Pinnacle Forum objective: to "Transform Leaders to Transform Culture." Merrill Oster, the founder of Pinnacle Forum, put the concept into practice, expanding the effort through many other faithful men and women seeking "to see God at the center of our culture." In particular, Os Hillman and Lance Wallnau have provided rich intellectual foundations for the efforts of Pinnacle Forum and similar organizations. Today, Pinnacle Forum is a nationwide organization having a positive impact on America's Spiritual Infrastructure via the Seven Mountains of Culture approach.

Now the real question is what about you, what about me? Are we operating within an existing movement to transform culture to the benefit of future generations? Are we "blooming where we are planted," providing positive influence in the mountain(s) of culture where we find ourselves? Similarly, are we listening to the Lord's promptings to craft our own vision to bring light and transformation to the cultural eclipses of our day? What is the noble cause that inspires our giftings, life experiences, vocational setting, and divine callings?

Then I heard the voice of the Lord, saying,
"Whom shall I send, and who will go for Us?"
Then I said, "Here am I. Send me!"
(Isaiah 6:8)

Resilient Nations Takeaways

RN 3A – As a brilliant and comprehensive synthesis of prior advancements in jurisprudence and the proper role of government (which was widely read and highly regarded in colonial America), Blackstone's body of legal theory and practice, totally consistent with natural and revealed law of God, was the blueprint upon which America's Founders relied as they sought to establish "a more perfect Union.

RN 3B – Understanding the philosophical and historical underpinnings of United States' law and government is essential to a proper interpretation of Constitutional and cultural issues and proper implementation of resulting policy. "Historical revisionism" in its simplest terms is the expedient omission or change of historical facts to fit a desired policy position.

RN 3C – Just as God's creation of the earth was an intentional and orderly masterpiece over which He granted man dominion, His establishment of three primary institutions (family, church, and state) to regulate the orderly affairs of men and nations was equally intentional.

RN 3D – God's intended role of government is to restrain evil and to promote righteousness while the complementary role of citizen includes submission and right living under the law of God and the law of man. This theme of subjugation to God-appointed government and leaders, as well as leaders and governments that ensure justice for the people, is replayed many times throughout the Old and New Testaments.

RN 3E – Thomas Paine rightly assessed that the nature of humanity requires a degree of external moderation. Government serves to restrain human vices, often necessitating the punishment of evil doers. This function of punishment is a necessary evil that should be administered at least cost and maximum benefit, implying a limited nature to government that avoids excessive intrusion or overreach into the lives of individuals, their communities, or their professional endeavors.

RN 3F – Man is subject to natural and revealed laws from God, and they are superior in obligation to any laws made by man. When governments or peoples fail to regard or uphold God's Natural or Revealed Law (such as the Ten Commandments), they subject themselves to the consequences of violating God's established order.

RN 3G – The albeit imperfect application of rules of international conduct, whether of the voluntary "consent-governed" variety or the customary international laws derived directly from "Natural Law," is an essential means of regulating interactions between nations and a reality which must be factored into "model nation."

RN 3H – Rules to govern interactions between individuals within a community, known as Municipal Law, are not transient or specific to a particular person, but permanent, uniform, and universal. As well, such rules are more than mere suggestions and carry the power of law for the willing and unwilling alike.

RN 3I – In the context of the Natural, Biblical, and Constitutional origins, governmental power exercised within the constraints of God-granted authority is legitimate and serves God's intended purpose of government. This is the type of government the Founders envisioned. Governmental power exercised beyond the bounds of God-given authority becomes abusive, overreaching, and tyrannical.

RN 3J – The most fundamental safeguard against abuse of power by our government is that "We the People" understand the authority which is granted to their government and the limits of power which are prescribed. It is extremely dangerous when the citizens of a free nation do not possess the knowledge or the interest to understand and perform their civic responsibilities.

RN 3K – The state exists to serve "We the People;" to secure for them Life, Liberty, and the Pursuit of Happiness. "We the People" are actually the Sovereign of our nation. This has immense implications when we consider the proper role of government in the lives of its citizens.

RN 3L – PURSUIT of Happiness implies a degree of effort, industriousness, and commitment to work towards one's goals. This pursuit brings out the best in people. In a political sense, "pursuit of happiness" is a democratic term connoting "equality of opportunity" whereas "happiness" unqualified would be a socialist term connoting "equality of outcome." Such a guarantee of happiness which does not include personal responsibility brings out the worst in people.

RN 3M – The "Seven Mountains of Culture" (Arts, Business, Education, Family, Government, Media, and Religion) are the cultural terrain on which public and private sector activities either empower or impede the everyday lives of "We the People." These are the sectors of influence which represent primary "battlegrounds" on which our nation's Spiritual Infrastructure is most at risk.

For Further Consideration

1. Further examine the concept of unalienable rights within the boundaries of love. How does a nation ensure such individual rights while maintaining national unity? How does a nation avoid the proliferation of militant rights groups who lay claim to their rights while depriving others of the same? What Biblical precepts might apply to this challenge?

2. When does a citizen determine that the government has so departed from its moral foundations that it is prudent and proper to actively resist? American revolutionaries had to wrestle with this dilemma, as did many others over the course of world history. How would you interpret the expression "one man's terrorist is another man's freedom fighter?"

Additional References

1. *Declaration of Independence.*
   http://www.archives.gov/exhibits/charters/declaration_tr
   anscript.html
2. *U.S .Constitution.*
   http://www.archives.gov/exhibits/charters/constitution.
   html
3. Blackstone, Commentaries of the Laws of England. Book
   The Fourth by Sir William Blackston, Knt; Printed by
   A. Straham, 1825.
4. Barton, David. *Original Intent.* Aledo, TX: Wallbuilders,
   Inc., 2005.
5. Beck, Glenn. *Glenn Beck's Common Sense.* New York, NY;
   Mercury Radio Arts/Threshold Editions, A Division of
   Simon & Schuster, Inc., 2009.
6. www.remnanttruth.blogspot.com, including some of Neil
   Markva's collected works.
7. Hillman, Os. *Change Agent.* Lake Mary, FL: Charisma
   House, 2011.
8. Pinnacle Forum. www.PinnacleForum.com.

4

National Historical Context:
The Rise and Fall of America

"We make men without chests and expect of them virtue and enterprise. We laugh at honor and are shocked to find traitors in our midst. We castrate and then bid the geldings be fruitful."
C.S. Lewis, *The Abolition of Man*

I recently received a simple prayer from a distinguished veteran, in this case a Korean War Veteran who suffered greatly on behalf of our nation, the South Korean nation, and his fellow soldiers. The cold was unbearable. The fighting was ferocious. The losses were horrendous. This veteran, and thousands like him over our nation's history, endured such hardship and bloodshed because they believed in America, in the values which America stands for. They relied upon the pillars of faith, family, and friends to help them have the courage to serve, and the courage to heal and become productive citizens of the greatest nation on earth. Today such veterans lament what they see in our country, what we highlight throughout the pages of *Resilient Nations*. Here is the "prayer worth a thousand words" this Korean War Veteran forwarded to me:

"Hi Lord, it's me.
We are getting older and things are getting bad here.
Gas prices are too high, no jobs, and food and heating costs too high.
I know some have taken you out of our schools, government, and even Christmas, but Lord I'm asking you to come back and re-bless America.
We really need you!
There are more of us who want you than those who don't!
Thank You Lord, I Love You."

In his simple way this veteran states the problem and he states the solution: Let us continue on our journey to give more definition to these problems of America today, as well as working toward solutions which include asking God to "come back and re-bless America."

In *Resilient Nations* we first introduced the concept of Spiritual Infrastructure, identifying ten critical subcomponents:

1. Adherence to Constitutional Foundations
2. Respect for the Rule of Law,
3. Retention of National History and Traditions
4. Basic Morality in Respect of God and Man
5. Healthy, Traditional Families as the Primary Building Blocks of Society

6. <u>Free Exercise and Relevance of Religion in Public and Private Venues</u>
7. <u>Unity, Diversity, and Civility</u>
8. <u>Moral and Practical Education of our Youth</u>
9. <u>Industrious, Resilient, and Engaged Citizenry</u>
10. <u>Spirit of Philanthropy and Volunteerism</u>

Using this Spiritual Infrastructure construct, we identified America as a resilient nation for over two hundred years, identifying relevant national events and resilient responses from 1740 to 1960. As a reminder, our U.S. timeline began in 1740 to reflect the Spiritual Infrastructure of that time which was so relevant to the Revolutionary Period and the formal establishment of our nation in 1776.

We then stepped back in time to view a global historical context regarding the rise and fall of nations. In particular we highlighted the fall of Rome and identified some "common denominators of decline." Similarly, we highlighted the history of Israel as a resilient nation and identified some "common denominators of national resilience." We saw that the Resilience Life Cycle© concept used in *Resilient Warriors* and *Resilient Leaders* is equally relevant when applied to the life of nations.

As a final stage setter, we identified God's design for nations, and then constructed "Model Nation" based upon God's natural and revealed law, and man's application of these fundamental Biblical concepts to a corresponding system of government. We demonstrated how America's Founders relied upon these precepts to shape our *Declaration of Independence* and our

United States Constitution, including the "unalienable rights" of Life, Liberty, and the Pursuit of Happiness. As well, we identified the type of "Statesmen" needed to lead the government in service of "We the People."

Now we apply these constructs to contemporary America, looking forward from the pivotal decade of the 1960s. The Book of Psalms questions:

> "If the foundations are destroyed,
> what can the righteous do?"
> (Psalm 11:3)

This is a legitimate question for all Americans, for "We the People," in these early years of the 21st Century. Ultimately in *Resilient Nations* (Chapters 5-9) we will wrestle mightily with this most critically important question: "...what can the righteous do?"

This Chapter 4, however, will first address the premise "If the foundations are destroyed." Some of our findings will be alarming, portending threat to the very existence of this nation, and most certainly predictive of a future way of life that we would not wish upon our children or grandchildren.

The Decline Becomes Apparent: 1960 - 2001

In stark contrast to the general trend of the United States' resilience from the 1700s forward (as depicted in Chapter 1), observe the precipitous decline which began in the 1960s.

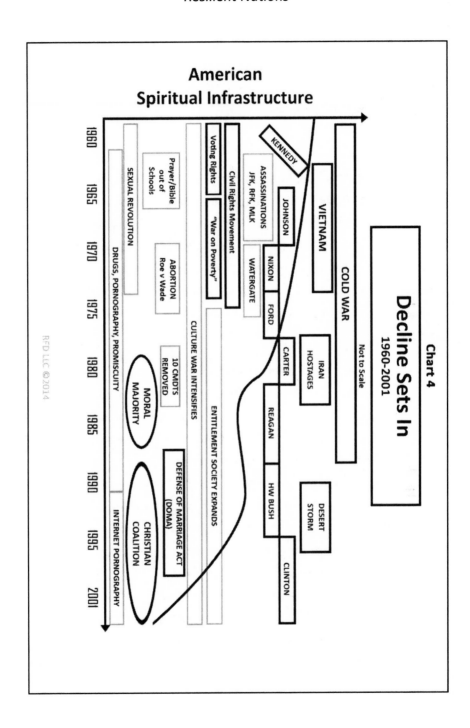

American
Spiritual Infrastructure

Chart 4

Decline Sets In
1960-2001

Not to Scale

1960   1965   1970   1975   1980   1985   1990   1995   2001

SEXUAL REVOLUTION

Prayer/Bible out of Schools

Voting Rights

Civil Rights Movement

"War on Poverty"

KENNEDY

ASSASSINATIONS
JFK, RFK, MLK

JOHNSON

VIETNAM

COLD WAR

DRUGS, PORNOGRAPHY, PROMISCUITY

ABORTION
Roe v Wade

NIXON

WATERGATE

FORD

CULTURE WAR INTENSIFIES

ENTITLEMENT SOCIETY EXPANDS

10 CMDTS REMOVED

MORAL MAJORITY

CARTER

IRAN HOSTAGES

REAGAN

DESERT STORM

HW BUSH

DEFENSE OF MARRIAGE ACT (DOMA)

CHRISTIAN COALITION

INTERNET PORNOGRAPHY

CLINTON

RFD LLC ©2014

Chart 4, *Decline Sets In 1960-2001* anecdotally tracks events which impacted Spiritual Infrastructure from 1960 to 2001. Detailed specifics related to many of the events are left for the reader's further investigation, but the causalities and trendlines are unmistakable.

Note that this decline starting in the 1960s is real, not contrived. Although the causative factors are numerous, it is indisputable that national morality, national will, national morale, national spirit of personal sacrifice, the strength of American families, and other elements of Spiritual Infrastructure all began a downward spiral during the 1960s. In *The De-Valuing of America*, William Bennett terms the period since the '60s "cultural warfare":

> *"The battle over culture reaches beyond art, music, poetry, photography, literature, cinema, and drama. The broader issue has to do with a growing realization that over the last twenty years or so the traditional values of the American people have come under steady fire, with the heavy artillery supplied by intellectuals. This all-out assault has taken its toll. In our time, too many Americans became either embarrassed, unwilling, or unable to explain with assurance to our children and to one another the difference between right and wrong, between what is helpful and what is destructive, what is ennobling and what is degrading. The fabric of support that the American people—families*

especially—could traditionally find in the culture at large became worn, torn, and unraveled.

Bennett continues by describing how these culture wars, largely fomented by intellectuals and liberal elites, who disdain fundamental American beliefs, impacted the psyche of the majority of God-fearing, patriotic Americans:

> *"In this period, many of us lost confidence in our right and our duty to affirm publicly the desirability of what most of us believe privately. As a result, we suffered a cultural breakdown of sorts – in areas like education, family life, crime, and drug use, as well as in our attitudes toward sex, individual responsibility, civic duty, and public service."*

First, a rapid fire rendition of the tumultuous 1960s in America, particularly for the benefit of those who did not live through them:

The decade quickly turned tragic for America. President John F. Kennedy assassinated. U.S. Senator and Presidential Candidate Bobby Kennedy assassinated. A lingering Vietnam War fought far away (except for its nightly presence on TV in American living rooms) with unclear national objectives and wavering commitment which resulted in loss of over 68,000 Americans and many more wounded physically and mentally for a lifetime. This war, ended in the early 1970s, left a gash in our national psyche which exists to this very day, along with tens of thousands of homeless Vietnam veterans under the bridges of America (roughly one third of America's total homeless population). The

Cuban Missile Crisis was but one indicator of a deepening Cold War fostered by Communist Totalitarians (especially the Soviet Union) and an Iron Curtain which became deeply rooted across Eastern Europe at the expense of freedom for millions.

The nation's century-old black civil rights struggle heated to a boiling point, progressing from non-violent marches and sit-in movements in Southern states, to urban rioting across the nation and the assassination of Reverend Martin Luther King, Jr., to the beginnings of a "black power" movement. While the Civil Rights Act and the Voting Rights Act represented significant legislative progress toward racial equality, the reality of deep-seated racial enmity (and poverty) could not be simply swept away by well-intended legislation. While progress continues to be made, the deep scars from this decade of racial strife remain evident to this day, analogous to the scars of Vietnam.

A sexual revolution combusted in America, fueled by drugs, birth control pills, and changing views of morality and authority. This resulted in unprecedented private and public promiscuity which struck to the very foundations of traditional marriage and family, soft pornography which grew into a hard-core and unrelenting master of millions across all sectors of society, and sexual perversion which today has ballooned to unforeseen proportions. To accommodate the nation's unbridled sexual appetite and the resulting outcomes, we justified the murder of millions of unborn babies each year (formalized by *Roe v. Wade* in 1973), all in the name of "choice" which was really a method of "convenience." Human life became cheaper. A culture of violence was birthed, even as birthing babies were being killed.

Humanist philosophies and secular progressive agendas which had been fomenting for decades began to have detrimental impacts on American life, such as when the long-standing religious practice of prayer in schools (*Engel v. Vitale*, 1962) was struck down by the courts.

"Great Society" welfare programs under the Democratic Johnson Administration instituted massive federal expenditures to help "the least among us." While perhaps well-intended and needed temporarily by many of the recipients, the unbridled Government largesse soon foist structural dependency among the poorest of Americans, feeding their human frailty for accepting handouts, eating away at their work ethic, tearing the fabric of their families, encouraging personal and public corruption, and creating a permanent welfare class in America. As well, these programs created expectations, primarily among the black community, that resulted in added frustration when conditions did not substantively change. Given these negative unintended consequences, this "War on Poverty" can be considered a failed social experiment.

Overall, this decade of the 1960s truly was tumultuous, in every sense. Fundamental values and standards of behavior were called into question like never before. Distrust in the government grew. A decade-long war with conscription forces greatly depleted national resources and manpower, fomented a strong anti-war movement, and resulted in blatant disrespect and antagonism toward fellow Americans (U.S. military personnel) involved in Vietnam. A revolutionary spirit abounded. Unlike the noble motives of 1776 revolutionaries, 1960-style revolutionaries cast off the bonds of civility, responsibility, morality, and national unity. This truly was a period of time when a vast number of Americans "did what was right in their own eyes." (Judges 17:6)

The 1970s represented a nation hung-over from the tumultuous 1960s. As mentioned, *Roe v. Wade*, a tragic decision by the U.S. Supreme Court, legalized abortion in the first six months of pregnancy. Distrust of government was reinforced by Vice President Spiro Agnew's resignation for tax evasion, soon followed by President Nixon's resignation under the likelihood of impeachment due to Watergate. Reaping seeds which had been sown in the 1960s, cultural indicators (as captured by Bill Bennett in *The Index of Leading Cultural Indicators*) all accelerated in the wrong direction: total crimes, violent crimes, murders committed by juveniles (particularly black males), drug use, illegitimate births, single-parent families, divorce rates, children involved in divorces, abortions, teenage suicide, rising education expenditures with plummeting student performance on Scholastic Aptitude Test (SAT) tests, rising welfare expenditures as poverty continued to rise, and many others. Energy dependence surfaced as a very real internal and external security issue with the 1973 Arab Oil Embargo. While President Nixon began the decade with significant foreign policy inroads with both China and Russia to reduce threats to world peace, President Jimmy Carter ended the decade with greatly reduced military expenditures and amnesty to Vietnam draft dodgers, creating real and perceived weakness toward growing world threats, culminating with the Iran Hostage Crisis beginning in November 1979, a failed rescue attempt (Desert One) in April 1980 (which was perhaps the first operation in what would become known as the Global War on Terror), and a Soviet wheat embargo and Summer Olympic boycott to counter their occupation of Afghanistan. Declines in the components of U.S. National power, to include Spiritual Infrastructure, were tangible and serious. U.S. morale and morality sank to new lows.

The 1980s have been termed by many as the "Reagan Revolution." Beginning with very high unemployment and high taxation from the Carter years, application of free market economic principles and sharp reduction in taxation allowed the decade to end positively with high economic growth and low unemployment. The malaise of the 1970s soon turned to relative optimism and national pride in the 1980s, symbolized by the "Miracle on Ice" (United States' men's hockey victory over the Soviet Union in the Olympic Games in Lake Placid, New York on February 22, 1980), release of the Iranian hostages after 454 days (notably just hours after the Reagan inauguration in January 1981), the U.S. military's successful rescue of students held prisoner by Marxists on the island of Grenada, continued gains in space and technology overall (particularly computers), and fostered ultimately by President Reagan's "The Best Is Yet to Come" confidence in America that was contagious and uplifting. On the downside, the Iran-Contra crisis highlighted a lack of governmental transparency and submission to Congressional oversight. The decade saw Global War on Terror worsen with the tragic loss of 241 Marines in the Lebanon barracks bombing in October 1983. The Supreme Court (*Stone v. Graham*, 1980) stripped the Ten Commandments out of U.S. public schools, one of many such efforts to remove religion from the public square. Given the import of this decision, let us do a brief excursion:

The majority opinion to deprive our nation's students of long-standing, visible, moral, and spiritual instruction on the walls of our public schools included the following:

> "...If the posted copies of the Ten Commandments are to have any effect at all, it will be to <u>induce the schoolchildren to read, meditate upon, perhaps to venerate and obey, the Commandments</u>. However desirable this might be as a matter of private devotion, it is <u>not a permissible state objective</u> under the Establishment Clause of the Constitution."

At best, this decision was "penny wise and pound foolish." Which of the Ten Commandments would we <u>not</u> want the school children of our land to "venerate and obey?" The Founder's intent certainly included such faith-based morality as a "permissible state objective..."; actually, they considered it essential to the operation of a democratic society. The minority opinion written by Justice William Rehnquist supported this sentiment:

> "<u>The Establishment Clause does not require that the public sector be insulated from all things which may have a religious significance or origin</u> . . . Kentucky has decided to make students aware of this fact by demonstrating the secular impact of the Ten Commandments."

Certainly high-profile Supreme Court decisions such as above have a deleterious impact on our nation's Spiritual Infrastructure, but activist federal judges which operate across the nation have an even greater impact. Representing "death by a thousand cuts," these judges (particularly those extremely liberal federal judges appointed by Presidents Carter, Clinton, and Obama) frequently support special interest groups to boldly redefine and suppress freedom of religion, gun ownership rights, and other fundamental Constitutional rights afforded to "We the People." We will discuss this further in our "unalienable rights" discussion in Chapters 5-7.

As the 1980s came to a close, the fall of the Berlin Wall and dissolution of the Soviet Union was a fitting triumph for President Reagan's "deterrence through strength" approach to national security, winning the Cold War without a major conflagration.

Now we review the period of the 1990s to America's Second "Day of Infamy" (mirroring President Roosevelt's reference to Pearl Harbor on December 7, 1941) at the Twin Towers on September 11, 2001.

With the exception of the one term Presidency of George H.W. Bush from 1989 to 1993 (notable for success in the 1990-1991 Desert Shield/Storm operation to remove Saddam Hussein from Kuwait, and for failure to keep his "read my lips, no new taxes" pledge), this decade was basically the Clinton era. While the decade was generally economically prosperous, there were numerous storm clouds hovering over America. Internally, the culture wars continued while financial corruption, savings and loan scandals, and immorality and deception in the White House

(Monica Lewinsky) reared their ugly heads. Television and the internet became increasingly toxic, with the ribald and crude *Simpsons* replacing the *Flintstones* and internet pornography becoming pervasive and addictive. The 1994 Republican landslide mid-term victory (ensuring a Republican-led House of Representatives for the first time in forty years) and frenetic execution of the promised Contract with America (orchestrated by Speaker Newt Gingrich) did not achieve its full potential largely because of ethics accusations directed at the Speaker, and because of the political prowess of President Bill Clinton. Parenthetically, mid-term elections in 2014 possess similar potential for a resurgence of limited government, fiscal conservatism, strong defense, and pro-growth policies.

Externally, a rapid succession of military interventions in Haiti, Panama, and Kuwait (in response to Saddam Hussein's blatant invasion) demonstrated that America had truly achieved unmatched military capability and joint service cooperation (primarily due to Reagan's defense buildup and the Goldwater-Nichols Act of 1986). With the demise of the Soviet Union and the Cold War stasis broken, the United States found itself the world's only remaining superpower with new global responsibilities and a new target on its back. Terrorism, both domestic and global, continued to grow as a primary threat to U.S. security: World Trade Center bombing (1993), Oklahoma City bombing (1995), Khobar Towers bombing of U.S Air Force personnel in Saudi Arabia (1996), the bombing of three U.S. Embassies in Africa (1998), the bombing of the USS Cole (2000, just eleven months before the Twin Towers attack on September 11, 2001), and the emergence of Usama Bin Laden (UBL) as the primary leader of a radical Islamist worldwide terror network. "Y2K" (the concern that embedded software around the globe would not successfully accommodate years beyond 1999) became a non-event at the stroke of midnight on December 31, 1999, but heightened global awareness of cyber threats which would loom larger every year as potential weapons of mass destruction.

America ended this era with a new President (former Texas Governor George W. Bush in a tightly contested and disputed victory over Democratic contender Vice President Al Gore) and a calm before the storm, one which would soon strike to the heart of America's financial center and the heart of all Americans.

The Decline Accelerates: 2001 – 2014

Chart 5 on the next page, *Decline Accelerates 2001-2014*, depicts the next era of discussion, ranging from 2001 to the present (2014).

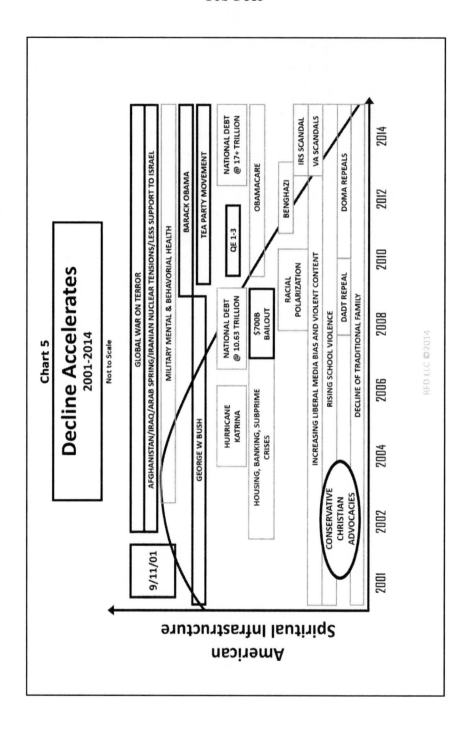

Chart 5

Decline Accelerates
2001-2014

Not to Scale

American Spiritual Infrastructure

9/11/01 · GLOBAL WAR ON TERROR · AFGHANISTAN/IRAQ/ARAB SPRING/IRANIAN NUCLEAR TENSIONS/LESS SUPPORT TO ISRAEL · MILITARY MENTAL & BEHAVORIAL HEALTH · BARACK OBAMA · TEA PARTY MOVEMENT · NATIONAL DEBT @ 17+ TRILLION · QE 1-3 · OBAMACARE · BENGHAZI · IRS SCANDAL · VA SCANDALS · DOMA REPEALS · GEORGE W BUSH · HURRICANE KATRINA · HOUSING, BANKING, SUBPRIME CRISES · NATIONAL DEBT @ 10.63 TRILLION · $700B BAILOUT · RACIAL POLARIZATION · INCREASING LIBERAL MEDIA BIAS AND VIOLENT CONTENT · RISING SCHOOL VIOLENCE · DADT REPEAL · DECLINE OF TRADITIONAL FAMILY · CONSERVATIVE CHRISTIAN ADVOCACIES

2001 2002 2004 2006 2008 2010 2012 2014

RFD LLC ©2014

148

The Bush Years

We all remember where we were on September 11, 2001 (9/11). You, no doubt, have your own searing memories. The human tragedy was overwhelming. The loss and serious injury of each family member, each coworker, and each neighbor struck deeply into the heart and soul of every American.

The new national "normal" was keyed to suspicion, prevention, and retribution in order to deter future attacks. The political, economic, social, and military impacts were also enormous.

On that now infamous day, I was huddled in Heidelberg, Germany, with the collective leadership of the Fifth U.S. Corps (V Corps) for a strategic offsite and leader development event. The first note reporting that a plane had hit the World Trade Center was passed to me by one of the Corps battle staff monitoring a news channel in an adjacent room. I passed the note along to Lieutenant General Scott Wallace (V Corps Commander at the time, and later Commander of the main effort in Operation Iraqi Freedom, followed by his four-star command of the U.S. Army Training and Doctrine Command), receiving a quiet nod very similar to the one by President George W. Bush as he read to an unsuspecting class of Florida children. With a second note came the realization that America was under attack. The V Corps immediately shifted gears to continuous vigilance, planning, and eventual execution of the initial assault into Iraq, followed by numerous rotations back to Iraq and Afghanistan over the next decade of war. After this day, V Corps was never the same, with many valiant soldiers paying the ultimate sacrifice to protect the home front. After this day, America was never the same, either.

Maintaining our focus on Spiritual Infrastructure, the 9/11 tragedy brought out the best in most Americans. National unity and commitment were at an all-time high. Communities drew together in candlelight vigils, prayer, and compassionate outreach for those with the most serious losses. Places of worship were overflowing. Police, Fire, and Rescue units from all around the country rushed to Ground Zero to help, inspired by the example of their fallen comrades. President George W. Bush, a war president from the very beginning, modeled leadership *in extremis*, galvanizing national will, and driving unprecedented integration of national resources to address the national security crisis. The goodness of America stood in stark contrast to the dark evil behind the insidious attacks.

As the embers of the World Trade Center cooled, so did the united clarity with which Americans had faced tragedy. All too soon, partisan bickering returned to the halls of Congress and the streets of America. Prayers to God quickly turned into special interest petitions. Among a number of economic harbingers, the granting of subprime mortgages to the underprivileged continued to address social welfare agendas, but undermined future economic security. While wartime funding increased government expenditures, the national debt grew disproportionately, uncharacteristic of a Republican administration. To their credit, the Bush administration remained doggedly and necessarily fixed on avoiding future such attacks by all means possible. This included preventive incursions into Afghanistan and Iraq, establishment of the USA Patriot Act (standing for *Uniting and Strengthening America by Providing Appropriate Tools Required to Intercept and Obstruct Terrorism*), and by reinvesting in the FBI and a new Department of Homeland Security. Gratefully, many subsequent terrorist plots were thwarted. The homeland remained safe, at least from external attacks. The wars in Iraq and Afghanistan increasingly taxed the resources, focus, and patience of a war-weary public. All the while, social media etched deeper into the psyche and relational patterns of the next generation, helping a charismatic, albeit inexperienced Presidential candidate capture the affections of a restless electorate.

The Obama Years

The erosion of America's Spiritual Infrastructure since the tumultuous 1960s is alarming in itself, but pales in comparison to the disastrous and swift Spiritual Infrastructure impacts resulting from just five short years of the Obama Administration. It is evident that a radical paradigm shift took place upon the election of President Barack Obama in 2008.

Let me revert to military terminology for a moment. The Germans have a term called *auftragstaktik* which refers to missions executed in accord with the "commander's intent." In their eyes, and consistent with U.S. military doctrine, a commander cannot prepare for every contingency on the battlefield, but should equip his subordinate leaders and formations with "intent" which guides their actions in the absence of specific orders. Hence, a leader's intent is far more relevant than his particular directives in a specific situation. The same applies to assessment of our current Administration. Does the Obama Administration intend to pursue a democratic process (albeit under the Democratic Party's umbrella of big government, expanding entitlements, pro-Union, et al) that aspires to govern better and uplift the American people, OR does it intend to fundamentally change the United States as President Obama said he would do, into a radically different form of government where socialistic tendencies have become unadulterated fact.

> ...a leader's intent is far more relevant than his particular directives in a specific situation.

President Obama's intent has become very clear. His popular mantra of "Hope and Change" has been clearly revealed to mean "hope in the government" and "change into a centralized machine which exercises control over every sector of American society." Unless you have been held captive in a liberal mainstream media bubble, you can probably recite President Obama's background as a devotee of anti-establishment activist Saul Alinsky (author of *Rules for Radicals)* as a Chicago community organizer who operated by those rules, as a lawyer for verifiably corrupt ACORN, as a willing consumer of Reverend Jeremiah Wright's anti-American vitriol for many years, and as an inexperienced U.S. Senator of less than three and a half years (with at least two of those spent campaigning for President) who was swept to the Presidency in the supportive arms of an adoring constituency and an equally adoring and unquestioning media. This background gives insight into the President's political, philosophical and ethical leanings, but his actions (and the actions of the Administration which carries out his intent) over the past five years clearly indicate that revolutionary change is the intent, and true hope in an improved American way of life is the victim.

While we will dive into specific policy issues in Chapters 5-7, consider the following supportable topline conclusions derived from my personal observation over the last five years. Former Speaker Newt Gingrich's book *To Save America*, as well as Jim Johnson's *Fracture Zone 2015*, listed in "Additional References" at the end of this chapter, provide useful data in support of these conclusions.

- **Partisanship and Divisiveness** Despite campaigning as a "Uniter in Chief," President Obama has been a divisive President, on the political front and on the social front. Politically, he is not inclined to engage with opposition leaders to gain mutual under-standing or compromise solutions, rather choosing inflammatory rhetoric at every turn. A most recent example in 2014 is the President's open declaration to use "the pen and the phone," seeking to flank duly constituted law and the will of "We the People" through their duly elected Congressional representatives. On the social front, he often fans the flames of class warfare and generates racial animosity (or affords the "civil rights industry" free rein to deepen racial hatred and suspicion) to garner popular support. While a serious and tragic incident, the President of the United States is counterproductive when he puts "more spin on the ball" by providing tactical commentary on the investigation of Trayvon Martin's death, particularly when in contrast to remaining silent on so many other issues of strategic importance that do merit his comments.

- **Economic Security** Incursion of national debt has taken on moral proportions. (The accrued national debt has more than doubled under Obama, and exceeds the national debt accrued by all other U.S. Presidents in history, saddling future generations with the bill.) This Administration has continued to grow already unsustainable entitlement programs and make unprecedented accommodations to special interest groups related to energy, healthcare, climate, gay rights, and others, suppressing economic growth and job creation. Unemployment, chronically high and even more problematic within certain demographics (particularly young black males), has grown demonstrably worse, despite Administration efforts to "spin" and change metrics midstride.

- **Health Care** Efforts to establish government-controlled universal health care (comprising one sixth of the U.S. Economy) have been disastrous, both in concept and in execution. This hole gets deeper and deeper, with every broken promise and executive order band aid applied to a terminal program. I discuss this more in Chapter 7.

- **Censorship** A mainstream media complicit with Obama Administration narratives, combined with specific suppression of conservative reporters who contest the party line. One well known example is James Rosen of FOX News who was subjected to State Department subpoenas as result of his reporting of a leak investigation.

- **War on Christians** It seems every day there is a new decision by a liberal activist judge in some state of the Union directing someone to take down that Cross, provide abortive care to your employees (despite your religious convictions), or offer services to same-sex couples in violation of your personal faith. The religious freedom pot is certainly boiling, and the predominant faith group getting scalded is Christianity, as in so many other regions of the world. There are certainly peace-loving Muslims, as well as other religions and "non-religions" in America, but isn't it ironic that the Obama Administration has been treating Muslims and atheists with kid gloves and Christians with an iron fist? In Chapter 6, we will discuss the "Devolution of Religion in America" which has greatly accelerated over the past five years.

- **Corruption** Some of the most notable examples of fraud in the Obama Administration include: ACORN Voter Fraud in the 2008 election that Attorney General Eric Holder refused to pursue, inability to account for billions in stimulus money, strong arming of bank officials to accept bailout money in order to gain greater control over bank assets, IRS targeting of conservative groups for political purposes, "sweetheart" government funding to government cronies, particularly to economically unviable companies like Solyndra.

- **Climate Change** Despite President Obama (State of Union speech in 2010 and more recently), Secretary of State John Kerry, and others declaring that "global warming is a scientifically settled argument," the Obama Administration cannot by fiat overrule what remains a very open question. Read Chapter 8 in *To Save America* for an in-depth discussion of the manipulation of scientific data which corrupted the U.N. Intergovernmental Panel on Climate Change (IPCC) report and other climate studies seminal to major national and international environmental policy decisions. While environmental stewardship is important, the "climate change industry" has become a political tool which this Obama Administration uses to gain greater control of its citizens, higher taxation of its businesses, and more pandering to special interests constituencies. As a final note, even if global warming were actually the threat postulated, green energy technologies are not adequate to address more than a small percentage of near-term energy demands. We need a realistic, comprehensive, long-term national energy strategy, one which would integrate energy benefits such as offered by the Keystone Pipeline, despite passionate (albeit unfounded) protestations by the Sierra Club and others.

- **War on Terror** The Obama Administration's deference to the Muslim community (to include radical elements seeking to destroy America) has been unwittingly misguided, or possibly worse, wittingly complicit. Consider the release of known terrorists from Guantanamo who later appeared in Afghanistan to kill more Americans, or the Justice Department's acceptance on staff of nine lawyers who actively defended Islamic terrorists, or the elimination of term "Global War on Terror" to protect Muslim sensibilities, or the dogged persistence that an inflammatory video was the real reason behind the killing of our U.S. Ambassador in Benghazi on September 11,

2012, or the fact that this is the first U.S. Administration to pursue such anti-Israeli rhetoric and policies. The killing of Usama Bin Laden has long since paled in light of the broader script.

- **Foreign Policy** The Obama Administration has been inept in foreign policy. With an "Apology Tour" as an opening statement to the World Community, President Obama has consistently denied "American exceptionalism" and portrayed weakness, ranging from the Global War on Terror incongruities listed above, to withdrawal of planned missile defense protection in Poland and the Czech Republic, to inept protest of Syrian atrocities by the Assad regime, to unwillingness to confront Iran regarding development of nuclear weapons, to clearly being outmaneuvered and outmanned by a defiant President Putin in the drama in Crimea during 2014.

While this could be a never ending litany, let me conclude this summary of the Obama years (at least through time of *Resilient Nations'* publication) with an excerpt from *To Save America* by Newt Gingrich. Maintaining that "the Left cannot tell the American people the truth about their goals and the way they operate," Gingrich queries what the American people would do if Harry Reid and Nancy Pelosi had been transparent in 2008 about their true intent:

"We are going to pass a $787 billion spending bill that no member of Congress had time to read, explode the deficit to unsustainable levels, seize control of private car companies, push for a massive energy tax, socialize the health system, sign an enormous number of earmarks, negotiate in secret with senators whom we will bribe to vote for a health bill their constituents oppose, and give the Environmental Protection Agency massive bureaucratic power to intimidate American businesses while dictating pay and bonus policy to dozens of companies. Oh, and our Justice Department will consistently favor protecting the rights of terrorists over the lives of Americans."

"We the People" would not have believed, and certainly not supported the magnitude and direction of these changes. They really did happen, however. Elections have consequences, and the 2008 trifecta of Obama, Reid, and Pelosi brought us disastrous consequences.

It is clear at this point that all but the most virulent Democrats (among them current House Speaker Nancy Pelosi and Senate Majority Leader Harry Reid), or the most ardent "Obamacrats" (including much of the main-stream media) recognize that the Obama Presidency has not headed America in the right direction and has not governed well.

Although many have characterized some of the actions referenced above as "impeachable," the realistic way ahead is that "We the People" make the 2014 mid-term elections a mandate on the failed policies of the Obama Administration, select principled "Statesmen" to replace self-seeking "Politicians," garner a united Republican majority in both Houses of Congress to redress some of the damage of the past five years, and set the conditions for election of a new President and an Administration that represent traditional American values in 2016. In addition to "stopping the bleeding" through the power of the ballot, *Resilient Nations* will prescribe specific mandates for "We the People," "We the Church," and "We the Statesmen" in Chapter 8 which will help us recover our true greatness as a nation.

We have now completed our overview of American history to the present, 1740 to 2014. Chart 6, *Macro Trendlines 1740-2014* depicts the aggregated Spiritual Infrastructure timelines to put the eras discussed into overall perspective. Note the summary comment on Chart 6 extracted from our initial *Resilient Nations* thesis (Chapter 1): "A critical assessment reveals that America's Spiritual Infrastructure is nearing bankruptcy. This constitutes a national security crisis."

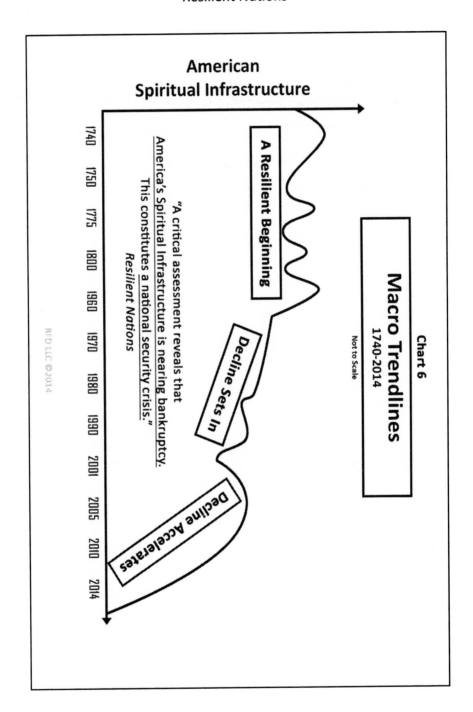

American
Spiritual Infrastructure

Macro Trendlines
1740-2014

Chart 6

Not to Scale

A Resilient Beginning

Decline Sets In

Decline Accelerates

"A critical assessment reveals that
America's Spiritual Infrastructure is nearing bankruptcy.
This constitutes a national security crisis."
Resilient Nations

1740 1750 1775 1800 1960 1970 1980 1990 2001 2005 2010 2014

RED LLC ©2014

Government "Gone Wild"

Before considering the options ahead for America, let us contrast "Model Nation" with something we will call Government "Gone Wild." (Chart 7, *Government "Gone Wild"* on next page)

While our current government overreach into every area of American's public and private lives does not match this model yet, it is certainly on the near horizon unless we make course corrections now.

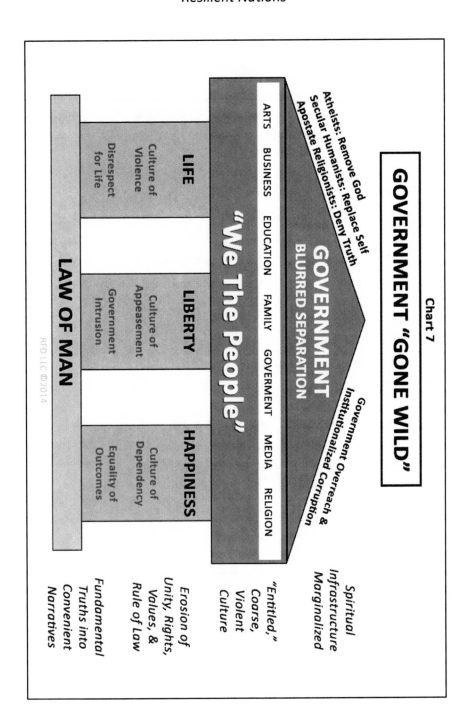

Chart 7

GOVERNMENT "GONE WILD"

Atheists: Remove God
Secular Humanists: Replace Self
Apostate Religionists: Deny Truth

ARTS BUSINESS EDUCATION FAMILY GOVERMENT MEDIA RELIGION

GOVERNMENT
BLURRED SEPARATION

"We The People"

LIFE
- Culture of Violence
- Disrespect for Life

LIBERTY
- Culture of Appeasement
- Government Intrusion

HAPPINESS
- Culture of Dependency
- Equality of Outcomes

LAW OF MAN

Government Overreach
Institutionalized Corruption

Spiritual Infrastructure Marginalized

"Entitled," Coarse, Violent Culture

Erosion of Unity, Rights, Values, & Rule of Law

Fundamental Truths into Convenient Narratives

RFD LLC ©2014

God's Law has been removed from the foundation. Remaining is the Law of Man which is dangerously close to the "Man of Law," meaning that a relativistic, secular humanist agenda becomes the "law" of the land. This allows fundamental truths from God's Law to be replaced with convenient lies. In short, America has lost its rudder of Truth.

Government has taken the position of primacy, maintaining strict control of "We the People," the "Seven Mountains of Culture" introduced in Chapter 3, and a dependency structure which robs initiative and feeds corruption. The result is an increasingly Godless and coarse, violent culture. In short, "We the People" are oppressed and lacking hope.

The Unalienable Rights are diminished, with Government encroachment upon Life, Liberty, and the Pursuit of Happiness. In short, tyranny replaces a Constitutional Republic.

Two Roads: A National Inflection Point

> I shall be telling this with a sigh
> Somewhere ages and ages hence:
> Two roads diverged in a wood, and I—
> I took the one less traveled by,
> And that has made all the difference.
> Robert Frost, *The Road Not Taken*

Chart 8, below, *The Road Not Taken*, illustrates America's "two roads" graphically.

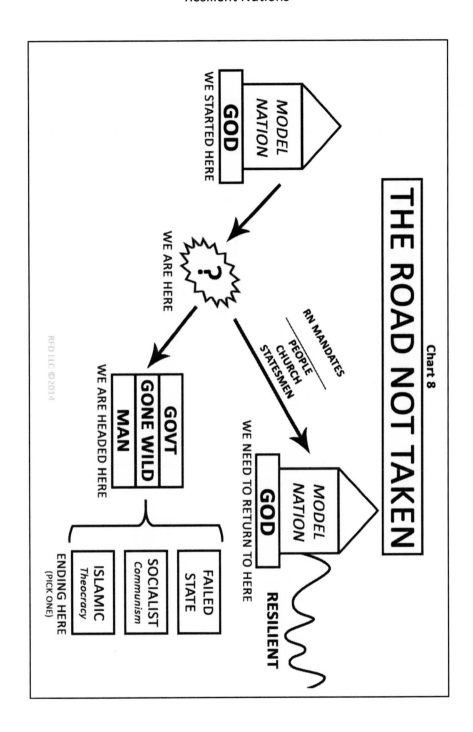

We have declined from "Model Nation" (Chart 3) to our current dysfunction, as described in Chapter 4 to this point, approaching Government "Gone Wild" (Chart 7). As with Robert Frost, we are now at an inflection point peering at two alternative futures: dissolution into Government "Gone Wild," beyond which the downward road leads to further decline and destruction resulting in three potential scenarios: chaos, anarchy, and a failed state (such as we described in the *Book of Eli)*, a Socialist state leading to Communism, or an Islamic theocracy with Sharia law; or the upward road, albeit steeper and fraught with challenge requiring commitment, which leads to national renewal, spiritual rearmament, and restoration of Life, Liberty, and Pursuit of Happiness. This upward road, although "less traveled" by most other nations, moves us back toward "Model Nation" and what God truly intended for the United States of America. This is how America regains its former greatness and endures as a resilient nation, observing the common denominators of national resilience we observed in Israeli history.

Chapters 5-9 identify how "We the People," "We the Church," and "We the Statesmen" put America back on this high road.

Gaining Altitude: America at a Crossroads

The orientation period (roughly eight weeks) for new arrivals at West Point is called "Beast Barracks." It is aptly named. The purpose of Beast Barracks is to immerse new cadets (hopeful to be "plebes" at the end of the summer) in the rigors of military life and forge a foundation for the subsequent four years of challenging academics, athletics, and military leadership training. One of the skills to be mastered during this time of indoctrination is marching, individually and in formation. From Day 1 the new cadets are marching everywhere and soon learn to conduct mass formation marching on "The Plain," observed by tourists and official visitors from around the world.

The summer before my first class (senior) year at West Point, I was assigned as the Adjutant for Beast Barracks, supporting the Cadet Commander who is known as the "King of Beast." The Adjutant handles personnel matters across the board, including the initial formation and accountability of troops for ceremonies. If you have observed many military parades, you have heard the command "Sound Adjutant's Call." You will know the Adjutant as the one who then struts (or runs) to the center of the Parade field, forms the troops (with a command such as "Bring Your Units to Attention") and takes the initial report from subordinate commanders. After these preliminaries, the Adjutant turns the formation over to the Commander and takes his place with the staff behind the commander.

The band sounded "Adjutants Call" to start yet another parade on a hot summer day during Beast Barracks in late July, 1971. Cadet Adjutant Dees marched briskly to the center of the field, a trek of maybe sixty yards, and directed "Bring Your Units to Attention." The parade went like clockwork until the long-awaited command "Pass in Review" (ending the torture of standing motionless in formation under the incessant pressure of the "tar bucket," the familiar cadet parade headgear which is sadistically uncomfortable). One company after another does their turns along the parade route, marching smartly, lining up for the all-important pass in front of the commander, his staff, and thousands of cheering civilians and military observers. The moving organism whispers to itself as it readies for the big moment: "steady men... too far ahead on the left... don't bounce... looking good... here we go." The unit commander commands "Eyes Right," simultaneously saluting the King of Beast with his saber as the guidon bearer snaps the unit guidon to a horizontal position with the unit designation showing on the waving flag. Simultaneously, the entire formation pivot their heads to the right "as one," connecting their eyes with the gaze of the reviewing Commander. It is a powerful moment. "Ready Front" commands the leader as their "moment of truth" is complete and they march the remainder of the parade route, eventually back to the cadet barracks and their next "chance to excel."

Company after company passed successfully. Then it happened. A cadet on the rear rank of one of the passing companies literally fell through the turf, rifle with bayonet and all. After a hushed moment as his company marches on, the cadet hoists his rifle out of the cavity and climbs out, just as if he were navigating the cadet obstacle course. Not to be left behind, he double times to rejoin his ranks.

What a surprise! How unexpected! That poor unsuspecting cadet! How did that happen?

Apparently in the early 1900s the Plain had been expanded with the dirt spoil from construction of a new building. Lore has it that this dirt was put on top of previous artillery battlements. After that, the Plain was used for decade after decade, still looking beautiful, still providing a fitting setting for such stately ceremonies—at least until July 1971. While the turf on top was lush and green, erosion of the soil underneath was slow and sure. With the rust and decay of the underlying "infrastructure" of the Plain, the inevitable finally happened.

Today we would know this as a "sinkhole" phenomenon. No doubt you have read about the hapless people whose homes suddenly disappear into a dark cavern under the ground, most notably in Florida. And no car lover can forget a real sinkhole tragedy in Bowling Green, Kentucky, when eight classic Corvettes were swallowed up by a sinkhole underneath the National Corvette Museum. Such sinkhole events don't seem to happen gradually or predictably. Suddenly the cataclysm happens. Unexpectedly the foundations give way. Then it is too late.

America is on borrowed time. The sinkhole impacts of American moral and spiritual erosion have been working under the visible surface of our nation for decades. The symptoms of such decline first became manifestly evident in the tumultuous 1960s, a decade where the normal ebb and flow of national challenges coupled with resilient recovery degraded into a steady decline in every area of Spiritual Infrastructure. Since the 1960s, we have been living on "residual resilience" which was purchased with blood, sweat, and tears by great Patriots that came before (statesmen, military defenders, fathers and mothers, business and civic leaders, spiritual role models, and citizens across our land). With the events of September 11, 2001, America entered into more than a decade of war and even more precipitous decline in Spiritual Infrastructure. Since the short-lived patriotism, unity, and dependence upon God of that "exogenous shock" in 2001, cracks in the American veneer have become even more evident:

burgeoning national debt, financial crisis, even greater partisan dysfunction in Congress and beyond, et cetera. With a "Hope and Change" agenda in 2008 until the present, the Obama Administration has not only been an unwitting accomplice, but also a witting antagonist in the dismantling of our nation's Spiritual Infrastructure and other elements of U.S. national power. The erosion has turned into a landslide. The sinkhole has begun to swallow up the future of America. *Hope* has turned into despair, and *Change* has turned into destruction of the "American Experiment" as we know it.

This puts America at a defining moment, a national inflection point. Will we now mirror a decadent Rome, falling subject to our lustful pursuit of secular idols, government largesse, and lack of vigilance to growing threats? Or will we mirror a resilient Israel, rediscovering our national values, becoming convicted of flawed policy and practice, identifying (and electing) God-honoring resilient leaders (Statesmen), and responding resiliently as a people and a nation to reverse course?

In the next three chapters, we investigate "what can the righteous do?" to win back America for future generations, specifically addressing Life, Liberty, and the Pursuit of Happiness. What can we do to take the high road which leads to national renewal, spiritual rearmament, and the America which our Founders and our God intended?

Resilient Nations Takeaways

RN 4A – <u>The decade of the 1960s truly was tumultuous</u>, in every sense. Fundamental values and standards of behavior were called into question like never before. Distrust in the government grew. Unlike the noble motives of 1776 revolutionaries, 1960-style revolutionaries cast off the bonds of civility, responsibility, morality, and national unity. This truly was a period of time when a vast number of Americans "did what was right in their own eyes." (Judges 17:6)

RN 4B – Reaping seeds which had been sown in the 1960s, <u>cultural indicators in the 1970s</u> all accelerated in the wrong direction: total crimes, violent crimes, murders committed by juveniles (particularly black males), drug use, illegitimate births, single-parent families, divorce rates, children involved in divorces, abortions, teenage suicide, rising education expenditures with plummeting student performance on Scholastic Aptitude Test (SAT) tests, rising welfare expenditures as poverty continued to rise, and many others. Declines in the components of U.S. National Power, to include Spiritual Infrastructure, were tangible and serious. National morale and morality sunk to new lows.

RN 4C – <u>The 1980s</u> have been termed by many as the "Reagan Revolution." Beginning with very high unemployment and high taxation from the Carter years, application of free market economic principles and sharp reduction in taxation allowed the decade to end positively with high economic growth and low unemployment. The malaise of the 1970s soon turned to relative optimism and national pride in the 1980s.

RN 4D – <u>The period spanning from 1989 into 2001</u> was generally economically prosperous, but ominous clouds hovered over America: corruption and scandal at the highest levels, continued cultural erosion, growth of terrorism, increased cyber threats, and highly disputed Presidential election results (*Bush v. Gore*, 2000) which left deeply rooted partisan bitterness on both sides. Many of these clouds erupted on and after 9/11.

RN 4E – <u>The 9/11 tragedy</u> brought out the best in Americans, at least temporarily. As the embers of the World Trade Center cooled, so did the unified clarity with which Americans had faced the crisis. Gratefully, many subsequent terrorist plots were thwarted. The wars in Iraq and Afghanistan increasingly taxed the resources, focus, and the patience of a war-weary public. Social media etched deeper into the psyche and relational patterns of the next generation, helping a charismatic albeit inexperienced Presidential candidate capture the affections of a restless electorate.

RN 4F – The Obama Presidency has not headed America in the right direction and has not governed well.

RN 4G – The realistic and desired outcome is that "We the People" will have made the 2014 mid-terms a mandate on the failed policies of the Obama Administration , will have selected principled "Statesmen" to replace self-seeking "Politicians," will have garnered a united Republican majority in both Houses of Congress to redress some of the damage of the past five years, and will have set the conditions for election of a new President and an Administration that represent traditional American values in 2016.

RN 4H — Current government overreach into every area of American's public and private lives is nearing a totalitarian outcome, unless we make course corrections now.

RN 4I — America is on borrowed time.   The sinkhole of American moral and spiritual erosion has been working under the visible surface of our nation for decades, beginning to swallow up the future of America.

RN 4J — America is at a defining moment, a national point of inflection.   Will we follow the path of a decadent Rome or a resilient Israel?

For Further Consideration

1. Look at a specific sub element of Spiritual Infrastructure and track it through the course of our nation's history.
2. Statesmanship makes a difference.   Each American Century has produced at least one great President in the persons of George Washington, Abraham Lincoln, and Ronald Reagan.   What characteristics made them great leaders and statesmen?

Additional References

1. Bennett, William J.   *The Index of Leading Cultural Indicators*. New York: Broadway Books, 1999.
2. Gingrich, Newt.   *To Save America*.   Washington, DC: Regnery Publishing, Inc., 2010.
3. Johnson, Jim. *Fracture Zone 2015*. Charleston, SC: 2013.

5

Respecting LIFE

"So choose LIFE in order that you may live,
you and your descendants."
(God to Moses and the Nation of Israel,
Deuteronomy 30:19b, all caps added)

For the next three chapters, we will examine the "Unalienable Rights" described in the second sentence of our *Declaration of Independence*:

> "WE hold these Truths to be self-evident, that all Men are created equal, that they are endowed by their Creator with certain unalienable Rights,-that among these are Life, Liberty, and the Pursuit of Happiness..."

Under each one we will describe the prevailing "culture" which impacts on that particular prescribed right of "We the People." Then we will select the "Top Three" issues within each chapter, highlighting a statement of the issue, Biblical precept relevant to the issue, and any policy prescriptions which warrant the attention of "We the People," "We the Church," and "We the Statesmen." The issues we highlight are complex and difficult to navigate politically and culturally, but the Founder's intent and Biblical wisdom generally provide clear moral responses (albeit hard) which lead to the highest good of mankind and obedience to God's Natural and Revealed Law. Each issue warrants a doctoral thesis, or an extensive book, or a passionate life pursuit to plumb the depths. *Resilient Nations* provides departure points (a basic orientation, a few statistics, and some Biblical guidelines) to frame these key issues impacting Life, Liberty, and the Pursuit of Happiness. Ideally, we together will not only be able to address key national issues, but also transform the way we think about and pursue solutions to national resilience and spiritual infrastructure. Chart 9, *Unalienable Rights*, on the next page, provides the "menu" for our journey in Chapters 5-7.

Unalienable Rights

Chart 9

LIFE	LIBERTY	PURSUIT OF HAPPINESS
Culture of Violence & Death	Culture of Appeasement	Culture of Dependency
"Respect For"	"Freedom From/To"	"Pursuit of"
1. Unborn	1. Threats	1. Education
2. Elderly	2. Government Intrusion	2. Prosperity & Work
3. Traditional Marriage	3. Religion	3. Health

A Culture of Violence and Death

"Zero Dark Thirty" was a powerful depiction of the raid on Usama Bin Laden's hideaway in Pakistan. The movie was very realistic, showing highly trained Navy Seals risking their lives, eliminating resistance, and ultimately accomplishing their mission. The extreme violence and graphic depictions of death were certainly tough medicine for the normal moviegoer, and perhaps even tougher for people with a security background (military, police, et al) who found themselves reliving some of their own traumatic experiences. Yet, during the movie, another group caught my eye. I later learned that they were members of a high school football team whose coach brought them for "a manly outing." In the reverent silence as this inspiring and sobering movie ended, with the credits still scrolling, I could hear one teenage player remark to another, "That wasn't so hot... *Grand Theft Auto* has more action than that!"

I suddenly had an unsettling realization. These young men, representing our current generation of American teens, did not appreciate that this was a true story. Usama Bin Laden represented <u>real evil</u> that killed <u>real people</u>, 3,000 of them in the Twin Towers alone. The Navy Seals are also <u>real warriors</u>, who bled <u>real blood</u>, who have <u>real families</u> (including teenage sons) that mourn their loss. Yet, these teens were captured in their virtual reality world where more death is better—it gives you a higher score on your video game. Killing is a measure of merit, easily accomplished with rapid bursts on a virtual automatic weapon. Ironically, the "joystick" becomes an object of death.

Such "desensitization" to violence, perversion, and death is shocking; yet this is "reality" for most Americans today (youth and adults alike).

The pot is now bubbling; the proverbial "frog in boiling water" is now trapped in a "CULTURE OF VIOLENCE AND DEATH."

> This American fixation on violence and death
> which is transforming our youth into "merchants of death"
> (perceived and real violence and killing)
> has heated up slowly but surely,
> fueled by a carnivorous media industry
> (video games, TV, movies, print, et al)
> for which profit trumps the future of our youth,
> and absentee parenting allows violence
> to fill the vacuum in our children's schedules and hearts.

The reality is that America's "culture of violence and death" is far more pervasive than just that which is evidenced in movie theatres or gaming rooms. When did this culture really take root? I would think when America (*Roe v. Wade*) sanctioned violence in the death of its own unborn children (abortion). Some would say that is the point at which God lifted His hand of protection to allow us to suffer the consequences of underwriting the death of humans in such a way. After this cheapening of human life, other forms of violence toward life perhaps became equally easy to justify: convenience killing of the elderly for "practical" considerations (euthanasia), killing oneself (suicide) because our own cheapened life does not seem worth living, prosecuting or accepting violence and exploitation directed at the vulnerable (human trafficking, sexual abuse, domestic violence, "knockout games," et al), and violence towards God's created order whether it be lack of environmental stewardship or efforts to "kill" God's fundamental institution for society and propagation of the human race, the traditional family (v. same-sex marriage, and other sexual perversions).

All of these are manifestations of a "culture of violence and death" which inevitably fuels subjective and self-serving factors of convenience, expediency, economic impact, and benefit to "The State." This was certainly true in ancient Rome, in the atheistic Soviet Union, in the totalitarian Nazi regime, and in George Orwell's *1984.* America is on the brink of a similar fate.

Let us look at how this "CULTURE OF VIOLENCE AND DEATH" undermines selected areas within the first unalienable right listed in our *Declaration of Independence*: LIFE.

Respecting the Unborn

> "Any country that accepts abortion is not teaching its people to love, but to use violence to get what they want. That is why the greatest destroyer of love and peace is abortion."
> ~Mother Teresa of Calcutta, National Prayer Breakfast, 1994

Consider the statistics below, one national and one local, to better understand the "scale" of abortion in today's America:

- "The death count of aborted infants in the United States alone is well over fifty-five million since 1973, when abortion became legal. That is more than the population of the three largest states combined—New York, California, and Texas!... The cost has been more than the loss of life. It has been socially divisive, morally destructive, and economically disastrous."

- "...the number of black babies killed by abortion totaled 31,328, while those born totaled 24,758, according to the New York City Department of Health and Hygiene. (CNSNews.com, 2012, underlines added) Regarding this latter New York City statistic, Reverend Bill Owens, president of the Coalition of African American Pastors (CAAP), commented at the National Press Club on February 25, 2014, when CNSNews.com asked about a report showing that more unborn black babies were aborted than born in New York City: "Something has to be done, and for this man, this administration to promote abortion is promoting murder. I'm talking about Obama and Holder. This society is becoming evil. Promote this organization [Planned Parenthood] that kills and put them in all in black neighborhoods—that's sick. And for Obama to support it shows he has no feelings toward little black children."

Some additional statistics from *The Issue is Life* by John Grant:

- "Approximately one out of four pregnancies in America is terminated by abortion.
- Slightly over half of all women having abortions are in their twenties and eight out of ten report a religious affiliation (43% Protestant, 27% Catholic, and 8% other religions).
- 41% of aborting women are white, 32% black, and 20% Hispanic.
- 98% of abortions are a matter of personal choice with only 1.7% for health of the mother and .3% resulting from rape or incest."

Abortion truly is one of the most divisive and destructive issues within America today—

One side maintains that life begins at conception; abortion represents murder deserving of the wrath of God and man, a "right to life" of the unborn which is unalienable under the Constitution. The opposing view declares a woman's "right to choose" as a fundamental woman's right over her body, despite moral and societal consequences. This pro-choice (what opponents would call "pro-abort") movement, a logical (albeit tragic) extension of the sexual revolution and women's activism beginning in the 1960s, has concertedly mobilized liberal academic, media, and political efforts to "change the narrative"— women should be able to choose, life begins at birth

(v. conception), abortion is often the most "practical" alternative (economic benefit, convenience, demands of parenting, even a "compassionate" means to reduce child abuse, et al).

Former Florida Senator John Grant's incisive book *The Issue is Life* is a valuable tool (See "Additional Resources") to understand the fundamental issues surrounding abortion, and identify ways that "We the People" can stop this blight across America. He maintains that the primary "enemy" is the abortion industry. Consider these statistics which identify the magnitude of the battle being waged:

- "From 2005 to 2006, Planned Parenthood, the nation's largest abortion provider, increased the number of abortions it performed from 264,943 to 289,650. With that increase, total revenue was over 1 billion dollars... This included taxpayer dollars in the form of government grants and contracts in excess of $336 million dollars. (Planned Parenthood Federation of America, Annual Report, 2006)"
- "Planned Parenthood lobbies our government to remove abortion restrictions in order to continue to assure future financial profits. In 2006, Planned Parenthood Political Action Committees spent 53.2 million dollars to adjust public policy. (Planned Parenthood Federation of America, Annual Report, 2006)"

Overall, the tragic statistics remain abundant and appalling.

> Overall, the tragic statistics remain abundant and appalling.

Pro-choice "intellectuals" attempt to rationalize this "holocaust" by any means. Partial birth abortion, the act of killing a late term baby in the birth canal (technically "not born") by pushing forceps into the baby's skull and sucking out the brains (previously supported at the State and Federal levels by President Obama), is a graphic example of the lengths to which the abortion industry will go. Gratefully, these irrational apologists for abortion can no longer hide behind science because of sonogram technologies which graphically demonstrate that life and "personhood" are established at conception. From a mental health perspective, the residual post-traumatic stress impacts (often called post-abortion syndrome) often last for a lifetime, visiting a sense of deep loss, depression, and inevitable guilt in the women who "choose" death for their unborn children. This aborted baby never leaves the mind and conscience of its mother, borne out by thousands of anecdotal post-abortion stories from grieving women. From an economic perspective, greying Baby Boomer entitlements (for which Social Security and Medicare are coming due) are outstripping revenue production by younger age groups in America, a problem that would be far less severe if we had not killed off younger generations of workers and tax- paying citizens.

A second part of the abortion tragedy is that there are many couples who cannot have their own baby, but who seek the fulfillment of together nurturing another human life through adoption. Is it not ironic to consider the exorbitant expenses and hardship such young couples experience to find a baby to adopt in Russia, or Africa, or the Far East, while around the globe we are killing a baby every two seconds, with America leading the way?

Adoption is far preferred to abortion.

God agrees: "Pure and undefiled religion in the sight of *our* God and Father is this: to visit orphans and widows in their distress, *and* to keep oneself unstained by the world." (James 1:27 italics added). An obvious way to "visit an orphan in distress" is adoption.

When all the specious arguments are blown away like chaff, the essential issue is LIFE, a precious commodity created and sustained by the Living God.

So what does God think about abortion?

Biblical Precepts Respecting LIFE of the Unborn

Psalm 139 states God's role in skillfully weaving us together in our mother's womb, starting with when he skillfully wrought our unformed substance into something fearfully and wonderfully made. Note that verse 16 also addresses the oft debated time of "when life begins:"

> [13] For You formed my inward parts;
> You wove me in my mother's womb.
> [14] I will give thanks to You, for I am fearfully and
> wonderfully made;
> Wonderful are Your works,
> And my soul knows it very well.

¹⁵ <u>My frame was not hidden from You,</u>
<u>When I was made in secret,</u>
And skillfully wrought in the depths of the earth;
¹⁶ <u>Your eyes have seen my unformed substance</u>;
And in Your book were all written
<u>The days that were ordained *for me*,</u>
<u>When as yet there was not one of them</u>."
(Psalm 139:13-16, underlines added)

Given that the conceived child (a living creature) is God's handiwork in the womb, one of God's Ten Commandments says directly: "<u>You shall not murder</u>." (Exodus 20: 13, underline added) Related to the seriousness of harming life in the womb, God also instructs in Exodus: "^{22a} If men struggle with each other and strike a woman with child so that she gives birth prematurely... ²³ But if there is *any further* injury, then you shall appoint *as a penalty* <u>life for life</u> ..." (Exodus 21: 22a, 23, underlines added)

Finally, children are a gift, an avenue to blessing, and a means for propagating the human race:

"Behold, children are a gift of the LORD, the <u>fruit of the womb is a reward</u>." (Psalm 127:3, underline added), and "^{28a} God blessed them; and God said to them, "<u>Be fruitful and multiply</u>, and <u>fill the earth</u>, and subdue it..." (Genesis 1:28a, underlines added)

Actions and Policies "Respecting the Unborn"

1. <u>Pursue Public Education Regarding Abortion And Alternatives To Abortion</u>. "My people are destroyed (literally) for lack of knowledge (about abortion)." (Hosea 4:6, parentheses added). Carol Tobias, president of the National Right to Life Committee (NRLC) states it well in her response to the previously mentioned report which showed falling abortion rates:

   > "... the resulting national debate and educational campaigns surrounding pro-life legislation should not be minimized when discussing the decline in abortion numbers. The more Americans learn about the development of the unborn child and the tragedy of abortion, the more they reject abortion as a legitimate answer to an unexpected pregnancy."

   One proactive step is to align with one or multiple pro-life advocacy groups in order to gain knowledge for self and others.

2. <u>Elect Pro-Life Representatives and Leaders</u> at every level who will "vote your values" and who will stop appointing activist judges who further liberal agendas (including abortion) in the courts.

3. <u>Support Pro-Life Legislative Initiatives</u> at Federal and State levels. An example is a proposed Congressional "Life at Conception Act" which declares unborn children as

"persons" covered by the 14th Amendment of the Constitution ("... *nor shall any state deprive any person of life...*"), legislatively flanking the *Roe v. Wade* judicial activism. Conservative pro-life majorities in the House and Senate (a possible result of the 2014 mid-terms, or beyond) could bring such legislation to pass, assuming "We the People" support grassroots movements in support of this and other pro-life legislative initiatives.

4. <u>Help Overturn The Affordable Care Act</u> (aka "Obamacare"). Chapter 7 will discuss this in greater detail, but the Obama Administration has been the most ardent pro-choice advocate of any administration in history. A provision being hotly contested before the US Supreme Court by Hobby Lobby and Conestoga Wood Specialties pertains to "contraceptive services," defined in Obamacare to include contraception, abortion, and euthanasia. As landmark legislation for the economic and cultural "transformation" of America, Obamacare has many imbedded provisions that counter a "culture of life."

5. <u>Keep Fighting</u>! (to overturn *Roe v. Wade*, and reinstitute pro-life policies in America) There are glimmers of hope with reports such as this from *Christianity Today* (February 8, 2014):

> "With abortion clinics closing at record rates as abortions hit near-record lows and state restrictions hit near-record highs, a respected report released today reveals that U.S. abortions have dropped to their lowest rate since 1973—the year the U.S. Supreme Court decided *Roe v. Wade*."

In the last chapter of *The Issue is Life* titled "The Good News: We are Winning," John Grant highlights the belief that *Roe v. Wade* will actually be overturned, as supported by a number of indicators: recent public opinion polls showing that pro-life now exceeds pro-choice, state legislatures enacting record numbers of abortion restrictions, numbers of abortions declining, use of Crisis Pregnancy Centers as an alternative to Planned Parenthood "counseling" is increasing... and most importantly, God is on the side of LIFE.

May "We the People," "We the Church," and "We the Statesmen" support LIFE by "Respecting the Unborn."

Respecting the Elderly

On a first level of consideration, "respecting the elderly" means to bestow dignity in thought, word, and deed to those in their last chapters of life.

> "Respecting the Elderly" means to bestow dignity in thought, word, and deed to those in their last chapters of life.

This certainly follows Biblical injunction beginning with one of the Ten Commandments which directs, "Honor your father and mother," and reinforced by verses such as, "You shall <u>rise up before the grayheaded and honor the aged</u>, and you shall revere your God; I am the LORD" (Leviticus 19:32, underline added), and "... <u>you must help the weak</u> (which includes the elderly) and remember the words of the Lord Jesus, that He Himself said, 'It is more blessed to give than to receive.'" (Acts 20:35, underline and parenthetical added). Such reverence for the elderly extends far beyond our own parents, and is clearly a desired Christian and American behavior, perhaps even more valued in countries where Confucianism and Buddhism have shaped the culture (such as Korea).

Consideration of the elderly brings us to the reality of death and dying. Growing old is not for cowards; it takes courage, perspective, and wisdom to grow old well, with dignity. These challenges are multiplied when a person becomes mentally or physically infirm to the point where their "quality of life" is so degraded that they (or others) question whether they should continue to live.

The Indian Journal of Medical Research provides a useful frame of reference:

> "Euthanasia encompasses various dimensions, from active (introducing something to cause death) to passive (withholding treatment or supportive measures); voluntary (consent) to involuntary (consent from guardian) and physician assisted (where physicians prescribe the medicine and patient or the third party administers the medication to cause death)... This debate cuts across complex and dynamic aspects such as legal, ethical, human rights, health, religious, economic, spiritual, social, and cultural aspects of the civilized society."

Dr. Jim Eckman addresses the topic further in "The Growing Acceptance of Euthanasia:"

"In Western Europe, euthanasia is increasingly easy and ethically acceptable... Many Europeans view euthanasia as a highly compassionate option that allows individuals to control their fate and that many now see it as a human right. In the US, current four states permit assisted suicide— Oregon, Washington, Montana, and Vermont. In all cases, the patient, not the doctor, administers the lethal dose. In the U.S. there is another euthanasia option being promoted by a group called Final Exit Network, a New Jersey-based nonprofit that advertises an 'exit bag'—a plastic hood that fits over the head and is fed by helium, resulting in a quick death."

> Growing old is not for cowards; it takes courage, perspective, and wisdom to grow old well, with dignity.

While euthanasia is not yet on the front page of U.S. papers, it is instructive to observe a number of nations where euthanasia policies have garnered substantive support: Australia, Belgium, Canada, Colombia, Germany, India, Israel, Italy, Japan, Luxembourg, The Netherlands, Russia, Spain, Switzerland, and The United Kingdom. We can be sure that this political, ethical, and spiritual debate will soon intensify and expand in America, given the "slippery slope" upon which our growing culture of violence and death places us.

> We can be sure that this political, ethical, and spiritual debate will soon intensify and expand in America...

Even today, such questions become very real for the children of aging parents who must wrestle with these end of life issues. I know I stood by my dying father's bedside for four months, watching every heartbeat, every oxygen percentage in the bloodstream, praying for a miraculous healing and yet also praying for God's mercy on a worn out body. I navigated the same with my dying mother and sister. These end of life considerations are fraught with ethical questions which suddenly become very raw and real for the family involved. Do we resuscitate? What about a ventilator and other life support? What medical directives do we put in place? What would our loved one want? What can we afford in terms of medical care? Do we mortgage the financial future of younger family members to sustain life at all costs? Maybe you have been in that situation yourself, wrestling with these same issues.

> End of life considerations are fraught with ethical questions which suddenly become very raw and real for the family involved.

These are tough questions that not only require human wisdom and endurance, but also guidance from our Creator God, the one who gave us LIFE and desires that we preserve this LIFE.

Biblical Precepts Respecting LIFE of the Elderly

Each of the verses below highlight <u>the value God places upon his human creation</u>, including physical LIFE which euthanasia destroys. As well, <u>God does not confer authority to man to take life</u> in this manner.

- [13] "You shall not murder. (Exodus 20:13) (Author note: Euthanasia can validly be considered as murder according to God's Law, and the predominance of man's laws has historically ruled the same.)

- [16] Do you not know that <u>you are a temple of God</u> and *that* the Spirit of God dwells in you? [17] <u>If any man destroys the temple of God, God will destroy him</u>, for the temple of God is holy, and that is what you are. (1 Corinthians 3:16,17, underlines added)

- [6] "<u>Whoever sheds man's blood</u>, By man his blood shall be shed, For <u>in the image of God He made man</u>. (Genesis 9:6, underlines added)

Nor does man have authority over <u>the time of death</u>:

- [1]There is <u>an appointed time for everything</u>. And there is a time for every event under heaven— [2] A time to give birth and <u>a time to</u>

die; A time to plant and a time to uproot what is planted. (Ecclesiastes 3:1,2, underlines added)

- [8]No man has authority to restrain the wind with the wind, or authority over the day of death; (Ecclesiastes 8:8, underlines added)

Of note, the Indian doctors cited above conclude their investigation with a strong argument for the humaneness of enhancing "palliative care" (helping those who are suffering better manage the pain physically, emotionally, and spiritually) instead of giving priority of focus and resources to ending life in these same patients. Certainly hospice care falls into this arena. From a Christian worldview, palliative care also includes the work of the Holy Spirit to comfort those in need, the Church to minister to those in need, and the individual Christian to be "Jesus with skin on" to those who are suffering with the physical, mental, and emotional ravages of old age, or any age for that matter. Those who escape the tomb of self to care for others in their dark days of life are also blessed richly through their obedience and service to others. As well, the individual sufferer has a wealth of faith resources (Scripture, prayer, meditation, and fellow believers) which allow one to "soar on eagle's wings" (Isaiah 40:31) above the greatest challenges in   life, including death and dying. The absolute best "palliative care" occurs when the person near death has full assurance of eternal life in heaven and a deep sense of God's presence with them:

"[54]But when this perishable will have put on the imperishable, and this mortal will have put on immortality, then will come about the saying that is written, 'DEATH IS SWALLOWED UP in victory. [55]O DEATH, WHERE IS YOUR VICTORY? O DEATH, WHERE IS YOUR STING?" ... [57]but thanks be to God, who gives us the victory through our Lord Jesus Christ." (I Corinthians 15: 54, 55, 57)

> The absolute best "palliative care" occurs when the person near death has full assurance of eternal life in heaven and a deep sense of God's presence with them.

There is abundant empirical evidence related to positive outcomes of faith in geriatric populations that validates reduced fear of death, greater perseverance and joy despite suffering, and even improved vital signs (pulse, blood pressure, cholesterol) in those who actively live their faith. For compelling research specifics, see Dr. Harold Koenig's comprehensive work, *The Healing Power of Faith*.

God in His infinite wisdom has created a rhythm of life which includes physical death. Although a difficult season of life for the dying person and for the often exhausted caregiver, this is also in God's economy. The practice of euthanasia which posits that human wisdom and modern technology are best suited to determine the means and timing of death is a dangerous "slippery slope" which leads to true depravity, and seeks to rob humans of humanity itself.

Actions and Policies "Respecting the Elderly"

1. Seek to care for the elderly in a home setting. Part of God's design and role for the traditional family included care for the elderly in a home setting as long as possible. Although a declining trend, this is a Biblical and humane way to "honor our fathers and mothers," particularly in light of the expense and questionable practices of many nursing homes today. While medical realities will sometimes not allow this home care to occur, the tragic rationale for "outsourcing the elderly" in today's American society is too frequently the familiar mantras of "choice, convenience, and practicality."

2. Discuss death and dying with your aging loved one in an informed and loving way. Have the hard conversations about medical directives before the person becomes incapacitated and on the brink of death. Recognize that there are no easy answers, but prayer, compassion, informed discussions with medical personnel, and the comfort and wisdom of the Scriptures and God's Holy Spirit will enable you to navigate this season of life successfully.

3. "We the Statesmen" promote life honoring policies. Resist pressure from "enlightened" interest groups who think they can social engineer death to the betterment of society; a practice which allows a "culture of violence

and death" to become even more pervasive and destructive.

May "We the People," "We the Church," and "We the Statesmen" truly support LIFE by "Respecting the Elderly."

> The practice of euthanasia which posits that
> human wisdom and modern technology are best suited
> to determine the means and timing of death
> is a dangerous "slippery slope"
> which leads to true depravity,
> and seeks to rob humans of humanity itself.

Respecting the Traditional Family

The traditional family, which some call the "natural family," is designed by God to be a giver of life to present and future generations. FOX News Commentator George Will concisely emphasized the importance of the traditional family (commonly defined as two parents, a husband and wife, along with possible children as a result of their own procreation or adoption) to American society: "Family is the primary transmitter of social capital—values, behaviors, worldview. Family is the primary determinant of life outcomes."

> Despite such importance and centrality to the future of
> America, the decline of the traditional American family
> has been precipitous over the last half century.

Charles Krauthammer, in an American Enterprise Institute lecture series in 1993 which is equally relevant in 2014, highlights an oft-cited survey of teachers in 1940 and 1990:

> "In 1940, a survey was taken of teachers asking them to list the five most important problems in school. They were: (1) talking out of turn; (2) chewing gum; (3) making noise; (4) running in halls; and (5) cutting in line.

> "Fifty years later, the survey was repeated. The 1990 list was substantially revised: (1) drug abuse; (2) alcohol abuse; (3) pregnancy; (4) suicide; (5) rape."

Krauthammer continues with an explanation:

> "One could cite a mountain of statistics. One could supply one's own anecdotal evidence. But this list will suffice to make the obvious point that <u>there has been an explosion of deviancy in American society over the last fifty years</u>. Things have gotten out of hand.

> "How have we dealt with that? Daniel Patrick Moynihan offers an arresting view in a recent essay in *The American Scholar* entitled "<u>Defining Deviancy Down</u>." His point is that deviancy—crime, broken homes, mental illness—has reached such vast and incomprehensible proportions that we have had to adopt a singular form of denial: <u>We</u>

<u>deal with the epidemic by simply defining away</u> <u>most of the disease</u>. We lower the threshold for what we are prepared to call normal in order to keep the volume of deviancy—redefined deviancy—within manageable proportions.

<u>"Since 1960, for example, the incidence of</u> <u>single parenthood has more than tripled</u>. It now afflicts—and anyone acquainted with the figures for poverty and the various social pathologies associated with single-parenthood knows that "afflicts" is the right word—more than one-quarter of all American children. <u>As the problem has</u> <u>grown, however, it has been systematically</u> <u>redefined by the culture—by social workers,</u> <u>intellectuals, and most famously by the mass</u> <u>media—as simply another lifestyle choice</u>. Dan Quayle (former U.S. Vice President and a Presidential candidate in 1992 who was publicly derided for his reference to the Murphy Brown TV sitcom as symbolic of a serious deterioration in American family values) may have been right, but Murphy Brown got the better ratings." (parentheticals and underlines added)

The erosive trends have only accelerated since 1990. In March 2014 Congressman Paul Ryan made similar observations about the importance of two-parent families and was immediately lambasted by civil rights activists as being "racist." No doubt feminists and gay rights activists will take a swing at him as well. The <u>single parent family statistics</u> cited that evening on FOX Special Report support Ryan's concern however: Black 72%, Hispanic 54%, and, for all Americans, 41%. <u>The bottom line is that children need a mom and a dad</u>.

In response to the Obama Administration's unfettered support of same-sex marriage initiatives, the Family Research Council maintains: "We believe Attorney General Holder is violating and trampling on the laws of 33 states where American citizens have voted to define marriage as between a man and a woman. Holder has told states they must recognize and protect all of the marital benefits of homosexual couples from other states that have redefined marriage."

The bottom line is that children need a mom and a dad.

Also addressing the same-sex agenda, D. James Kennedy and Jerry Newcombe have provided a well-researched and Biblically grounded analysis in *What's Wrong with Same-Sex Marriage?* Although written before some of their worst fears about government support of the same-sex agenda were realized via activist court decisions and Justice Department directives, here are their valid and well-supported "Top Twelve Reasons We're Opposed to Same-Sex Marriage":

1. God opposes homosexuality.
2. Same-sex marriage (and same-sex conjugal relations) goes against the natural order.
3. It goes against all of recorded history.
4. It will hurt children.

5. It cheapens marriage.
6. Same-sex marriage will unleash a legal nightmare. (which we are now observing)
7. It will sink the culture from civilization to barbarism.
8. It destabilizes all of society.
9. It opens Pandora's Box in the legalization of all sexual perversion. What's next?
10. It will hurt women for many reasons, including polygamy.
11. Same-sex marriages can produce no natural offspring.
12. Same-sex marriage will criminalize Christianity.

As an indicator that these cultural battles are causing soul-searching within the Church, note the 2014 reversal by World Vision regarding support of homosexuals within their organization, posted by the American Family Association:

> "As you may know by now, World Vision yesterday reversed its decision to allow for two 'married' men (or women) to work for them. This came less than 48 hours after the organization's first press release saying they were fine with 'married' homosexuals working for their ministry because it promoted 'unity' in the church, according to CEO Richard Stearns.

> "In yesterday's reversal announcement, World Vision president Richard Stearns states:

'Today, the World Vision U.S. board <u>publicly reversed its recent decision</u> to change our employment conduct policy. The board acknowledged <u>they made a mistake</u> and chose to <u>revert to our longstanding conduct policy</u> requiring <u>sexual abstinence for all single employees</u> and <u>faithfulness within the Biblical covenant of marriage between a man and a woman.</u>'

"World Vision changed its position because it received an avalanche of discontent from their supporters who sponsor children around the globe through their organization. It's still very disconcerting that one of the largest Christian charities in the world made this kind of decision in the first place. It just goes to prove what I have said before, the spiritual and cultural war on the great moral issues of our time is being waged both within and without the church." (underlines added)

It is difficult to understand such governmental unwillingness to acknowledge the primary causes for our societal erosion, or to recognize that much of the solution involves resurrecting the traditional family.

Add to this "gay rights" activists who not only seek rights for homosexuals, bi-sexuals, and transgenders, but also <u>seek to destroy the traditional family as a way to legitimize same-sex</u>

marriage and other sexual perversions.   As much as possible, I will minimize use of the word "gay," recognizing it as an effort by the homosexual community to characterize their behavior in a more positive light. "Defining Deviancy Down" has certainly occurred regarding sexual perversion with efforts to "normalize" deviant behavior such as homosexuality, sex with minors, gender transformation, polygamy, human sexual trafficking, and even bestiality. As well, the converse is also true: "Defining Deviancy Up" attempts to redefine "family" and separate it from long standing religious and societal roots, as well as labeling individuals who hold to traditional values as "intolerant bigots."   As with Rome, good has become evil, and evil has become good.

Since the sexual revolution in particular, the homosexual agenda in America has been the result of concerted planning, determined undermining of traditional values in key organizations such as the National Education Association (NEA) or the American Psychiatric Association (APA), and well-resourced public relations campaigns to change the reality and perception of sexual perversion in America. For greater details regarding these matters, I recommend *The Homosexual Agenda* produced by Alan Sears and Craig Osten at the Alliance Defending Freedom (ADF).

It is important at this point to emphasize that respect for all people, including the homosexual community, is fundamental to Christian belief and practice.   Franklin Graham, President of the Billy Graham Evangelistic Association (BGEA) and Samaritans Purse, summarized this well in a recent interview with Piers Morgan. Paraphrasing, he said God made Adam and Eve. We have male and female "plumbing" as well as many other differences. We can't redefine what God gave us. Believing in these truths is not anti-gay, or homophobic. From God's perspective, homosexuality is sin. Adultery is sin. Murder is sin. Our loving God can forgive all of these through a personal acceptance of Jesus Christ, confession of that sin, and repentance.

> You have probably heard the familiar mantra "hate the sin, but love the sinner." This is certainly what Jesus did, and likewise how Christians and non-Christians alike should behave toward homosexuals.

The traditional family also continues to be under attack by feminist activist groups. This is not an argument about the respective value of men and women as God's created beings, as members of God's family institution, or as contributors to society via work, volunteerism, and philanthropy. Simply put, men and women are different. God made them that way— physically, mentally, spiritually, emotionally, relationally. As stated earlier, children need a mom and a dad. A prominent female news announcer on a popular morning show recently asserted, "Women can do anything men can do, and often better." This is a lie, a false expectation, that often draws women away from their God-given giftings to seek areas of contribution that are outside their true calling as uniquely created beings. The assertion that a woman can do anything a man can do is wrong. Just as a man cannot do everything a woman can do. Related to the traditional family, can a woman mentor and mold a young man the way a loving father can do? No. Can a man provide the innate nurture and compassion that a woman manifests for the child that she shared life with for nine months and brought into this world? Of course not. God's master design for the traditional family brought together two people, male and female, designed to complement one another in every regard. Any departure from this breaks the divine mold.

Emphasis upon traditional marriage in no way minimizes the value or potential of women. In fact, the opposite is true. Kathleen and I saw this first-hand when I was an instructor at the U.S. Military Academy (West Point) during the years when young women were just beginning to attend. Some were well-suited to a singular focus as a military officer (which many women are very qualified for), but most (sooner or later) would identify a disconnect between their chosen career path and their desire to be a "mommy." They often felt a deep yearning to invest in the future of their own children, a unique "calling" which God built into women. Many would come to Kathleen in a quiet moment to express their dilemma with very heartfelt emotions. Many left the Academy to pursue other dreams, and many female Academy graduates ultimately migrated into more traditional roles as mothers and wives, while pursuing their military careers or as a new (and refreshing) next season of life. Ironically, radical feminists have historically demeaned women who pursue traditional roles for which God created them, with or without the trappings of a parallel career in the workplace.

Even for traditional families that are weathering the assaults mentioned above, there is a self-inflicted threat, caused by parents (single or in tandem) who deny their children of love and time in order to chase their "pots of gold" (whatever form that takes). Given that *Resilient Nations* is dedicated to future generations, let me look at the traditional family from a child's perspective. Just as with ancient Israel, America of today is bowing down to many idols which are foreign and inimical to America's Godly heritage. Just as when Israelites caused their sons and their daughters to pass through the fire to Molech (an ancient Ammonite idol to which parents sacrificed their children ... for more context, see Leviticus, 1 & 2 Kings, and Jeremiah), many Americans today are symbolically doing the same with their children.

A friend recently recounted a conversation with a highly paid, upwardly mobile, young business professional, a harried young man who was tired, discouraged, even desperate. Explaining his forlorn spirit, he talked about the 24-hour business cycle (enabled by "the cloud"), his constant travels, his wife's similar schedule in her professional endeavors, the fact that his only contact with his children were infrequent visits to pack a new bag or an infrequent Internet call, and frustration that his children were being "single parented" by a nanny that both parents were paying to raise their children. This represents today's "American Dream" and America's fixation upon a modern day Molech (the idol of status, money, work, pleasure, and "more things") for which we are sacrificing our children. Although the single parent nanny is harmful enough, such absentee parenting actually results in the children being raised by decadent cultural role models, indoctrinated by humanistic schools, and steeped in a pervasive media environment that glorifies violence, sensuality, and materialism.

Hence, the traditional family is under attack from intertwining racial, sexual, feminist agendas which are often supported by biased liberal public policy, combined with parental absenteeism within traditional families. The net effect is destroying the primary building block of society, the traditional family which God established as foundational in America and nations across the globe.

Let us review what God says about the traditional family.

Biblical Precepts Reflecting LIFE of the Traditional Family

Some representative passages which undergird traditional marriage and family:

- <u>Regarding heterosexual marriage partners</u>, "For this reason a man shall <u>leave his father and his mother</u>, and be <u>joined to his wife</u>; and they shall <u>become one flesh</u>." (Genesis 2:24, underlines added)
- <u>Regarding God's plan for marital function and harmony</u>, Ephesians 5 contains key concepts: "[22] Wives, *be subject* <u>to your own husbands</u>, as to the Lord. [23] For the husband is the head of the wife, as Christ also is the head of the church, He Himself *being* the Savior of the body.
  [25] <u>Husbands, love your wives</u>, just as Christ also loved the church and gave Himself up for her,

³³ Nevertheless, each individual among you also is to <u>love his own wife</u> even as himself, and the wife must *see to it* that she <u>respects her husband</u>." (Ephesians 5:22, 23, 25, 33, underlines added)

- <u>Regarding sexual purity in marriage</u>, "Marriage *is to be held* in honor among all, and the *marriage* bed *is to be* undefiled; for fornicators and adulterers God will judge." (Hebrews 13:4)

Consistent with this last verse on sexual purity, God also speaks clearly on sexual perversion. From the Old Testament:

- "If *there is* a man who lies with a male as those who lie with a woman, both of them have committed a detestable act; they shall surely be put to death. Their bloodguiltiness is upon them." (Leviticus 20:13)
- "...just as Sodom and Gomorrah and the cities around them, since they in the same way as these indulged in gross immorality and went after strange flesh, are exhibited as an example in undergoing the punishment of eternal fire." (Jude 1:7, underline added) Read Genesis 19 for a full account of this cautionary tale from Sodom and Gomorrah.

From the New Testament:

- "[24] Therefore God gave them over in <u>the lusts of their hearts to impurity,</u> so that their bodies would be dishonored among them. [25] For they <u>exchanged the truth of God for a lie,</u> and worshiped and served the creature rather than the Creator, who is blessed forever. Amen. [26] For this reason <u>God gave them over to degrading passions;</u> for their <u>women exchanged the natural function for that which is unnatur</u>al, [27] and in the same way also <u>the men abandoned the natural function of the woman</u> and burned in their desire toward one another, <u>men with men committing indecent acts</u> and receiving in their own persons the due penalty of their error." (Romans 1:24-27, underlines added)
- "[9] Or do you not know that the unrighteous will not inherit the kingdom of God? <u>Do not be deceived; neither fornicators, nor idolaters, nor adulterers, nor effeminate, nor homosexuals,</u> [10] <u>nor thieves, nor *the* covetous, nor drunkards, nor revilers, nor swindlers, will inherit the kingdom of God.</u> [11] Such were some of you; <u>but you were washed, but you were sanctified, but you were justified in the name of the Lord Jesus Christ and in the Spirit of our God.</u>" (I Corinthians 6:9/11, underlines added)

Although the homosexual lobby might declare or prefer differently, the Biblical injunctions are clear. God created man and woman as uniquely different, established the marriage relationship between them, and provided guidelines which lead to maximum fulfillment and joy, as well as procreation of the human race. Beginning with the Garden of Eden, this marital relationship was marred with sin which includes sexual perversion. God hates and judges sin. God loves sinners, to the degree that He sacrificed His Son, Jesus, so that sinners might live, and be washed, and experience abundant life. God models love to all, including the homosexual community. We should do the same.

Actions and Policies "Respecting LIFE of the Traditional Family"

1. <u>Seek to model God's plan for the traditional family in your own home</u>. Align with Joshua's proclamation, "As for me and my house, we will serve the Lord." Resist the temptation to sacrifice our children to modern day idols.
2. <u>Resist attacks on traditional marriage in public and private forums</u>. Stay informed. Align with family advocacy groups. Support Defense of Marriage Act (DOMA) initiatives.
3. <u>Support family friendly legislation</u>. For instance, tax structure for many years has dis-incentivized marriage and children. Support tax incentives for child care, some of which have bi-partisan support in the US Senate.
4. <u>Protect Client and Therapist Freedom of Choice</u> Regarding Sexual Orientation Change Efforts (SOCE). There are active efforts in a number of states, which particularly

impact on Christian counselors, making it illegal to engage in SOCE counseling. See www.frc.org/socetherapyban for a good overview of this issue.

5. <u>Model love for the homosexual community</u>. Seek to understand the heartfelt needs of those engaged in this lifestyle, as well as their family members and associates who struggle with how to affirm their loved one without compromising their own values.

May "We the People," "We the Church," and "We the Statesmen" support LIFE by "Respecting the Traditional Family."

The traditional family is under attack from intertwining racial, sexual, feminist agendas which are often supported by biased liberal public policy, combined with parental absenteeism within traditional families. The net effect is destroying the primary building block of society, the traditional family which God established as foundational in America and nations across the globe.

Other Threats to LIFE

While we have chosen three key issues (abortion, euthanasia, and homosexuality) which threaten LIFE for present and future Americans, the list is obviously much longer. A few other areas for your own consideration:

- **Respect for Self contrasted with Suicide**

  Suicide statistics, particularly among America's teens, continue to rise. As well, our military, a reflection of society at large, has experienced historically high suicide rates within the past decade. These trends illustrate a "cheapening of life" in the eyes of many individuals, with causal factors that are generally driven by relational factors: relationship with God, and relationships with others. For a deeper dive,   I suggest starting with the American Foundation for Suicide Prevention at www.afsp.org.

- **Respect for Others contrasted with Blatant Disregard for Others**

  This category covers a spectrum of concerns ranging from basic civility (such as respect and manners between individuals for which William Wilberforce crusaded, along with elimination of the slave trade) to human trafficking at the most severe end of the spectrum, with phenomenon such as the "Knockout Game" (recent "game" by predominantly young black males attempting to strike a single blow to "knock out" an unsuspecting passerby) and sexual trauma (rape, incest) somewhere in between.

Each of these manifestations of disrespect is destructive. Perhaps the worst, human trafficking is a truly pernicious global blight. The UN Definition of Human Trafficking includes "control over another person for the purpose of exploitation including prostitution, forced labor, slavery and servitude, and removal of organs;" and I would add breeding of babies for commercial purposes. I refer readers to www.thea21campaign.org for a comprehensive and passionate exposé of this insidious exploitation of women in particular. As well, Dr. Diane Langberg, one of the world's foremost experts on human trafficking and sexual trauma, has an excellent video on YouTube at www.**youtube**.com/watch?v=jWm9Xkc8C_k.

- **Respect for Others Contrasted with School Violence**

Certainly with the onslaught of high-profile and deadly school shootings across America, one must address the primary causes. Some would argue that a "gun culture" drives this trend. I subscribe, however, to the notion that "people, not guns, kill people." There are some logical restrictions to be placed on guns for public use (such as military assault weapons), but those that see this "cause celeb" as a means to deprive Americans of their Second Amendment Rights is misguided and oppositional to Constitutional intent.

The news accounts of school expulsions for young school children (usually boys) making a "gun" with their fingers illustrate the irrational backlash, while there is little mainstream discussion about how "matters of the heart" and violent video games are even more central to school violence. If the current Spiritual Infrastructure of the United States was as strong as in the 1850s or the 1950s (in which guns were prevalent and respected), then school violence would not be the issue it is today.

- **Respect for God's Creation Contrasted with Pollution**

    Although climate change remains a debatable phenomenon, one which has been highly politicized and even corrupted, the fact remains that God left us as custodians of a beautiful creation. Environmental stewardship is a moral and societal responsibility. This responsibility must be exercised wisely and pragmatically, however.

    It is ironic that "Save the Seals" and "Save the Whales" are battle cries heard far more frequently than "Save the Babies." As well, "Green energy," often taken hostage by environmental activists, has not yet led to economical and scalable technologies which can satisfy appreciable energy demands. Failure to ease American energy dependencies on foreign oil by approving energy enhancements such as the Keystone pipeline is the "environmental tail wagging the dog." For more information regarding environmentally responsible energy policy, see

    http://csis.org/program/energy-and-national-security.

Each of these "additional threats" to LIFE in America are just as real as the three highlighted in this chapter. They all live on "Mainstreet USA," representing in most cases toxic combinations from the drug culture, the pornography industry, youth criminality, racial and gender discrimination, media promotion of violence and disrespect for persons, special interest groups which often fan the flames, and an abandonment of traditional values in American society, starting with the family. The net result is a growing "culture of violence and death."

Our collective imperative is to return to the Culture of Life which our Founder's and God intended.

Gaining Altitude: Returning to a Culture of LIFE in America

> *"A red rose is not selfish because it wants to be a red rose.*
> *It would be horribly selfish if it wanted all the other flowers in the garden to be both red and roses."*
> -Oscar Wilde

We began this chapter by looking at the pervasive and worsening CULTURE OF VIOLENCE AND DEATH
in today's United States, one which counteracts the unalienable right of LIFE that is God-ordained and precious to the American way of life.

Using key areas related to LIFE, we illustrated the depth of the issues we face as a nation. As well, we clearly addressed Biblical precept relevant to these areas and provided actions and policies respecting LIFE, aimed at strengthening our nation's Spiritual Infrastructure and spiritual rearmament. Finally, we provided a sobering snapshot of many other serious areas where LIFE is losing to VIOLENCE AND DEATH. Before departing this chapter, let us "gain altitude" to once again view these issues through God's eyes.

The Apostle Paul in the Book of Romans well addresses the responsibilities of Godly citizens. You may recall our use of Romans Chapter 13 to illustrate a citizen's responsibility to their ordained government. Romans Chapter 8 provides a key principle which summarizes our current dilemma in America:

"For the mind set on the flesh is DEATH,
but the mind set on the Spirit is LIFE and peace."
Romans 8:6, (caps added)

America has its mind set on the flesh. In essence, a selfish pursuit of rights, pleasures, and domination of others. We see the results in every dark corner of American life—disrespect and violence is a selfish pursuit of control, rape is a selfish search for power, murder is the ultimate act of selfishness. Hypocritically cloaked in the relativistic idol of TOLERANCE, many Americans pursue their self-interests at the expense of others, with special-interest groups fanning the flames of controversy and resentment to likewise further their own self-interests. Our current government adds additional fuel to the fire. The results of this American mind set on the flesh are hatred, division, class warfare, violence, and DEATH.

America has its mind set on the flesh.

Conversely, the mind set on the Spirit is LIFE and peace. Americans must again move from selfishness to selflessness. Addressing the negative impacts of selfish thinking, Nobel Prize winner Alexander Solzhenitsyn observed the following:

"It is not because the truth is too difficult to see that we make mistakes... we make mistakes because the easiest and most comfortable course for us is to seek insight where it accords with our emotions—especially selfish ones."

Americans must again move from selfishness to selflessness.

More to the point, Jesus said, "For even the Son of Man did not come to be served, but to serve, and to give His life a ransom for many." (Mark 10:45) This spirit of service to others is integral to our Spiritual Infrastructure and the renewal of our nation.

America's "mindset" must change if we are to save this nation. Romans 12 also talks about changing mindset: "And <u>do not be conformed to this world</u>, (FLESH) but <u>be transformed by the renewing of your mind</u>, (SPIRIT) so that you may prove what the will of God is, that which is good and acceptable and perfect." (Romans 12:2, underlines and caps added) Applied nationally, the ultimate solution is for Americans to set our minds on the Spirit in order to achieve what God's will is for this great nation, beginning with spiritual rearmament, leading to a Third Great Awakening.

In summary, America must return to a Culture of LIFE.
It will take a miraculous move of God in each citizen,
in each community, in each church and corporation,
and in each statesman who walks the
halls of legislatures around this country.

Next we look at the second unalienable right prescribed in the *Declaration*, LIBERTY.

Resilient Nations Takeaways

RN 5A – The American fixation on violence and death which is transforming our youth into "merchants of death" (perceived and real violence and killing) has heated up slowly but surely, fueled by a carnivorous media industry (video games, TV, Movies, print, et al) for which profit trumps the future of our youth, and absentee parenting which allows violence to fill the vacuum in our children's schedules and hearts.

RN 5B – Abortion truly is one of the most divisive and destructive issues within America today. The tragic statistics remain abundant and appalling, a "holocaust" by any measure.

RN 5C – Adoption is far preferred to abortion.

RN 5D – The Bible speaks clearly about the sanctity of human life in the womb, the origin of life at conception, and the imperative to help orphans, including parentless babies.

RN 5E – "Respecting the Elderly" means to bestow dignity in thought, word, and deed to those in their last chapters of life.

Growing old is not for cowards; it takes courage, perspective, and wisdom to grow old well, with dignity.

RN 5F — The political, ethical, and spiritual debate over euthanasia will soon intensify and expand in America, given the "slippery slope" upon which our growing culture of violence and death places us.

RN 5G — "End of life" considerations are fraught with ethical questions which suddenly become very raw and real for the family involved. The absolute best "palliative care" occurs when the person near death has full assurance of eternal life in heaven and a deep sense of God's presence with them.

RN 5H — The practice of euthanasia which posits that human wisdom and modern technology are best suited to determine the means and timing of death is a dangerous "slippery slope" which leads to true depravity, and seeks to rob humans of humanity itself.

RN 5I — You have probably heard the familiar mantra "hate the sin, but love the sinner." This is certainly what Jesus did, and likewise how Christians and non-Christians alike should behave toward homosexuals.

RN 5J — The traditional family is under attack from intertwining racial, sexual, and feminist agendas which are often supported by biased liberal public policy, combined with parental absenteeism within traditional families. The net effect is destroying the primary building block of society, the traditional family, which God established as foundational in America and nations across the globe.

RN 5K – In addition to abortion, euthanasia, and homosexuality, there are many other threats to LIFE in the America God and our Founding Fathers intended.

RN 5L – Hypocritically cloaked in the relativistic idol of TOLERANCE, many Americans pursue their self-interests at the expense of others, with special interest groups fanning the flames of controversy and resentment to likewise further their own self-interests. Our government of recent adds additional fuel to the fire. The results of this American mind set on the flesh are hatred, division, class warfare, violence, and DEATH.

RN 5M – America must return to a Culture of LIFE. It will take a miraculous move of God in each citizen, in each community, in each church and corporation, and in each statesman that walks the halls of legislatures around this country.

For Further Consideration

1. In ancient Rome "good became evil, and evil became good." Consider how the concept of "Defining Deviancy Up" applies to an area of American societal erosion. As well, look at "Defining Deviancy Down" for the same area.
2. The concept of LIFE is supremely important to God and to our nation's Founding Fathers. Identify another issue (drawn from "Other Threats to Life" in this chapter, or another source) which also threatens LIFE? Analyze the current status, relevant Biblical precepts, and actions and policies to better "respect LIFE" in this area.

Additional References

1. Grant, John. *The Issue is LIFE*. Atlanta, GA: Mindshift Publications, 2013.
2. Koenig,Harold G. *The Healing Power of Faith*. New York, NY: Touchstone, 1999.
3. Sears, Allen and Craig Osten. *The Homosexual Agenda*. Nashville, TN: B & H Publishing Group, 2003.
4. Kennedy, D. James and Jerry Newcombe. *What's Wrong with Same-Sex Marriage?* Wheaton, IL: Crossway Books, 2004.
5. www.thea21campaign.org. A21: Abolishing Injustice in the 21st Century.
6. www.afsp.org. American Foundation for Suicide Prevention.
7. www.frc.org. Family Research Council.
8. www.afa.net. American Family Association.
9. http://csis.org. Center for Strategic and International Studies.
10. Dr. Diane Langberg YouTube videos on "A Christian Response to Human Trafficking and Sexual Abuse" at www.youtube.com/watch?v=jWm9Xkc8C_k.

6

Securing LIBERTY

"FREEDOM IS NOT FREE"
Engraved on Korean War Veterans Memorial
Washington, DC

LIBERTY is not given—it must be purchased. The price of external security for the United States is often the blood of the sons and daughters of America, spilled in conflicts near and far. The price of domestic liberty is governmental responsibility by "We the Statesmen" and civic responsibility by "We the People," including government provisions for peace and tranquility, and principled lives that govern from within. We will address how we "Secure LIBERTY," but first we look at a prevailing "culture of appeasement."

A Growing Culture of Appeasement

We have identified "tolerance" as a 21st Century idol in America. The toleration clause basically means "anything goes," but ironically justifies labeling those who disagree as "bigots," often with some modifier such as racist, or fascist, or religious. Instead of engaging in valid debate, or "agreeing to disagree," character assassination is the customary debating tactic. Not very tolerant!

Applying the concept to foreign affairs, tolerance takes the form of appeasement, the notion that anything is preferable to confronting a bad actor on the world stage, a confrontation which might require the use of military force or other levers of national power. In September 1938 British Prime Minister Neville Chamberlain sought a path of appeasement, crafting a "deal" (*Anglo-German Declaration*) with Adolf Hitler that would curtail his territorial appetite (Czechoslovakia and beyond). Responding confidently to the cheers of a hopeful populace, Chamberlain stated, "My good friends, for the second time in our history, a British Prime Minister has returned from Germany bringing peace with honour. I believe it is peace for our time."

Less than a year later in September 1939, Hitler's "Blitzkrieg" rolled through Poland and soon France. The British were soon evacuating their dead and wounded from a place called Dunkirk. Once again world history illustrated graphically that <u>a path of appeasement in the face of evil leads to disastrous outcomes</u>. Freedom is not free and Western allies, including the United States, were soon to pay the price.

On the international stage, appeasement occurs when a national leader does not "walk softly and carry a big stick" (as with President Teddy Roosevelt), or ensure "Peace through Strength" (as with President Ronald Reagan). President Reagan further observed "None of the wars in my lifetime came about because we were too strong... our military strength is a prerequisite for peace." Real or perceived weakness on the world stage encourages adventurism by global "bullies" with preventable outcomes that must be remedied at a very high cost. As of this writing, Russia's Vladimir Putin has not been deterred by the indecisive signals sent by President Obama. With a wide range of inducements to adventurism (a "red line" in Syria that was not enforced, seeming apathy toward the killing of a U.S. Ambassador in Libya, massive military drawdowns of U.S. armed forces due primarily to internal debt and growing entitlements, a weak negotiating posture regarding Iranian nuclear weapon development, and others), Putin has seen nothing from the U.S. (and its Allies) to deter him from a forced takeover of Crimea, and whatever may follow that. Terrorists are no doubt similarly emboldened by weakened U.S. military posture, U.S. release of prisoners from Guantanamo Bay Detention Center in Cuba to rejoin the fight in Afghanistan and Iraq, treatment of terrorists as criminals instead of enemy combatants, et cetera. Such tolerance and appeasement on the international stage endanger LIBERTY. At every turn, potential aggressors can well question if the United States is willing to pay the price for continued freedom.

Just as the U.S. State Department promulgates this culture of appeasement internationally, other departments of government lead the way in carrying out the Obama Administration's intent on the home front. Applying the concept to domestic affairs, appeasement takes a subtle twist.

To appease the masses, government provides handouts which create widespread dependency addiction. To appease the unemployed, government provides ever-increasing unemployment benefit extensions which erode work ethic and self-respect. To appease the Muslim community, we classify Major Nidal Hassan's murderous jihadist rampage at Fort Hood in April 2014 as "workplace violence" instead of terrorism. To appease illegal immigrants, government provides costly social services and even releases   ones who have committed serious crimes. We use "catch and release" enforcement practices as a tolerant way to deal with thousands illegally entering our country each month, some of whom are known terrorist infiltrators. To appease special interest groups, government offers favorable legislation and executive orders in return for their support at the ballot box. To appease partisan political support, our government turns a blind eye to voter intimidation by the Black Panthers (and organizations like them such as ACORN) and serious allegations of voter fraud in every state of the Union. To appease those who have lost their moral bearing, government comes full circle back to promote tolerance which sacrifices moral absolutes and exalts deviant behavior.

As this culture of appeasement plays out in many ways, always aimed at asserting more government control, "We the People" suddenly find ourselves surrounded by government, in fact "oppressed" by such intrusion into our public and private lives. Chapter 4, including the *Government "Gone Wild"* chart, previously described this serious challenge of government overreach.

With every appeasement, the Spiritual Infrastructure of the United States is further weakened. Our nation becomes a "paper tiger" in the eyes of adversaries and an "oppressive tyrant" in the eyes of "We the People."

With a deep-rooted culture of appeasement in today's America, how do "We the People," "We the Church," and "We the Statesmen" secure the LIBERTY which God and our Founder's intended?

With every appeasement, the Spiritual Infrastructure of the United States is further weakened. Our nation becomes a "paper tiger" in the eyes of adversaries and an "oppressive tyrant" in the eyes of "We the People."

Securing Freedom from External and Internal Threats

"Come, let us wipe them out as a nation,
that the name of Israel be remembered no more.
For they have conspired together with one mind;
Against You they make a covenant."
(Psalm 83:4)

The quote above reminds us that some things do not change – just as with Israel, there are nations and movements who seek to "wipe the U.S. out as a nation." As we stated in Chapter 3, God's fundamental role of government is "to restrain evil and to promote righteousness." At the first level of application, this means defending the country from external and internal threats using all the elements of national power introduced in Chapter 1 (Political, Military, Economic, Social, Infrastructure, and Information Systems).

External Threats

Regarding external threats, the <u>political</u> element of national power is essential for developing strong Allies with shared interests, enabling American enterprise globally, and shaping conditions to deter potential adversaries. From a geo-political perspective, the United States has committed at least two major strategic blunders since the Obama Administration assumed leadership in 2009. The first is "hitting the RESET button" with Russia. Secretary of State Hillary Clinton strolled right into the den of a wounded and angry Russian Bear, presenting them with the golden opportunity to begin their reclamation of the former Union of Soviet Socialist Republics (U.S.S.R.). This Russian agenda, and America's impotence, have been patently obvious in the ongoing humanitarian crisis in Syria, as well as March 2014 machinations over Ukraine.

The second major strategic blunder was the highly publicized "pivot to the Pacific." This pivot established unrealistic expectations among Allies and potential Adversaries in the region, creating future vulnerabilities and providing one more example of rhetoric overriding resources. Even if the pivot was an appropriate reprioritization of U.S. efforts to counterbalance growing Chinese influence, it was unwise to trumpet it as a major foreign policy and military initiative. Particularly when such a pivot is accompanied by our national naiveté regarding Chinese military aspirations and aggressive economic policies, the pivot is dead on arrival. It becomes one more instrument of appeasement rather than deterrence. In geographical terms, the region's "tyranny of distance" swallows up military resources just like the search for Malaysian Airlines Flight 370 swallowed up search assets from seven nations during March and April and beyond in 2014.

Appeasement: unrealistic expectations, future vulnerabilities, and rhetoric overriding resources...

The second challenge related to this Pacific pivot is the "opportunity cost" of drawing focus and resources away from critical geographies such as Russia, the Middle East, and Africa. Such signals of a pivot "away from" Europe and the Western Hemisphere sent shock waves through the NATO (North Atlantic Treaty Organization, begun in 1949) Alliance and other bi-lateral relationships in the region. The reality is that U.S. presence cannot be an "either Europe/Africa or the Pacific" proposition. Deterrence of global threats and fortification of worldwide allies requires both.

These two geo-political blunders, combined with a perceived withdrawal of traditional U.S. support for Israel and U.S. incompetency in navigating crises such as Syria, do not "set the conditions" for stable and peaceful relationships around the globe, or for fighting an integrated Global War on Terror (GWOT).

Regarding GWOT (a term that was banned as detrimental to Muslim sensibilities by the Obama Administration), our nation's "new normal" since 9/11 (the September 11, 2001 attacks on The Pentagon and New York World Trade Center) requires constant vigilance and considerable expenditure of national resources. Terrorism is an asymmetric threat which holds us hostage both internationally and domestically. It is naïve to suggest that the United States is "winning," yet it is laudable that hundreds of classified attempts have been thwarted since 9/11, including any cataclysmic events to match the scale of 9/11. There are no easy solutions on this one, particularly since the terrorist organizations and actors who seek the destruction of America are passionate to the point of martyrdom, technologically savvy, and tactically adept. Will the next technique of terrorism directed at the U.S. be cyber, nuclear, biological, chemical, explosive? Or all of the above?

These external threats place our military at even greater risk at the same time that domestic priorities (which are driving expenditures far beyond prudent economics or stewardship) are forcing disinvestment in the military element of national power. The Military Officers Association of America summarizes the trend in defense budgeting which places U.S. foreign policy and military capability to deter and, if necessary, decisively prevail at extreme risk. An April 2014 article by Alan W. Dowd in *Military Officer* provides some useful bottom lines, quoted below (underlines added):

- "...<u>waging war is far more costly</u> than maintaining a military capable of deterring war."

- "...in the middle of World War II, Winston Churchill offered his opinion: 'If we had kept together after the last war, if we had taken common measure for our safety, <u>this renewal of the curse need never have fallen upon us</u>.'"

- "Today defense spending is under 15 percent of the federal budget and 3.5 percent of the GDP (and falling). In fact, <u>we could eliminate the entire defense budget and turn the Pentagon into a megamall, and yet we still would face a budget deficit</u>—and wouldn't even be putting a dent into the $17 trillion debt."

- "<u>The nearly $1 trillion in cuts to the projected defense spending</u> between now and 2021—$500 billion in sequester cuts plus $487 billion in cuts ordered in 2010—might make sense if peace were breaking out around the world. But we know the very opposite to be true."

- "As the US declaws itself, <u>China's military-related spending</u> has skyrocketed from $20 billion in 2002 to around $180 billion a decade later... <u>Russia's military spending</u> spiked 25% in 2012."

- "...fewer troops, fewer ships, fewer planes, less modernization, and less training translate into <u>slower reflexes, a shorter reach, and a smaller role for the U.S.</u>"

According to Congressman Randy Forbes' public information website, such cuts to the military budget will shrink the military to an Army at insufficient pre-9/11 levels, the smallest Navy in over 100 years, an Air Force with roughly one third of current fighters and bombers, and the smallest Marine Corps in five decades.

A decade-plus of continuous warfare has created tremendous "maintenance" backlogs in every military system, particularly personnel. Combined with the need to reshape and prepare the force to address growing future threats, this is a "perfect storm" for our military, and our nation. The price of such a precipitous military drawdown will be paid in blood, either the result of a major miscalculation with a belligerent nation state, or the "death by a thousand cuts" from continual terrorism.

> The price of such a precipitous military drawdown
> will be paid in blood, either the result of a major miscalculation
> with a belligerent nation state, or
> the "death by a thousand cuts" from continual terrorism.

An area which bridges external and internal threats to U.S. national security is immigration. While we won't address this comprehensively, a few comments are in order. While there are admittedly complex issues regarding how to sensitively handle the human challenges resulting from long-standing dysfunction in U.S. immigration policy and execution (ranging from human trafficking, to labor resources, to family considerations, to equity for those seeking legal immigration, to the nexus with an ongoing war on drugs, to the tremendous challenges within the law enforcement community for humane enforcement), <u>it is nevertheless a primary task of government to secure national borders</u>. As one example of government blatantly ignoring this responsibility, consider the Justice Department's shocking release of undocumented immigrants with criminal records, from a report released in March 2014 by the Center for Immigration Studies, a conservative think tank that studies immigration patterns:

> "The Obama administration in 2013 released nearly 68,000 undocumented immigrants who had criminal records—many of them in New York and New Jersey, according to a new review of immigration data. "

Immigration reform will definitely be a critical issue in the November 2014 Congressional elections, the November 2016 Presidential election, and beyond. A minimum essential requirement is secure borders, both to prevent external infiltration threats and internal domestic impacts.

Internal Threats

In addition to the external and internal threats fostered by dysfunctional immigration policy and execution, internal threats to our national security fall into four categories: terrorists operating within the U.S., racial discord, lawless disrespect for others, and apathy. Many have also said that our national debt is the biggest security issue the U.S. faces, but I will save that topic for Chapter 7 when we discuss "Pursuing a Prosperous Future."

Terrorists Operating within the U.S. While this is not a classified venue allowing for full discussion of past or ongoing challenges of terrorists operating within U.S. borders, an unclassified example will make the point. One clear terrorist tactic is to infiltrate and assimilate into U.S. society, particularly within Muslim or Kurdish enclaves in the U.S. which provide sanctuary to embedded "sleeper cells." Consider the "Lackawanna Seven" in Lackawanna, New York which was discovered in the wake of 9/11. In short, this was a group of young male American citizens who grew up in the U.S. in a tight-knit Arab community with Yemeni roots. The men were "radicalized" over time by Muslim extremists, to the point where they eventually were providing tangible support to Al Qaeda from U.S. soil. A biography of one of the Lackawanna Seven reads as follows:

"Yasein Taher was voted 'friendliest' by his 1996 graduating class at Lackawanna High School. Five years later, in the spring of 2001, he was in an Al Qaeda training camp attending military lectures and learning how to use a Kalashnikov.

"The 25-year-old former soccer team co-captain married his high school sweetheart, a former cheerleader. Friends said Taher became more interested in Islam as he entered his early twenties. When he returned from the camp in Afghanistan, relatives said he appeared less devout, going out to nightclubs again and shaving his beard.

"Taher worked at a collection agency and had attended a local community college. He was living with his mother at the time of his arrest. He pled guilty in May 2003 to providing material support to

Al Qaeda, and was sentenced to an eight-year prison term in December 2003."

This biographical sketch gives us appreciation of how insidious this problem is, how difficult it is to truly identify this type of internal threat. Further research, as well as classified investigation, will reveal that this scenario is not unique; in fact, there have been many such instances of "sleeper cells" and active terrorism sympathizers who were compromised by good law enforcement work and an alert public. And those are only the ones we know about. Whether a sleeper cell such as the Lackawanna Seven, or a Boston Marathon bomber, or Major Hassan at Fort Hood, or numerous other terror incidents either planned or perpetrated within U.S. borders, these internal threats to our national security are very real. The challenge becomes doubly difficult when our government lacks clarity and commitment regarding such internal terrorist threats.

Racial Discord Many (including African-American pastors) across America are asking "Why are we so angry?" Consider the March 2014 incident in Detroit when an older white man, Steve Utash, got out of his car to check on a young African-American child who he hit when the child stepped into the street. He was then brutally and inexplicably beaten by African-American youth and men. This resulted in a charge of "ethic intimidation" for a 16- year old African-American youth, along with a number of even more serious charges for other participants in the unnecessary and unprovoked beating. Under state statute,

> "...a person is guilty of ethnic intimidation if that
> person maliciously, and with specific intent to

intimidate or harass another person because of that person's race, color, religion, gender, or national origin causes physical contact with another person; damages, destroys or defaces personal property; threatens any of those acts; or if there is cause to believe any of those acts will occur."

Such an ethic of ethnic intimidation and violence by African-American youths only worsens when high profile African-American public figures put even more "spin on the ball," often validating these angry young African-Americans and failing to seriously deal with the root causes of their behavior.

Although the inauguration of America's first African-American President held promise that America was turning another corner in the needed evolution of racial harmony and equity in the U.S., the reality is that President Obama, Attorney General Eric Holder, and the ever present "Civil Rights Industry" (personified by Reverend Jesse Jackson, as well as Reverend Al Sharpton and his National Action Network) have done nothing but fan the flames of racial animosity.

Consider these remarks by President Obama to the National Action Network in April 2014: "The right to vote is threatened today in a way that it has not been since the Voting Rights Act became law nearly five decades ago." Attorney General Eric Holder enflamed the same African-American special interest group by inferring that he and the President were being treated unfairly by Congress because of their race, essentially playing "the race card." None of this inflammatory rhetoric is based upon fact, nor is it beneficial to the future of America. Instead of addressing systemic and cultural issues such as violence among African-American youth, the preponderance of African-American babies born to unwed mothers, father absenteeism, a pervasive culture of dependency and entitlement which seeks to game the system instead of promoting working for a living, and inordinately high African-American unemployment, these very leaders who hold the power to model and promote positive change in and for the African-American community of America are counter-productively fanning the flames of racial antagonism. They have become part of the problem, instead of the solution.

This pattern of denial and defensiveness regarding systemic issues within America's African-America culture is endemic and worsening. As a result, racial discord and tensions in America are approaching a level not experienced since the 1960s. Prayerfully, this tension will not boil over into another cycle of inter-racial violence which only drives the roots of bitterness deeper. Regrettably, we will likely reap the consequences of the discord we have been sowing—"Do not be deceived, God is not mocked; for whatever a man **sows**, this he will also **reap**." (Galatians 6:7, bold added)

While there is much progress still to be made for African-Americans and other racial and ethnic minorities, the answer does not lie in inciting further bitterness and hatred. We must not place partisan political gain above the true welfare of the African-American community. Ironically, this has been the norm for the Obama Administration.

Martin Luther King, Jr. was a seminal figure in American history—an American Hero in many ways. While a force for non-violent protest against the many racial inequities in the 1960s, he was also a symbol of racial reconciliation, working with a broad range of people and constituencies, to include teaming at one point with Billy Graham to emphasize the spiritual nature of America's racial tensions. I venture to say he would not approve of the Black Panther tactics that followed his death, or of the present day "race industry" that only exacerbates racial tensions. The Civil Rights Act of 1964 and the Voting Rights Act of 1965 were useful tools to rein in systemic prejudice. These were battles fought and won on the streets of Selma, on the National Mall in Washington, in the Birmingham jail, and after the crack of an assassin's bullet.

Many others like Martin Luther King, Jr. have also fought the good fight to right basic wrongs in American culture and politics: Justice Clarence Thomas, Alan Keyes, Congressman Alan West, former Secretary of State Condoleezza Rice, Dr. Benjamin Carson, and others who have persevered through racial inequities to become fitting role models for African-Americans. Such positive examples have produced increasing acceptance and empowerment of African-Americans in every walk of life and leadership in this nation, moving from the simple absence of oppression to the presence of increasing opportunity for African-Americans. While further progress is still needed, we collectively need to "lay down our guns" and focus on the remaining tasks of forgiveness, reconciliation, and continued progress together. As in Ecclesiastes 3:3 ("A time to kill and a time to heal; A time to tear down and a time to build up."), it is time for America's racial discord to be transformed into racial reconciliation, a time to heal and to build up.

The enemy is no longer systemic prejudice in an America trapped in the vestiges of a slavery mentality. America has worked hard to repent of its "original sin" of slavery, and if anything has "overcorrected" to the detriment of African-Americans (witness the "Great Society" which created an addiction to entitlements). Now the primary threat to African-American progress is a continued denial of the systemic cultural challenges (fatherless families, youth violence, dependence mentality, structural poverty, et al) that exist within the African-American community itself. In his March 10, 2014, speech in observance of the 50th Anniversary of the Civil Rights Act, President Obama stated, "With effort and courage, people who love their country can change it." As an invaluable gift to future generations, "We the People," "We the Church," and "We the Statesmen," including the African-American community, must collectively muster the effort and courage to candidly address and demonstrably improve the racial climate in America.

> It is time for America's racial discord to be transformed into racial reconciliation, a time to heal and to build up.

Lawless Disrespect for Others When reflecting on the dual vision of William Wilberforce (1759-1883) to stop the slave trade and reinstitute civility in society, I have sometimes felt that "manners" were a trivial cause when compared to the gross injustice of the slave trade. Further reflection leads me to a different conclusion, however. Civility can be defined as "polite, reasonable, and respectful behavior." Such behavior, ideally learned in the home at a young age, begins in small ways with simple expressions of respect to others: "Thank you. I am sorry, will you forgive me? How can I help you? Please pass the butter." The problem is that when such civil behavior is not learned and respected at a young age, the manifestations grow worse in time, ultimately resulting in a spirit of lawlessness that displaces respect for others with selfish pleasure-seeking violent behavior towards others, and lawlessness that is only restrained by a high probability of getting caught. The reality in a democratic society is that if every person does not possess an "inner policeman," then there will never be enough policemen to restrain the coarse behavior and violence that a lawless populace can inflict upon fellow citizens.

Consistent with America's growing culture of coarseness and violence, lawless disrespect for others continues to rise. For starters, consider the dialog one hears on public transportation. As an example, the "F" word is rampant in modern American vocabulary, often used to disrespect others. Or how about the alcohol-induced, riotous celebrations or protests of defeat at sporting events in America? Rome didn't hold a candle to some of today's woeful disregard for the safety and serenity of fellow citizens. Consider the University of Arizona riots in March 2014 when their team lost to Wisconsin in the NCAA basketball tournament. Of greatest concern is that the student's target of outrage became the local police, symbols of authority who were pummeled with beer cans, firecrackers, and utter disrespect. It is alarming when students have so little self-control that they brazenly ignore law enforcement officials and put property and persons at risk, all because of a basketball outcome.

If every person does not possess an "inner policeman,"
then there will never be enough policemen
to restrain the coarse behavior and violence
that a lawless populace can inflict upon fellow citizens.

Regrettably, this scenario of alcohol abuse and blatant disrespect for authority replays itself when college students migrate for "Spring Break," a drunken celebration of college students "gone wild" at numerous venues in the U.S. and Mexico. These gatherings glamorize lawlessness, tax local police resources, and deepen the moral rift across America by further normalizing coarseness, drunkenness, lewdness, and immoral acts. "Knockout Games," already discussed in "Culture of Violence" in Chapter 5, represent even one more escalation of lawless disrespect and random violence directed at others.

Ultimately, this lawless disrespect for others is also directed at God. Although these verses from Romans 1:28-32 apply to many of the areas we have discussed thus far, perhaps this is a fitting place to highlight the consequences of the lawlessness, immorality, and disrespect for God and others so prevalent in America today:

> "[28] And just as they did not see fit to acknowledge God any longer, God gave them over to a depraved mind, to do those things which are not proper,

[29] being filled with all unrighteousness, wickedness, greed, evil; full of envy, murder, strife, deceit, malice; *they are* gossips, [30] slanderers, haters of God, insolent, arrogant, boastful, inventors of evil, disobedient to parents, [31] without understanding, untrustworthy, unloving, unmerciful; [32] and although they know the ordinance of God, that those who practice such things are worthy of death, they not only do the same, but also give hearty approval to those who practice them."

Such behavior by so many of "We the People" is not only blight on our land, but also a very real internal threat to our national security.

Apathy "The feeling of not having much emotion or interest" is the way Merriam-Webster defines apathy. Apathy particularly constitutes an internal threat when citizens are passionate about wrong things (such as lawlessness, immorality, and narcissistic self-fulfillment) and apathetic about right things (such as civic duty, selfless service, respect for others, and moral behavior). As you probably recall from Chapter 2, apathy was a stage in Tytler's cycle of national decline.

In a July 11, 2011 article on "Apathy in America: The Neglected Duty of Civic Awareness," Chuck Colson (who served with President Nixon as White House Counsel 1969-1973, served prison time for his involvement with Watergate, and subsequently became a leading Christian leader and thinker) states the following:

"An informed public is essential to the notion of self-government. We need to be able to make educated political decisions. That means—at a minimum—knowing who our representatives are and what they stand for. The whole process of representative democracy collapses without our participation. (Hence, apathy is a true threat to our continued existence as a nation.)

"The complaint is often heard that bureaucrats in Washington are a power-hungry elite who pay little attention to those who elected them. And that's exactly what is happening. But the reason is not so much that the politicians are ignoring us. It is because we the public are studiously ignoring them.

"We cannot hold our elected officials accountable if we do not know who they are or how our political system operates. It's called civic responsibility—a great American tradition (one of the elements of Spiritual Infrastructure defined in Chapter 1). In times past civic duty—or civics—was taught to our young people as a required course in high schools across the land. These days civics is an option, often ignored.

"Christians ought to set an example and take a cue from the Scriptures. Government is not to be despised or ignored. Along with the family and the church, Government is one of the three institutions ordained by God." (underlines and parentheticals added)

In a *US Observer* website article, "Apathy in America Today," J.M. Appleton echoes a similar theme regarding the national threat posed by apathy:

"When spoken of in regard to the over-all "health" of any nation, <u>apathy amongst its citizens is very much like a cancer that spreads nefariously</u>... the destruction it causes leaves the body weakened and susceptible to a plethora of deadly diseases that can sooner or later mean the end.

"<u>The only therapy for apathy is to remain involved or to increase your current involvement, keeping a watchful and critiquing eye on the actions of our elected and appointed officials....then speaking up and out when discrepancies are found.</u>

"Is it too late for the U.S.A.? Only time will tell for certain, <u>but if our course remains the same and if we as a people in general don't set down the game controller, or T.V. remote, or alcoholic beverage and turn our attention to matters of GREAT importance</u>... we (like Caesar's Roman Empire) might be spoken of through history books in 'past tense' and that my friends would be a dirty and crying shame." (underlines added)

> Apathy particularly constitutes an internal threat
> when citizens are passionate about wrong things (such as
> lawlessness, immorality, and narcissistic self-fulfillment) and
> apathetic about right things (such as civic duty, selfless service,
> respect for others, and moral behavior).

Biblical Precepts for "Freedom from Threats"

Regarding equality and unity across races and genders, Galatians 3:28: "There is neither Jew nor Greek, there is neither slave nor free man, there is neither male nor female; for you are all one in Christ Jesus."

Regarding proper use of freedom, Galatians 5:13: "For you were called to freedom, brethren; only do not turn your freedom into an opportunity for the flesh, but through love serve one another."

Regarding the consequences of sowing discord, immorality, and lawlessness, Galatians 6:7: "Do not be deceived, God is not mocked; for whatever a man sows, this he will also reap."

Actions and Policies Securing "Freedom from Threats"

1. <u>Fight proposed military cuts</u> which will jeopardize U.S. ability to deter adversaries, decisively win necessary conflicts, continue to prosecute the war on terror, defend the homeland, and render support in times of national disaster.

2. <u>Reform immigration</u>, with a first priority to securing America's borders.

3. <u>Seek true racial reconciliation</u>. Work with moderate African-American leadership (including pastors) to define a pathway of resolution to deep-seated racial challenges in America.

4. <u>Fight apathy in self and others</u>. Promote civic participation, volunteerism, and philanthropy. Be an informed, values voter—electing the right "statesmen" to govern, and holding them accountable to "We the People."

Securing Freedom from Government

Recall the Thomas Paine quote we used in Chapter 3 which included the following:

> "Society in every state is a blessing, but <u>government even in its best state is but a necessary evil; in its worst state an intolerable one</u>..."

For this reason, the Constitution establishes "enumerated powers" for the federal government to perform on behalf of "We the People." The Founders recognized the importance of <u>limited government</u>. All powers not enumerated are reserved for lower level government and for "We the People" directly (to include private sector endeavors). For many years the federal government has reached far beyond the enumerated powers intended by the Constitution. This "government overreach" has grown monumentally since 9/11, and most significantly with the Obama Administration. This encroachment into every area of American life is, in Thomas Paine's words, becoming "intolerable," robbing "We the People" of unalienable LIBERTY.

By doing an internet search on "enumerated powers," you can gather significant background quickly. For instance, Wikipedia enumerates all of the powers granted to the federal government in the Constitution:

"The Congress shall have Power

To lay and collect Taxes, Duties, Imposts and Excises, to pay the Debts and provide for the common Defense and general Welfare of the United States; but all Duties, Imposts and Excises shall be uniform throughout the United States;

To borrow on the credit of the United States;

To regulate Commerce with foreign Nations, and among the several States, and with the Indian Tribes;

To establish a uniform Rule of Naturalization, and uniform Laws on the subject of Bankruptcies throughout the United States;

To coin Money, regulate the Value thereof, and of foreign Coin, and fix the Standard of Weights and Measures;

To provide for the Punishment of counterfeiting the Securities and current Coin of the United States;

To establish Post Offices and Post Roads;

To promote the Progress of Science and useful Arts, by securing for limited Times to Authors and Inventors the exclusive Right to their respective Writings and Discoveries;

To constitute Tribunals inferior to the Supreme Court;

To define and punish Piracies and Felonies committed on the high Seas, and Offenses against the Law of Nations;

To declare War, grant Letters of Marque and Reprisal, and make Rules concerning Captures on Land and Water;

To raise and support Armies, but no Appropriation of Money to that Use shall be for a longer Term than two Years;

To provide and maintain a Navy;

To make Rules for the Government and Regulation of the land and naval Forces;

<u>To provide for calling forth the Militia</u> to execute the Laws of the Union, suppress Insurrections and repel Invasions;

<u>To provide for organizing, arming, and disciplining, the Militia</u>, and for governing such Part of them as may be employed in the Service of the United States, reserving to the States respectively, the Appointment of the Officers, and the Authority of training the Militia according to the discipline prescribed by Congress;

<u>To exercise exclusive Legislation</u> in all Cases whatsoever, over such District (not exceeding ten Miles square) as may, by Cession of particular States, and the acceptance of Congress, become the Seat of the Government of the United States, and to exercise like Authority over all Places purchased by the Consent of the Legislature of the State in which the Same shall be, for the Erection of Forts, Magazines, Arsenals, dock-Yards, and other needful Buildings; And

<u>To make all Laws which shall be necessary and proper</u> for carrying into Execution the foregoing Powers, and all other Powers vested by this Constitution in the Government of the United States, or in any Department or Officer thereof." (termed the "necessary and proper" clause which

has been used to justify necessary and unnecessary
laws and programs)

These enumerated powers from the Constitution, along with some granted in Amendments (such as the 16th which provided the power to tax income), comprise the extent of federal government authority. One quickly notices that broad areas such as health care, education, gun control, long term entitlement programs, and environmental regulations are not powers enumerated to the federal government.

Enumerated powers have always been an area of tension and debate (strict constructionists v. loose constructionists). Building on Post-9/11 security changes, post-2008 economic injections by government, Obamacare, and now executive orders to flank the Congress with a phone and a pen, the Obama Administration has overreached enumerated powers to unprecedented levels.

Of even greater concern, recent reports suggest that the Obama Administration is also using government powers to enhance their political welfare. The ongoing "IRS Scandal" is one of the most prominent examples, uncovering IRS suppression of 501 (c) (3) organization applications by groups considered politically unfavorable, particularly those aligned with the TEA Party ("Taxed Enough Already"). Subsequently, other irregularities were uncovered including IRS agents caught telling customers to vote Democratic. While President Obama and bi-partisan critics at first proclaimed that these illegal and irresponsible practices would be stopped and persons held accountable, the Administration and Democratic Congressional leadership have quickly "obfuscated" the issue and "slow rolled" any accountability efforts by Congress.

The hole keeps getting deeper. Similar to the Administration's dissembling that a videotape was the cause of the attack on our U.S. Consul in Benghazi and the murder of our U.S. Ambassador to Libya Christopher Stephens, the Administration initially claimed that the growing IRS scandal was only the work of rogue agents in the IRS Kansas City office. President Obama's assertion that "there is not a smidgen of corruption in the IRS" has likewise proven false. Whether these illegal political activities by the IRS were part of a grand strategy at the highest levels of the U.S. Government remains to be determined.

While such government intrusion undermines market economies and creates many unintended negative consequences, scenarios such as the ongoing "IRS Scandal" also undermine Americans' basic trust in government and in those they have elected to represent them. This further weakens the Spiritual Infrastructure of the United States, specifically the first sub element:

> <u>Adherence to Constitutional Foundations</u>
> *Contrasted with political operatives, special interest groups, and activist judges for whom the Constitution is not sacrosanct, for whom the ends often justify the means, for whom separation of powers, checks and balances, and other principles of American government are only observed when*

supportive of partisan agendas. (from *Resilient Nations*, Chapter 1)

Actions and Policies for Securing "Freedom from Government"

1. Support the "Enumerated Powers Act" which would require all legislation before Congress to set forth the specific Congressional authority to enact such legislation.
2. Support efforts to identify and curtail existing laws and practices by the federal government which clearly exceed their Constitutional granted authorities. Repeal of Obamacare (to be discussed in Chapter 7) would be an obvious example.

Securing Religious Freedom

Recall the third of our key sub elements of Spiritual Infrastructure related to religious freedom:

"Free Exercise and Relevance of <u>Religion in Private and Public Venues</u>"

Contrasted with efforts to restrict the "Freedom of Religion" wording of the Constitution to mean "freedom of worship," isolating religion to a private matter not to be discussed or applied in the public square; complicated by witting and unwitting non-Constitutional interpretations of "Separation of Church and State" which conveniently serve anti-religion agendas.

The wording is important. Note that it does not merely say "Freedom of Worship" (a term of recently used by President Obama to apparently shrink the domain of religion). Note that our definition also refers to public venues, what some would call the "public square." As we laid out Spiritual Infrastructure timelines in Chapters 1 and 4, we noted both positive (1740-1960) and negative (1960+) impacts on America's Spiritual Infrastructure, including specific freedom of religion inflection points. We will not repeat these many examples here, but will rather dive into specific challenges and strategies for maintaining the Freedom of Religion which God and our Founding Fathers intended. The "Additional Resources" section of this chapter has a number of excellent books and websites that allow one to dive much deeper into this critical issue.

The U.S. Constitution is a good place to begin our discussion of Freedom of Religion, an essential ingredient of LIBERTY. The "Religious Clauses" of the First Amendment consist of the "Establishment Clause" ("Congress shall make no law respecting an establishment of religion") and the "Free Exercise Clause" ("or prohibiting the free exercise thereof"). The establishment clause basically means that Congress cannot establish a national religion, nor can it prefer one religion over another. The free exercise clause basically means that Congress cannot make laws which prevent a person from exercising the dictates of their particular religion. While there are understandable complexities of application of these clauses that our courts and legislators have wrestled with since the Constitutional Convention, there have also been invalid interpretations that have threatened true Freedom of Religion.

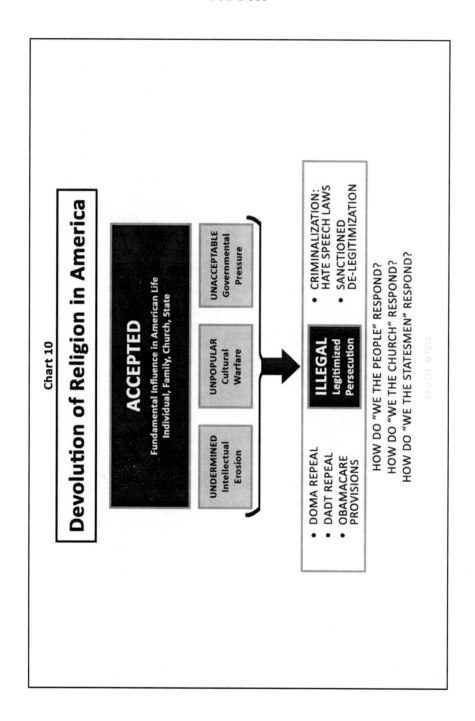

Chart 10

Devolution of Religion in America

ACCEPTED
Fundamental Influence in American Life
Individual, Family, Church, State

UNDERMINED
Intellectual
Erosion

UNPOPULAR
Cultural
Warfare

UNACCEPTABLE
Governmental
Pressure

ILLEGAL
Legitimized
Persecution

- DOMA REPEAL
- DADT REPEAL
- OBAMACARE PROVISIONS

- CRIMINALIZATION: HATE SPEECH LAWS
- SANCTIONED DE-LEGITIMIZATION

HOW DO "WE THE PEOPLE" RESPOND?
HOW DO "WE THE CHURCH" RESPOND?
HOW DO "WE THE STATESMEN" RESPOND?

Threats to Religious Freedom

Devolution of Religion in America

Chart 10 on the opposite page, entitled *Devolution of Religion in America*, provides the big picture. A brief explanation is in order: from the founding of this nation until the 1960s, religion was <u>accepted</u> as a fundamental influence in American life, recognized as relevant and beneficial to individuals, families, the Church, and the State. As indicated on our Spiritual Infrastructure timelines, forces seeking to discredit religion during the entire 20th Century coalesced in the 1960s along three primary avenues: intellectual erosion (fomented by humanists, progressives, and other philosophies of man) which <u>undermined</u> the basis for religion, cultural warfare in every marketplace of society (later to be discussed as the "Seven Mountains of Culture") which made religion <u>unpopular,</u> and governmental pressure and rulings which effectively made religion <u>unacceptable</u> (removal of school prayer, Ten Commandments, et al). As the predominant faith in America, Christianity received the most pressure to conform to increased secularization of America.

While seeming to provide the Muslim religion "most favored status," the Obama Administration moved rapidly to take the devolution of traditional religion one step further. Legislation and executive orders such as the Don't Ask Don't Tell (DADT) repeal in the U.S. Military, aggressive efforts at the state and national levels to roll back the Defense of Marriage Act (DOMA), unfettered support of the gay activist agenda (wrongly labeled as gay "rights"), continuing pursuit of the Employment Non-

Discrimination Act (ENDA), and efforts to classify Biblical teaching as "hate speech" have moved America closer to making religion not just unpopular or unacceptable to many in the culture, but also <u>illegal</u>. This would result in legitimized persecution of Christians and others, as we are already seeing with unprecedented frequency in the Middle East (Iraq, Iran, Syria, et al) and Africa, primarily at the hands of Muslim perpetrators. Parenthetically, one must ask why President Obama has allowed the U.S. Ambassador-at-Large for Religious Freedom position to remain vacant for over a year, particularly with such heightened persecution of Christians and others worldwide.

Prayerfully, this latter stage of overt religious persecution will not become reality in America. "We the People," "We the Church," and "We the Statesmen" must recognize the seriousness of this erosion of religion in general and Christianity in particular within our own borders and beyond. It is time to stand up. As David Lane, leader of the American Renewal Project, would exhort, "Will a Gideon or Rahab the Harlot please stand?" (referring to Gideon in Judges 6-8 and Rahab in Joshua 2 and 6 as courageous and faithful Biblical figures who stood up against daunting odds to change the course of history)

> **It is time to stand up!**

Separation of Church and State Mythology

Consider the mantra "separation of church and state," which is increasingly used as rationale for "protecting" the state from the incursion of the church, legitimizing the prohibition of religious practices in the public square, directly violating the Free Exercise clause. The reality is that the term "Separation of Church and State" is never used in the *Declaration of Independence* or the *Constitution*. It was actually used by Thomas Jefferson in a letter to the Danbury Baptists in 1802, intended to convey that there should be "a wall" which protects the church from the state, not vice versa. "Separation of Church and State" has become the primary bludgeon of judicial activists, anti-religion crusaders, and unwitting influencers in every sector of society across our land. Supreme Court Justice William Rehnquist summarized it well:

> "The wall of separation between church and state is a metaphor based on bad history, a metaphor which has proven useless as a guide to judging. It should be frankly and explicitly abandoned."

To examine this area further, I recommend Mat Staver's *Take Back America* and David Barton's *Original Intent* which also includes the following warning about judicial activism related to religious freedom:

> "In their own words, the Supreme Court has become 'a national theology board,' 'a super board of education,' and amateur psychologists on a "psycho-journey." The result has been

<u>a virtual rewriting of the liberties enumerated in the Constitution</u>.

"A direct victim of this judicial micromanagement has been the religious aspect of the first Amendment. For example, the Court now interprets that Amendment under: a "Lemon Test" absurdly requiring religious expression to be secular, an "Endorsement Test" pursuing an impossible neutrality between religion and secularism, and a "Psychological Coercion Test" allowing a single dissenter to silence an entire community's religious expression." (underline added)

Hence, the myth of "Separation of Church and State," perpetuated and expanded by liberal judicial activism, has created an environment which is prejudicial against freedom of religion in America.

Governmental Obstruction

Ironically, the government which is charged by the U.S. Constitution to ensure free exercise of religion in America is one of free exercise of religion's primary impediments. While the erosion of religious liberties occurred over the entire 20th and now the 21st Century, the Obama Administration has become a witting accomplice in the process. Without repeating examples provided earlier, issues range from suppression of religious expression at the U.S. Air Force Academy, to forcing employers to violate religious conscience via Obamacare (such as with Hobby Lobby and the Sisters of Mercy cases pending before the Supreme Court), to consistent bias against religion by the Holder Department of Justice. President Obama himself manifested disdain for religion in unguarded comments which stated: "... it's not surprising then they get bitter, <u>they cling to guns or religion or antipathy to people who aren't like them</u> or anti-immigrant sentiment or anti-trade sentiment as a way to express their frustrations."

This governmental influence over free exercise appears in more subtle ways as well. Take for instance the Bush White House Office of Faith-Based and Community Initiatives which became Faith-Based and Neighborhood Partnerships (FBNP) under President Obama. While seeming to be an innocuous change, this reshaping transferred much of the previous emphasis on faith to "neighborhood partnerships" (weaving in since-discredited ACORN and other Democratic "community organizers"). It is very difficult to find validation of religion as one "surfs" the FBNP websites associated with each Department of Government. While our government seeks to secure as many resources as possible from the faith-based community, religious faith is not an inherent value of the Obama Administration or the liberal establishment which supports it.

Anti-Religion Special Interest

Other threats to religious freedom are special interests, committed to removing every vestige of faith or religion from American public life. The most notable of these secular and often rabid anti-religion special interest groups are the Freedom from Religion Foundation (FFRF, www.ffrf.org), the American Civil

Liberties Union (ACLU, www.aclu.org), the American Humanist Association (AHA, www.humanistlegalcenter.org), the Secular Coalition for America (SCA, www.secular.org), the Americans United for Separation of Church and State (AU, www.au.org), and the Military Religious Freedom Foundation (MRFF, www.militaryreligiousfreedom.org). Such groups, increasingly organized and technologically savvy, continually "patrol" the public square to identify and remove religious practice. Their primary tool is litigation, of recent quite effective in tandem with activist federal judges and complicit (or naïve) leaders across all "Seven Mountains of Culture" (Arts & Entertainment, Business, Education, Family, Government, Media, and Religion).

Gratefully, there are a number of Christian and faith-based organizations which provide a counterbalance to these groups who seek the demise of Christianity (and other faith groups) in America through "death by a thousand cuts" (thousands of lawsuits and road blocks to free exercise across the nation). Some of the more visible Christian advocacy groups who are "fighting the good fight of faith" every day in our courts and in the public square are Alliance Defending Freedom (ADF, www.alliancedefendingfreedom.org), the American Center for Law and Justice (ACLJ, www.aclj.org), the Becket Fund for Religious Liberty (www.becketfund.org), the Liberty Counsel (LC, www.lc.org), the Liberty Institute (LI, www.libertyinstitute.org), Wallbuilders (www.wallbuilders.com), and the Family Research Council (FRC, www.frc.org). The Congressional Prayer Caucus Foundation (CPCF, www.cpcfoundation.com) does a tremendous service to communities of faith by consolidating religious freedom information and resources at the national, state, and local levels, as well as working with other national prayer organizations to mobilize continual intercession on behalf of our nation.

Rise of the "Nones"

One other trend (and possibly a threat) influencing religion in America is the "Rise of the Nones." Time magazine's March 12, 2012, cover story, *10 Ideas that are Changing Your Life*, states "the fastest-growing religious group in the U.S. is the category of people who say they have no religious affiliation. Sometimes called "the nones" by social scientists, their numbers have more than doubled since 1990; major surveys put them at 16% of the population." The "Nones" are not necessarily against religious faith, but they do appear to resist traditional forms of religious expression. Newly-inducted Arizona Congressional Representative Kyrsten Sinema recently became the first professing "None" in Congress.

While the "Nones" are indisputably rising, there is considerable debate regarding the significance of this trend, ranging from serious impacts on organized religion in America to simply another social trend largely driven by generational differences which is an opportunity for the church to be relevant in new ways to true seekers. In Randy Newman's "Integration Points" blog on this topic, he cleverly highlights a quote illustrating vehement religious doubt and skepticism, later revealing the author to be C.S. Lewis, written before he became one of the world's greatest Christian thinkers and apologists. This provides useful perspective regarding the potential of each "None" as they wrestle with their own spirituality and religious expression.

Somewhat related to the "rise of the nones" are prevalent "politically correct" efforts to marginalize religion by relegating it to a minor subset of the larger universe of "spirituality." I have seen this particularly up close in the military. Because of the charged atmosphere surrounding "religion," many military leaders and program directors try to finesse the "spiritual" dimension of their comprehensive fitness and resilience programs by quickly injecting that "spiritual means a lot more than religion." Others simply exclude anything with religious connotation from their programs. Despite the high relevance of religious practice to our troops, current unwillingness by military leadership to appropriately acknowledge and resource the spiritual fitness component of comprehensive fitness does a great disservice to troops and families, depriving them of the very resources which will assist with the pervasive mental and behavioral health challenges the military faces. I am confident there is far more empirical and anecdotal evidence regarding the benefits of religion to challenges of suicide, depression, posttraumatic stress, marital harmony, recovery from addictions, moral injury, et al than for most other techniques being tried in the military today. Regrettably, the preponderance of faith-based protocols does not get a legitimate hearing or resourcing.

Every troop and military family member possesses a spiritual dimension, and religion is still the primary way in which troops and families exercise their spirituality. Troops getting ready to go in harm's way don't worry about being "politically correct;" they want to be "God correct." They will unashamedly hold hands and pray together with words like, "God, you are our Rock, our Fortress, our Deliverer... the strong tower to whom we can run" (Psalm 18), or the 23d Psalm, or the 91st Psalm (also known as the "Soldier's Psalm").

So it is in every other sector of American society. Religion remains the primary way in which Americans express their spirituality. Religion, particularly Christianity as the predominant American faith group, still makes a huge difference in the foxhole, in the factory, and in the family. Such religious faith, empowered by religious freedom, is a tangible benefit to individual Americans and to society at large.

> Religion, particularly Christianity as the predominant American faith group, still makes a huge difference in the foxhole, in the factory, and in the family.

Benefits of Religion in America

Just as with the cycles of resilience in Israel, America has periodically rediscovered religious values, become convicted about flawed policy and practice, responded to the direction of God-honoring resilient leaders ("Statesmen"), and reversed course individually and nationally. This has resulted in true national renewal and spiritual rearmament. While we pray for another Great Awakening in America, we must also recognize the daily benefits that religion affords. These often occur with one citizen, one family, one statesman, one organization at a time. They also occur in faith communities across America—the churches, parishes, synagogues, and other places of worship—

which impart values, fight isolation, afford a venue for service, serve as refuge in storms of life, and instill hope.

Consider Dr. Harold Koenig's (Duke University Center for Spirituality, Theology, and Health,) depiction of our nation's "religious coping" during national stress on <u>September 11, 2001</u> (www.spiritualityandhealth.duke.edu),

1. Talking with others (98%)
2. **Turning to religion (90%)**
3. Checked safety of family/friends (75%)
4. Participating in group activities (60%)
5. Avoiding reminders (watching TV) (39%)
6. Making donations (36%)
(Bold emphasis added)

Dr. Koenig further asserts, "Hundreds of quantitative and qualitative studies report similar findings in persons under stress, especially in minorities." Religious faith is truly an "anchor for the soul" for Americans in travail, but the impacts go far beyond national or personal disasters. Faith makes an empirical, scientifically validated, real difference in the everyday lives of the vast majority of American citizens, regardless of race, gender, age, or particular challenge or opportunity they face. For further validation of this assertion, I direct readers to Dr. Koenig's extensive and highly reputable research regarding the efficacy of faith in every walk of American life.

Actions and Policies to Secure Religious Freedom

1. **Heterogeneous Accommodation**. A common approach to navigating religious issues is to "homogenize" the tenets of multiple faiths down to the lowest common denominator which neither offends, nor truly benefits, the recipients. For example, programs which include a Christian world view are often deemed "out of bounds" because they might offend the sensibilities of non-Christians. An alternative approach, which we will call "heterogeneous accommodation," retains the distinctives of each faith (including "nones," free thinkers, atheists, et al) and provides "best practice" to each faith group in a given population (such as the military, businesses, schools, et cetera), allowing them to maximize spiritual benefit within the construct of their particular world view. In essence, heterogeneous accommodation allows each faith group to celebrate and grow from their own respective best faith practices instead of focusing on what other faith groups might be doing. In a military context, this means Chaplains, para-church organizations, lay faith group leaders, and local worship communities enhance spiritual fitness via best Protestant, best Catholic, best Jewish, best Islamic, best Hindu, et al, faith practices for those respective segments of the military population. Exercise of Christian best practices (prayer, Bible study, fellowship, and outreach) by a Christian does not inherently deprive other faiths of their right to exercise spirituality in accordance with their own world view and faith practices.

2. "We the People" must support (with our time, talents, and treasure) the efforts of Religious Freedom organizations such as listed in this chapter, as well as serving as "cultural scouts" to identify impediments to religious free exercise. Strongly oppose legislation or societal pressures which undercut religious expression in America.

3. "We the Statesmen," as well as leaders across the Seven Mountains of Culture (Arts & Entertainment, Business, Education, Family, Government, Media, and Religion), serve as modern day Nehemiahs to rebuild our Spiritual Infrastructure, particularly regarding "Free Exercise and Relevance of <u>Religion in Private and Public Venues</u>."

4. "We the Church" must seek to be relevant to the issues of our day, being "innocent as doves and wise as serpents." The role of the Church will be discussed more in Chapter 8, along with the unique role for pastors, priests, rabbis, and other religious leaders across America.

Gaining Altitude: Securing LIBERTY for All Americans

We have discussed the importance of securing LIBERTY, one of the unalienable rights afforded to "We the People" in our *Declaration of Independence* and one of the Constitutional responsibilities of government. Our overview began with identification of a Culture of Appeasement, and then extended to three key domains of LIBERTY: Freedom from External Threats (global adversaries, terrorism, and immigration) and Internal Threats (terrorists within the homeland, lawless disrespect, racial discord, and apathy), Freedom from Government Oppression, and Freedom of Religion.

Knowing that "freedom is not free," we recognize that policy and practice must match rhetoric if we are to remain the freest nation on earth. As a general approach, it is seldom an effective use of resources to try to sway the "radicals" in a particular interest group. In the case of militant Muslim extremists such as Al Qaeda, they must be identified and killed, or they will kill us. Likewise it is seldom productive to attempt to reason with radical Muslim interest groups such as the Council for American and Islamic Relations (CAIR). Any productive engagement with Muslims will be with moderates who are willing to live and let live, assuming such Muslim moderates have the courage to defy their own radicals. One such Muslim moderate with courage and vision is Dr. Zhudi Jasser, author of *A Battle for the Soul of Islam: An American Muslim Patriot's Fight to Save His Faith*. (see Additional Resources)

In the case of special-interest <u>radicals</u> (race activists, gay activists, environmental activists, feminist activists, abortion activists, et al), the best strategy again is to <u>marginalize the radicals</u> by discrediting their own hateful practices and lack of tolerance for the rights of others, and <u>engage the moderates</u> to craft policy and practice that don't require the destruction or oppression of one population in order to meet the needs of another.

At one more level of collaboration with moderates, we must address political compromise. While it is important for "We the Statesmen" to adhere to personal and political core values, they must be willing to work with moderating statesmen on the other side of the aisle to "break the back" of America's deep economic and societal issues. The current challenge is that President Obama, formerly the most liberal voting U.S. Senator in Congress, is the embodiment of the most radical elements of the Democratic Party. As we have seen with the Obama Administration, as well as the Democratic leadership of Nancy Pelosi and Harry Reid "going it alone" (even during the years when they had a majority in both Houses), this has led to the Obamacare fiat that continues to flounder because of lack of bi-partisan support, unrequited stimulus and deficit spending resulting in unprecedented national debt, and further division and stalemate. To cite a counter-example from both "sides of the aisle," President Lyndon Johnson and President Ronald Reagan were never weak-kneed about their own core political positions, but they were masters of persuasion and creative compromise, a key trait for true statesmen who make life better for "We the People."

As a final note, it is important for "We the People," "We the Church," and "We the Statesmen" to stay on a positive agenda, avoiding "rabbit trails" that prevent a transformational message from reaching the intended audience. Franklin Graham of Samaritans Purse models this well, staying on the "middle C" of the gospel without fixating on the vitriol which is thrown at him. Congressman Randy Forbes is a similar role model in the political sphere.

In the case of special interest <u>radicals</u> (race activists, gay activists, environmental activists, feminist activists, abortion activists, et al), the best strategy again is to <u>marginalize the radicals</u> by discrediting their own hateful practices and lack of tolerance for the rights of others, and <u>engage the moderates</u> to craft policy and practice that don't require the destruction or oppression of one population in order to meet the needs of another.

We now move to our final unalienable right: Pursuit of HAPPINESS.

Resilient Nations Takeaways

RN 6A – Thomas Paine rightly assessed that the nature of humanity requires a degree of external moderation. Government serves to restrain human vices, often necessitating the punishment of evil doers. This function of punishment is a necessary evil that should be administered at least cost and maximum benefit, implying a limited nature to government that avoids excessive intrusion or overreach into the lives of individuals, their communities, or their professional endeavors. wisdom to grow old well, with dignity.

RN 6B – With every appeasement, the Spiritual Infrastructure of the United States is further weakened. Our nation becomes a "paper tiger" in the eyes of adversaries and an "oppressive tyrant" in the eyes of "We the People."

RN 6C – The price of a precipitous military drawdown will be paid in blood, either the result of a major miscalculation with a belligerent nation state or the "death by a thousand cuts" from continual terrorism.

RN 6D – <u>Immigration reform</u> will definitely be a critical issue in the November 2014 Congressional elections, the November 2016 Presidential election, and beyond. A minimum essential requirement is secure borders, both to prevent external infiltration threats and internal domestic impacts.

RN 6E – Internal threats to our national security fall into four categories: terrorists operating within the US, racial discord, lawless disrespect for others, and apathy.

RN 6F – While further progress is still needed, we must collectively "lay down our guns" and focus on the remaining tasks of forgiveness, racial reconciliation, and continued progress together. As in Ecclesiastes 3:3 ("A time to kill and a time to heal; A time to tear down and a time to build up."), <u>it is time for America's racial discord to be transformed into racial reconciliation, a time to heal and to build up</u>.

RN 6G – Regarding <u>lawless disrespect for others</u>, if every person does not possess an "<u>inner policeman</u>," then there will never be enough policemen to restrain the coarse behavior and violence that a lawless populace can inflict upon fellow citizens.

RN 6H – Apathy particularly constitutes an internal threat when citizens are passionate about wrong things (such as lawlessness, immorality, and narcissistic self-fulfillment) and apathetic about right things (such as civic duty, selfless service, respect for others, and moral behavior).

RN 6I – In the case of special interest <u>radicals</u> (race activists, gay activists, environmental activists, feminist activists, abortion activists, et al), the best strategy again is to <u>marginalize the radicals</u> by discrediting their own hateful practices and lack of tolerance for the rights of others, and <u>engage the moderates</u> to craft policy and practice that don't require the destruction or oppression of one population in order to meet the needs of another.

RN 6J – While it is important for "We the Statesmen" to adhere to personal and political core values, they must be willing to work with moderating statesmen on the other side of the aisle to "break the back" of America's deep economic and societal issues.

RN 6K – It is important that "We the People," "We the Church," and "We the Statesmen" stay on a positive agenda, avoiding "rabbit trails" that prevent a transformational message from reaching the intended audience.

For Further Consideration

1. Dive deeper into the dangers of an apathetic populace. One of the checks and balances within the American system of government is an informed public which constrains governmental excesses. Conversely, a subservient and uninformed populace compliant to

ever increasing government control will soon find itself encased in tyranny.

2. Consider the "Devolution of Religion in America." As asked on Chart 10, how do "We the People," "We the Church," and "We the Statesmen" respond? How would "heterogeneous inclusion" help to accommodate varied faith "best practices" without violating the establishment and free exercise clauses?

Additional References

1. Reed, Ralph. *Awakening.* Brentwood, TN: Worthy Publishing, 2014.

2. Staver, Mathew D. *Take Back America*. Orlando, FL: New Revolution Publishers, 2011.

3. Barton, David. *Original Intent: The Courts, the Constitution, and Religion*. Aledo, TX: Wallbuilders Press, 2013.

4. Jasser, Zhudi. *A Battle for the Soul of Islam: An American Muslim Patriot's Fight to Save His Faith*. New York, NY: Threshold Editions, 2012.

5. www.LC.org. Liberty Counsel: Restoring the Culture by Advancing Religious Freedom, the Sanctity of Human Life and the Family.

6. www.Wallbuilders.com. Wallbuilders: Presenting America's forgotten history and heroes with an emphasis on our moral, religious, and constitutional heritage.

7. www.ColsonCenter.org. The Chuck Colson Center for Christian Worldview: Proclaim Truth, Train Leaders, and Collaborate with Like-Minded Organizations.

8. www.cpcfoundation.com. Congressional Prayer Caucus Foundation (CPCF): Alarmed by the concerted effort to remove God from every vestige of government and to silence the voice of millions, CPCF is at the center of a growing network of national, state and local leaders who are protecting our right to be a nation that prays and trusts in God. CPCF is mobilizing leaders and citizens who are committed to prayer and action. [Note: This website is very useful consolidation of resources and website references regarding the defense of religious liberties.]

9. www.spiritualityandhealth.duke.edu Duke University Center for Spirituality, Theology, and Health.

10. www.LUOnline.com/IMR Liberty University Institute for Military Resilience: Nation's first faith-based institute to promote resilience and address the pervasive and persistent mental and behavioral health issues of our nation's military, veterans, and their families.

7

Pursuing HAPPINESS

⁹ What profit is there to the worker from that in which he toils?
¹² I know that there is nothing better for them than to rejoice
and to do good in one's lifetime;
¹³ moreover, that every man who eats and drinks
sees good in all his labor—it is the gift of God.
(Ecclesiastes 3:9, 12, 13)

Early one morning I found myself with some unusual "idle time" in the Nashville airport. Walking past the entrance to the Transportation Security Agency (TSA) checkpoint, I noticed an elderly African-American lady scurry up, looking very dignified in her well-pressed volunteer clothes. Her apparent duty was to serve at the volunteer desk just outside the security checkpoint, answering any questions for harried travelers, and imparting a final dose of Nashville hospitality to departing visitors of "Music City USA." Drawn by her sense of dignity and purpose, I walked over to the volunteer desk as Mrs. Doris Francois was getting settled. I knew there was probably a powerful life story behind this dignified elder and I was right. Beginning the conversation with something like "You are really up early!" I spent the next thirty minutes hearing about a fascinating life that I knew had to appear in the pages of *Resilient Nations*.

Doris Francois was brought up Catholic, in New Orleans, poor, the eldest of five children. She was very involved in healthy activities as a child—competing in basketball all over the city with the Catholic Youth Organization, playing the piano, and singing in small operettas. Her grandfather, one who had a significant impact on her life, played jazz music in New Orleans. In her early years of schooling, Doris threw herself into learning, despite the decrepit text books with pages torn out and marred with writing.

Early on she wanted to be a missionary or a nun. Most women at that time would be a teacher, an office assistant, or work at the Post Office. Despite the odds, and after praying the Lord would direct her path, Mrs. Francois decided she wanted to be a doctor—this would be her "pursuit of happiness." While persisting with her medical education, she worked part-time for $3 per shift and car fare (7 cents for street car and bus to get to her job). Wanting to attend a good medical university up North, she was told she had many strikes against her as a woman, poor, colored, Catholic, entering a field dominated by males, and being hearing-impaired. Many predicted she would fail, yet Doris Francois stayed the course to become a medical doctor, a pediatrician. Her subsequent distinguished medical career allowed her to be the hands and feet of the Great Physician in varied children's hospitals, internal medicine and family practices, community-based clinics, and State of Tennessee care facilities for disabled clients.

Interestingly, Doris Francois married in 1963 as racial tensions were heightening and the government was preparing to launch Great Society social programs in America which would initially help but eventually condemn millions to social and economic dependency. She was not lured into complacency, an entitlement mentality, or racial antagonism, however. With her cardiologist husband, she would make house calls for those who couldn't come during the week or didn't have the money. They also made opportunities available for other young people by providing funding for education, books or lunch money, or helping them improve in their studies.

Retired since 2000, Mrs. Francois at age 78 still volunteers and makes a difference in someone's life every day, now working with the Flying Aces volunteer group at the Nashville airport for over ten years. The pearls of wisdom which flow from her years of caring for others read like the Proverbs: "Do not exploit people. There are no failures, just challenges in life. Be kind and good to people and you will have impacted them in a positive way. Do what you are passionate about. Be self-sufficient and independent. Learn from your experiences every day. Always wake up being grateful." This is sage advice from one who could have easily succumbed to the lure of dependency and entitlement.

Her reflections on the current status of America are equally profound. In her own words: "We don't seem to share and care for people and their welfare, racing on the fast track of selfish pursuits. Taking prayer out of schools has impacted our national morality. Loss of discipline and respect in the family, as well as preoccupation with cell phones and 24/7 media, has robbed us of the ability to play and worship together. So many are learning to take the road of least resistance, seeking whatever is pleasurable for the here and now. So many brilliant and talented young people whose minds should be prepared to lead us in the subsequent decades are being poisoned by privileged living for the moment, with the acquisition of material things defining their successes so that caring for their neighbor and others has been discarded. Drugs and pornography have become the real weapons of mass destruction in our children's minds." She has certainly put her finger on the Spiritual Infrastructure challenges of America in 2014 and beyond.

Doris Francois' ultimate advice to America in 2014 turns to the power of personal faith: "Pray and ask God to lead you. It is not about religion, but about what is in your heart. Love and respect the individual, not knowing when you may be touching God Himself."

Maybe you, too, will be privileged to meet Doris Francois one day. It would be worth a trip through the Nashville airport. She is an inspiring example of one who could easily have spent her life homeless, poverty stricken, dependent on handouts, and bitter at the world about her. I'm sure you appreciate the realities she navigated as a young African-American woman in the 1950s forward. Yet, she fought to be educated, worked hard, contributed greatly (to the health care others), forgave much, loved many, spoke kindly, and fostered unity in her pursuit of happiness. She benefited from hand-up opportunities, but never depended on handouts. She pursued happiness in true American fashion – and certainly achieved it.

> ... she fought to be educated, worked hard, contributed greatly (to the health care others), forgave much, loved many, spoke kindly, and fostered unity in her pursuit of happiness. She benefited from hand-up opportunities, but never depended on handouts. She pursued happiness in true American fashion – and certainly achieved it.

A Culture of Dependency

In her early adult years, Doris Francois certainly fit the underprivileged economic and societal profile of one who could easily get stuck in a life of dependency. But she did not, choosing instead the passionate pursuit of a good education, a commitment to hard work, and the dedication to build a healthier America, both personally and professionally. Today she is more the exception than the rule. As with the culture of appeasement discussed in Chapter 6, a "culture of dependency" is pervasive in America and operates at two levels.

On the individual level, it takes the form of depending on the government to provide life support in the form of food stamps, long-term unemployment benefits, and even healthy school lunches. America has just passed a dependency tipping point where less than half of our citizens actually pay taxes. In defining an "American Entitlement Society," Jim Johnson states the dilemma well in *Fracture Zone 2015*:

> "... dependence on entitlement transfers of wealth from the government and a pervasive attitude that Americans are due entitlement benefits. Over the past twenty years, federal spending on means-tested entitlements has risen to 16% and the number of Americans living in a household receiving aid rose 161%. Sociologists pinpoint four key cultural trends that lead to the entitlement society: self-esteem movements, celebrity culture, emerging media, and the credit bubble."

In his 1935 State of the Union Address, President Franklin D. Roosevelt succinctly addressed the impact of welfare "entitlements" on our Spiritual Infrastructure: "Continued dependence upon welfare induces a <u>spiritual disintegration fundamentally destructive to the national fiber</u>. To dole our relief in this way is to administer a narcotic, <u>a subtle destroyer of the human spirit</u>."

Jim Johnson furthers this point that entitlements foster dependency:

> "Some amount of social safety net is necessary. America must take care of citizens in need, but not at costs that bankrupt her. Unemployment benefits payouts have increased over 400% in the last 5 years. Social Security Disability payments

and healthcare entitlements have skyrocketed. Loopholes in our tax code are hidden entitlements. Return to historic growth rates and increased employment is the path to providing for the needs of all Americans."

At the national level, a "culture of dependency" is also at play within every sector where the government seeks to assume undue responsibility for that which individuals or local communities should be rightly responsible. In the case of our economy, the government uses debt to fund ever expanding entitlement programs which engender popular support from recipients. A "bail-out" mentality has become pervasive, creating deeper dependency on government. Examples are the bail-out of private entities, such as auto companies (some would say "GM" has become "Government Motors"), and the use of public financial "bailouts" such as the Quantitative Easing (QE) actions following the economic crisis of 2008. As mentioned in Chapter 6, even if the defense budget were totally zeroed out, government entitlement programs would still incur annual deficits and certainly prevent reduction of the 17+ trillion dollars of cumulative national debt. In *Fracture Zone 2015*, Jim Johnson summarizes this government addiction to debt as follows: "Trillions of dollars of liabilities accumulate as we reduce free market practice and Washington commits billions of precious tax dollars to control and manipulate the markets.

America's culture of financial dependency is serious; mirroring a culture of dependency in every sector of society where government has reached into people's lives to provide "help" which quickly turns into addiction, dependency, and demotivation. After many "hits" of government entitlements intruding into areas where the <u>industriousness of "We the People"</u> and <u>old-fashioned free-enterprise capitalism</u> are the best remedies, too many Americans now possess an entitlement mentality, addicted to "something for nothing." As with post-Communist nations (recall our story about the Bulgarian President: "The people don't have a will to work"), many Americans today have lost their will to work, trapped in a dependency mentality created by sustained feeding at the trough of government largesse.

Wouldn't we rather take the path of Mrs. Doris Francois? She certainly understands what it means to pursue happiness, and in large measure she obtained it for herself and others.

We now look at three specific Pursuits of HAPPINESS foundational to "The American Dream": A Better Future (Education), A Prosperous Future (The Economy and Work), and A Healthy Future (Health Care).

Pursuit of a Better Future: Education

Aristotle once said, "All who have meditated on the art of governing mankind are convinced that the fate of empires depends upon the education of youth." Our nation's Founders certainly appreciated this truism and integrated it into the fabric of our fledgling nation. While education is a very complex topic that could consume volumes, it is relevant to R*esilient Nations* in two regards: 1) Constitutional Guidelines Concerning Education, and 2) Religious Freedoms within Education.

Constitutional Guidelines Concerning Education

Related to the Spiritual Infrastructure subcomponent "Adherence to Constitutional Foundations," the Constitution makes no mention of public education. The Tenth Amendment to the Constitution reserved to the States everything not delegated to the federal government and not specifically prohibited to the States. <u>Hence, the function of public education is a STATE role</u>. This was generally adhered to until the 1950s when an activist judiciary granted the federal government far greater powers over public education, and the 1960s when Great Society programs, supported by a very proactive Congress, stimulated a six fold increase in federal education spending in the next twenty years.

Apart from a slight withdrawal of federal education spending and associated regulations during the Reagan years, this trajectory of increasing federal intrusion into public education has continued, with even greater acceleration during the last Bush Administration and now the Obama Administration, wresting ever more control from the States.

The current debate relates to Common Core (formally the Common Core State Standards Initiative, CCSSI), developed under the auspices of the National Governors Association (NGA) and the Council of Chief State School Officers (CCSS). Common Core was developed without state legislative or parental input. Parenthetically, the passage and implementation of Common Core was out of the same playbook as the Affordable Care Act (aka Obamacare) and Obama economic stimulus programs (quantitative easing, et al), all characterized by rushed federal legislation precluding debate and passed before stakeholders knew what it contained, followed by roughshod implementation of regulations rife with special interest agendas that can be rightly called "Trojan horses."

From my reading of Common Core at www.CommonCore.org and exposure to numerous Common Core debates and analyses of national education policy (beginning with assessments at the Industrial College of the Armed Forces in 1991), I make a few top-level observations:

- Centralized federal public education which is controlled by special interests <u>cuts parents and local communities out of the process</u>.
- The goal of higher standards is commendable, but <u>one size does not fit all</u> and the <u>standards are not consistently higher</u>. All children are different, with varied gifts and maturation rates.
- <u>All locales in which the children live and go to school are different</u>, even within the same city.
- The intent of the law may be noble, but <u>the implementing regulations written by liberal special interests require objectionable curriculum topics</u> which include pornography, gender identity training, revisionist history, and overly complicated and directive methods for basic math procedures, among others.
- Related to the above, <u>home schooling and private schools are unduly disadvantaged</u> by Common Core standards which are starting to permeate SAT/ACT testing.

- <u>Classroom implementation</u> has been unsatisfactory, frequently inconsistent, confusing, and frustrating for teachers.
- Outcomes for federally-controlled public education <u>have not been empirically validated</u>.
- <u>Some States are backing away</u> from their Common Core commitments, recognizing that despite risking loss of federal monies, they can set their own standards without federal involvement.
- <u>The underlying issue of substandard teachers</u> which are perpetuated by teacher unions is not being substantively addressed.

In summary, I would conclude that Common Core (along with related programs and regulations) is the educational equivalent of Obamacare and Quantitative Easing (QE), again epitomizing Government "Gone Wild" (discussed in Chapter 4). *Common Core*, formulated to correct deficiencies in *No Child Left Behind*, has taken us further in the wrong direction regarding adherence to Constitutional foundations and true educational effectiveness.

The Stop Common Core (www.StopCommonCore.com) website provides additional strong rationale for radical reform or replacement of Common Core.

Religious Freedoms within Education

While public education reform involves many other considerations, the second area pertaining directly to Spiritual Infrastructure is religious freedom, specifically "Free Exercise and Relevance of Religion in Public and Private Venues," as well as

"Moral and Practical Education of our Youth." Our nation's Founders recognized that the Judeo-Christian foundations of America inherently contained the ethical, moral, and spiritual underpinnings critical to an educational system that would help America become the greatest nation on earth.

Lest there be any doubt regarding the Christian beginnings of American education, consider the following from David Barton's *Original Intent*:

- "The American settlers, having been exposed to the Reformation teachings, believed that the proper protection from civil abuses in America could be achieved by eliminating Biblical illiteracy." (pg 86)
- "The inseparability of Christianity from education, whether public or private, was evident at every level of American education." (pg 87)
- Harvard, William & Mary, Yale, Princeton, Dartmouth, Kings College (name later changed to Columbia), and Queens College (name later changed to Rutgers) were but many examples of the religious origin and purpose of our nation's universities. (pp 87-91)

We have already addressed historical turning points in our nation's Spiritual Infrastructure, specifically the removal of prayer from our public schools in 1964 and the removal of the Ten Commandments in 1980. Since those seminal court rulings which began the erosion of religious freedoms in our nation's schools, the culture wars in our nation's schools have been incessant. Fast forwarding to the present, consider a representative example from the Alliance Defending Freedom (ADF, www.AllianceDefendingFreedom.org):

> "Government agencies are discriminating against Christian colleges in student aid grants and trying to force them to abandon Biblical beliefs while accepting unbiblical behavior. Furthermore, the Obama Administration's abortion pill mandate could force Christian colleges to abandon their beliefs or pay potentially bankrupting fines. Left unprotected from these assaults, Christian universities could be:
>
> - Forced to compromise their Biblical values and accept a secular worldview.
> - Unable to educate Christian teachers and leaders to impact the culture.
> - Driven to bankruptcy, forced to close their classroom doors."

Of recent, we must add the pressure on Christian universities to recognize same-sex "marriage" and domestic partner benefits.

ADF also addresses the guerilla warfare against Christians which is pervasive on secular college campuses:

> "The secular worldview now dominating at many formerly Christian and virtually every state university exposes many Christians and campus ministries to discrimination and hostility. Thousands of students have chosen to avoid such

antagonism by pursuing degrees at Christian colleges and universities. And now these Christian schools are also feeling pressure—this time from the government—to abandon their Christ-centered mission, and compromise with the secular culture."

Such warfare in the classrooms and campuses of America occurs every day and at every grade level across our land. Gratefully, organizations such as Alliance Defending Freedom, Liberty Counsel, Liberty Institute, American Center for Law and Justice, and others are available to assist.

In reality, American education has not truly discarded religion; it has just embraced counterfeit religions such as humanism, secular progressivism, and hypocritical toleration of deviancy, poor substitutes for the deep religious roots upon which American education was built.

At this point, we must ask "How is that working for you, America?" What metrics should we use? Continued degradation of morality as evidenced by disrespect, lack of civility, school bullying, violence, and mass shootings? Geometric increases in federal spending without substantive improvement in student performance? Woeful Science, Technology, Engineering, and Math (STEM) rankings (addressed in our Introduction)? Or how about the recent "Nation's Report Card" which revealed the following:

- "America's high school seniors <u>lack critical math and reading skills</u> for an increasingly competitive global economy.

- Only about one quarter are performing proficiently or better in math and just 4 in 10 in reading. <u>And they're not improving</u>...
- Scores on the 2013 exam in both subjects were <u>little changed from 2009</u>, when the National Assessment of Educational Progress was last given to 12th-graders.

(underlines added)

> In reality, American education has not truly discarded religion; it has just embraced counterfeit religions such as humanism, secular progressivism, and hypocritical toleration of deviancy, poor substitutes for the deep religious roots upon which American education was built.

While spin masters try to find silver linings in such results, the reality is that our nation's educational system is failing our most precious assets. We are not providing our nation's children with sufficient moral or academic training to allow them to succeed as workers or responsible citizens. Even now we are reaping what we have sown.

Biblical Precepts for Pursuing a Better Future: Education

Proverbs 1 is a treatise on the benefits of and means to wisdom. Verses which directly apply to education:

- Regarding the <u>benefits of education</u>: "[3]To receive instruction in wise behavior, righteousness, justice, and equity; [4]to give prudence to the naïve, to the youth knowledge and discretion."

- Regarding the <u>benefits of being a lifetime learner</u>: "[5]A wise man will hear and increase in learning, and a man of understanding will acquire wise counsel."
- Regarding the <u>origin of true knowledge</u>: "[7a]The fear of the Lord is the beginning of knowledge."
- Regarding the <u>primary educators of youth</u>: "[8]Hear, my son, your <u>father's instruction</u> and do not forsake your <u>mother's teaching</u>; [9]Indeed, they are a graceful wreath to your head and ornaments about your neck."

Proverbs 4:13 further describes the <u>critical importance of education</u>: "Take hold of instruction; do not let go. Guard her <u>for she is your life</u>." (underlines added)

King Solomon in Proverbs also observed, "Do you see a man skilled in his work? He will stand before kings; he will not stand before obscure men." (Proverbs 22:29) <u>Education helps one acquire the skills which achieve excellence in work and other life endeavors</u>. This excellence equips one to exercise influence at the highest levels of government and society.

Actions and Policies Pursuing a Better Future through Education

1. **Return control of public education to the States**, with limited involvement by the federal government.

2. **Revise or replace *Common Core*** to remove imbedded secular progressive agendas. Basic learning standards are useful, but not when accompanied by pervasive efforts to indoctrinate children and youth in marginal and often inappropriate and detrimental special interest issues.

3. **Reverse ongoing efforts to excise religion from public education.** While avoiding coercion or state-sponsored religion, recognize, appreciate, and enable free exercise of religion by all students.

4. **Reward excellence in the classroom by teachers**. Change faculty longevity rules that impede removal of substandard teachers. Break long standing teacher union cartels that perpetuate poor performance, inefficiencies, and cost effectiveness.

5. **Reward excellence in the classroom by students.** Change the "everyone gets a trophy" culture that does not reward excellence for fear that underperformers will feel "discriminated" against.

Pursuit of a Prosperous Future: The Economy and Work

One of the Spiritual Infrastructure subcomponents included <u>an industrious citizenry,</u> in contrast to the story we told earlier about the Bulgarian President's statement that "The people don't have a will to work." While the economy is often considered an element of national power separate from Spiritual Infrastructure, it has such an impact on work and workers that we must also consider the macro aspects of our national economy as having a direct impact on work and workers, families, and every American citizen. We will address this first, seeking to identify enduring principles versus a barrage of fleeting statistics that seem to change (and generally get worse) every day.

The American Economy

After interpreting the Egyptian Pharaoh's dream in Genesis, Chapter 41, Joseph provided an economic forecast for the nation:

> "²⁸ It is as I have spoken to Pharaoh: God has shown to Pharaoh what He is about to do. ²⁹ Behold, <u>seven years of great abundance</u> are coming in all the land of Egypt; ³⁰ and after them <u>seven years of famine</u> will come, and <u>all the abundance will be forgotten</u> in the land of Egypt, and the <u>famine will ravage the land</u>. ³¹ So the abundance will be unknown in the land because of that subsequent famine; for it *will be* very severe." (Genesis 41:28-31, underlines added)

Note that Joseph did not render an overly optimistic forecast based on faulty out year assumptions that seldom materialize (as is the case with current U.S. economic projections). He accurately predicted forthcoming economic hardship. As a result of Joseph's fiscal prudence, including austerity measures which built reserves for coming hardships, the nation of Egypt was spared and provided for surrounding nations and peoples, including Joseph's very own family.

Contrast Joseph's fiscal conservatism which saved the nation of Egypt with our nation's current loose monetary policies which arguably have us on the brink of economic cataclysm. Despite Obama Administration claims of victory over the 2008 economic crisis, a sobering assessment from Jim Johnson, author of *Fracture Zone 2015,* brings us closer to the truth:

> "Washington has <u>fully nationalized housing finance</u>, and now <u>needs ever-larger liquidity from debt markets in order to survive</u>. Simultaneously, the Federal Reserve and Treasury have managed to <u>reduce interest rates to their lowest levels ever</u>, despite vastly expanding the money supply, <u>running enormous deficits</u> and receiving warnings and credit downgrades. How long can they maintain imbalanced debt markets? <u>If Washington loses market confidence and interest rates rise, the crisis will become a storm. </u>" (underlines added)

This rampant deficit spending and the burgeoning national debt are clearly ticking time bombs that may explode in our generation, but will most definitely wreak havoc on our children and grandchildren.

From a Spiritual Infrastructure perspective, the most profound observation regarding the economy is that <u>capitalism must be constrained by morality</u>. We have seen this theme in so many other facets of Spiritual Infrastructure. Left unconstrained and without a moral governor, basic human tendencies toward greed become the very pit which swallows up the noblest of intentions—yet one more reason why a strong Spiritual

Infrastructure is so critical to the America which God and our Founders put in place.

> This rampant deficit spending and the burgeoning national debt are clearly ticking time bombs that may explode in our generation, but will most definitely wreak havoc
> on our children and grandchildren.

I refer the reader to Leo Tolstoy's parable *How Much Land Does A Man Need?* for further discussion of the relationship between morality, capitalism, and human consumption.

> Left unconstrained and without a moral governor, basic human tendencies toward greed become the very pit which swallows up the noblest of intentions—yet one more reason why a strong Spiritual Infrastructure is so critical to the America which God and our Founders put in place.

The American Worker

Clearly, workers are subject to the broad ebbs and flows of our nation's economy, but they also have individual responsibilities that are even more relevant to their eventual success or failure in a vocation and in life overall. We have sufficiently discussed the pervasive entitlement mentality that afflicts so many of our nation's workers. Regrettably, the

American "work ethic" has increasingly gravitated from industriousness to sloth, from "going the extra mile" to complying with lowest common union standards, from an "honest wage for an honest day's work" to gaming welfare systems to work the least amount possible.

Gratefully, there are many counterexamples of diligent workers who still demonstrate the qualities which made America great. Let's look at some of these critical success factors for American workers which contribute to our nation's Spiritual Infrastructure.

The sequence begins with the knowledge that <u>work is a sacred act</u>. The Apostle Paul exhorted, "Whatever you do, <u>do your WORK heartily as for the Lord</u> rather than for men, knowing that <u>from the Lord you will receive the reward</u> of the inheritance. <u>It is the Lord Christ whom you serve</u>." (Colossians 3:23, 24, capitalization and underlines added) This spiritual rationale behind work generates passion, commitment, and a spirit of service, all of which lead to a more industrious worker and a more productive work force.

Recognition of the <u>principle of sowing and reaping</u> also changes the work dynamic. Galatians 6:7 states clearly, "Do not be deceived, God is not mocked; for whatever a man sows, this he will also reap." Paul further states in Thessalonians, "For even when we were with you, we used to give you this order: <u>if anyone is not willing to work, then he is not to eat</u>, either." (2 Thessalonians 3:10, underlines added) Put in context of America today, all citizens should seek to work (sow) for their own benefit and for the benefit of society. Able citizens who do not "pull their weight" by working cannot rightly expect the government   to "foot the bill." Our country will inevitably reap the negative consequences of massive welfare programs which underwrite worker apathy and irresponsibility.

Given the principle of the sacred nature of work, and the principle of sowing and reaping, we next look at the <u>principle of preparation and diligence</u>, likewise essential for a strong work ethic. In this case, we simply observe the ant:

> [6] Go to the ant, O sluggard, <u>Observe her ways and be wise</u> (learn from others, don't be a deceived sluggard),
> [7] <u>Which, having no chief, Officer or ruler</u> (demonstration of initiative and honesty, even when "the boss" is not watching),
> [8] <u>Prepares</u> her food in the summer *And* <u>gathers</u> her provision in the harvest (diligence in preparation, a "stitch in time").
> [9] <u>How long will you lie down, O sluggard</u>? When will you arise from your sleep?
> [10] "A little sleep, a little slumber, A little folding of the hands to rest"—
> [11] <u>Your poverty will come in like a vagabond</u> And your need like an armed man (the consequences of not sowing diligence, of not having a "will to work").
> (Proverbs 6:6-11, underlines and parentheses added)

Finally, we highlight the <u>principle of stewardship</u>, meaning loosening our grip on the fruits of our labors so that God can multiply them for His purposes in us and others. This means having the right motives behind our work. Jesus encouraged diligence, readiness, and responsible work in many of His parables, but ultimately He addressed underlying motives. In Luke 12:15, He warned, "Beware, and <u>be on your guard against every form of greed</u>; for not even when one has an abundance does his life consist of his possessions." (underline added) Jesus followed with a cautionary parable about a rich man with a very successful business who builds bigger and bigger barns to store his riches, becoming totally fixated on "more" without any redeeming purpose for incessant accumulation. Jesus concludes this parable in Luke 12:21 with, "So is the man who stores up treasure for himself, and is not rich toward God." After even another parable about heavenly priorities, He summarizes the principle in Luke 12:34: "<u>For where your treasure is, there your heart will be also.</u>" (underline added)

This principle of stewardship also includes doing the right things with the money which we earn through work. Americans are captive to credit—college debts, credit card debts, and mortgages far beyond our means. Proverbs 22:7 highlights the trap, "The rich rules over the poor, and <u>the borrower *becomes* the lender's slave</u>." Immediately following our obligations to the government cited in Romans 13, we are reminded, "<u>Owe nothing to anyone</u> except to love one another; for he who loves his neighbor has fulfilled *the* law." (Romans 13:8, underline added) Presumably, if individual Americans were able to rein in their appetite for things they cannot afford, as well as managing the money they do have, then they would probably be emboldened to expect the same of their government.

To summarize, essential traits for American workers include the sanctity of work, the principle of sowing and reaping, preparation and diligence, and stewardship. It is equally important for parents to model and inculcate these principles in their children. In *Resilient Leaders*, we defined *integrity* as the *"seamless integration of faith, family, and profession* (work) *into a God-honoring life message."* Work is an important dimension of life. Children who develop a solid work ethic at a young age are far more likely to become productive people, workers, and citizens, demonstrating true integrity in every dimension of their lives.

> ... if individual Americans were able to rein in their appetite for things they cannot afford, as well as managing the money they do have, then they would probably be emboldened to expect the same of their government.

> ... essential traits for American workers include the sanctity of work, the principle of sowing and reaping, preparation and diligence, and stewardship.

Biblical Precepts for Pursuing a Prosperous Future: The Economy and Work

Some Biblical passages previously referenced are included here for completeness:

> "There is precious treasure and oil in the dwelling of the wise, but a foolish man swallows it up." (Proverbs 21:20)

> "[9]Honor the Lord from your wealth and from the first of all your produce; [10]So your barns will be filled with plenty and your vats will overflow with new wine." (Proverbs 3:9, 10)

> "He who tills his land (works) will have plenty of food, but he who follows empty pursuits will have poverty in plenty." (Proverbs 28:19, parenthetical comment added)

> "Whatever you do, <u>do your WORK heartily as for the Lord</u> rather than for men, knowing that <u>from the Lord you will receive the reward</u> of the inheritance. <u>It is the Lord Christ whom you serve.</u>" (Colossians 3:23, 24, capitalization and underlines added)

> "Do not be deceived, God is not mocked; for whatever a man **sow**s, this he will also reap." (Galatians 6:7)

"For even when we were with you, we used to give you this order: <u>if anyone is not willing to work, then he is not to eat</u>, either." (2 Thessalonians 3:10, underline added)

As with Paul in the verses above, Jesus encouraged diligence, readiness, and responsible work in many of His parables, but ultimately He addressed underlying motives. In Luke 12:15 He warned, "Beware, and be on your guard against every form of greed; for not even when one has an abundance does his life consist of his possessions." Jesus followed with a cautionary parable about a rich man with a very successful business who builds bigger and bigger barns to store his riches, becoming totally fixated on "more" without any redeeming purpose for incessant accumulation. Jesus concludes this parable in Luke 12:21 with, "So is the man who stores up treasure for himself, and is not rich toward God." After even another parable about heavenly priorities, He summarizes the principle in Luke 12:34: "<u>For where your treasure is, there your heart will be also.</u>" (underline added)

Actions and Policies for Pursuing a Prosperous Future

1. **Support a Balanced Budget amendment** to the Constitution, first insuring that national bi-annual budgets do not run in deficit, and followed by reduction of aggregate national debt.
2. **Press for entitlement reform** which ensures long term sustainability for Social Security and reduces unfunded liabilities.
3. **Promote pro-growth** revenue and taxation policies.

Pursuit of a Healthier Future: Health Care Reform

Health is so very important to each of us. Of all the possible deprivations of life, chronically poor health or serious disease (physical, mental, emotional) is perhaps the most debilitating. Pursuit of a healthier future involves action at a number of levels. Beginning with the individual, each of us has been given a body, mind, and soul which need to be nurtured and trained. Related to the culture of dependency, far too many Americans seek to have the medical system "fix" them, rather than placing greater upstream effort on health promotion and comprehensive personal fitness™ which was introduced in *Resilient Warriors*. This comprehensive fitness covers the broad range of physical, mental, spiritual, emotional, and relational fitness derived from the Great Commandment (Mark 12:28-31). Within each category lie very specific fitness practices including exercise, diet, consumption, hygiene, techniques for emotional regulation, friendship activities, spiritual disciplines, mental exercises, et al. Such individual commitment to healthy lifestyle is a first critical step in pursuing a healthier future. Ideally, one's individual diligence and "health ethic" minimize time spent in doctor's offices and on operating tables.

The next level is the "health care system" which is comprised of patients, caregivers and providers, insurers, and regulators. This complex milieu of players and interactions provides daunting challenges to national, state, and local leaders in the public and private sectors who are charged with collectively providing quality healthcare. Effective health care reform has eluded many previous Democrat and Republican attempts, as well as bi-partisan efforts over many decades (with highly visible efforts by President Roosevelt in 1944, President Truman in 1948, and First Lady Hillary Clinton in the 1990s). The crux issues in any health care reform effort are access, affordability, and quality. The Obama Administration's latest effort via the Affordable Care Act (aka Obamacare) has surpassed all previous attempts at health care reform, seeking to achieve universal health care for all Americans (a noble goal) and to place one sixth of the U.S economy (the existing health care proportion) under government control (a somewhat nefarious goal).

Without discussing the "jot and tittle" of Obamacare, it can readily be concluded that the motives were not consistent with principles of limited government, constitutionally enumerated powers, and transparency. Perhaps even more nefarious is that Obamacare seems to intentionally break the health care relationship between employer and employee, giving the government even more control and creating serious economic impact on small businesses and job creation.

Further, the means of Obamacare was a unilateral "powerball" legislative process without popular or legislative consensus, and the methodology of implementation was dysfunctional with regulatory overreach which far exceeded the original scope of the law. Political rhetoric has quickly succumbed to reality: patients were not able to keep their plans or their doctors, many of the new mandated policies were not cheaper or better, the economics are not affordable or feasible, many previously insureds have lost coverage, and a relatively few uninsureds have obtained coverage. Overall, Obamacare has not worked, it has broken more than it has fixed, and headed us in the wrong direction with the wrong motives, means, and methodology.

Jim Johnson provides a useful summary of current U.S. health care status in *Fracture Zone 2015*:

> "National Healthcare. Inefficient government control will be extended to an additional 15% of our economy. Government management is expanding into the most intimate aspects of our lives. American's cost of healthcare has risen uncontrollably for many years. The purported 'savings' from nationalizing medicine come from estimating projected healthcare costs for everyone, regardless of whether they ever would have been paid or not. Once again, this was never foreseen as a legitimate function of government."

Perhaps an equally useful harbinger of the risks of continuing the Obamacare experiment is the ongoing Department of Veterans Affairs (VA) health care scandal involving over fifty VA facilities and uncovering significant fraud, waste, and abuse. One St. Louis VA whistleblower diagnosed the situation as "moral blindness." At the time of *Resilient Nations'* publication, this scandal grows larger by the day, with bi-partisan outcry increasing, ironically contrasted with lethargic and indecisive corrective action by President Obama. "We the People" are rightly exorcised that our nation is defaulting on the health care which our nation's veterans so urgently need and have rightly earned through their sacrificial service.

The broader implication of this VA scandal is a picture of the U.S. health care system under Obamacare a decade from now: bureaucratic government control and gross inefficiencies, ever increasing consumption of taxpayer dollars, lack of competition leading to unsatisfactory delivery of care, institutional corruption, and gross lack of patient confidence in the compassion or competence afforded to them.

Before leaving the subject of Obamacare and U.S. health care reform to your further research (ample statistics abound), I must mention Dr. Ben Carson. Coming from humble beginnings (similar to Mrs. Doris Francois, whose story we related at the beginning of this chapter), Dr. Carson rose to world renown as a brain surgeon. He possesses a powerful Biblical worldview and articulates truth in a winsome and compelling way, to include his powerful message at the National Prayer Breakfast in Washington, DC. Dr. Carson is quite possibly the man-of-the-hour regarding health care reform, possessing deep professional expertise in the health care field, along with the vision and character required to effect such change. As Chairman of "Save Our Healthcare," he is providing leadership to "a national citizens" effort to hold Washington accountable, re-center the healthcare debate around doctors and patients, and begin to answer the question of "What's next?" – because real reform is absolutely vital. I encourage you to follow his efforts.

A final level of health care impact is cultural and political. As an example, just as the drug and sex revolution in the 1960s had detrimental national health impacts, recent liberalization of marijuana distribution policy at the state and national levels will negatively impact our nation's long term health posture. While the use of medical marijuana is a valid debate, the legalized recreational use of marijuana will no doubt have serious second and third order impacts, particularly on our nation's youth. Congressman Earnest Istook noted the contradiction between President Obama's claims in New Yorker magazine that marijuana is not worse than alcohol or cigarettes, and the White House's own Office of National Drug Control Policy which maintains that marijuana has many serious and lasting impacts on users. While we will not discuss this arena further, the reality is that cultural trends and politically expedient social positions also have very tangible health consequences.

Biblical Precepts for Pursuing a Healthier Future

Regarding care for one's body as a sacred duty, "Or do you not know that <u>your body is a temple of the Holy Spirit</u> who is in you, whom you have from God, and that you are not your own?" (I Corinthians 6:19)

Regarding the linkage between mental and emotional health and healthy physical outcomes, "A joyful heart is good medicine, But a broken spirit dries up the bones." (Proverbs 17:22)

Regarding the health benefits of civility and gracious speech, "Pleasant words are a honeycomb, Sweet to the soul and healing to the bones." (Proverbs 16:24)

Regarding moderation in consumption, "Whether, then, you eat or drink or whatever you do, do all to the glory of God." (1 Corinthians 10:31)

Regarding health benefits of religious devotion and right living, "Be not wise in your own eyes; fear the Lord, and turn away from evil. It will be healing to your flesh and refreshment to your bones." (Proverbs 3:7, 8)

Regarding the importance of spiritual fitness (godliness) to complement physical training in achieving positive health outcomes, "[7] But have nothing to do with worldly fables fit only for old women. (referring to earlier verses addressing frivolous pursuits) On the other hand, <u>discipline yourself</u> for the purpose of godliness; [8] for <u>bodily discipline</u> is only of little profit, but <u>godliness is profitable for all things</u>, since it holds promise for the present life and *also* for the *life* to come." (1 Timothy 4:7, 8, underlines added, parenthetical note added)

Note that our earlier discussion (Chapter 5 regarding the benefits of religious practice) detailing Dr. Harold Koenig's work at the Duke Center for Spirituality, Theology, and Health, as well as the work of many other medical researchers empirically demonstrate the valid health benefits of each of these Biblical injunctions.

The Bible also provides ample guidance regarding the honest and effective management of health care. *Resilient Leaders* discusses many of the leadership principles and practices which lead to excellence in organizations and activities, including the U.S. health care system.

Actions and Policies for Pursuing a Healthier Future

1. **Repeal the Affordable Care Act** It is not consistent with fundamental American values and economic principles. The complexity of the law, along with the overreaching government regulations in support of the implementation make it unfixable. Establish a phased approach to meet prioritized reform objectives with bi-partisan participation, rather than attempting a unilateral "grand fix."

2. **Focus health care reform efforts on what is truly broken** (care for uninsured disadvantaged Americans, tort and insurance reform, inefficiencies and soaring costs in the health care system, and fraud and abuse in Medicare reimbursement procedures). Allow the private market system to maximize benefits of competition in health care costs and quality. Ensure that doctor-patient and patient-insurance provider relationships are not fractured by government intervention.

3. **Promote Biblically-based health promotion** based on responsible diet, exercise, and physical, spiritual, and mental health practices which enhance long term preventative health and well-being.

Gaining Altitude: Noble Self-Sufficiency

In 2007 Kathleen and I were at the Moi Air Base Chapel in Nairobi, Kenya. Recognizing the criticality of "faith in the foxhole" for Kenyan military personnel, the presiding chaplain had sponsored a lay training program to teach basic evangelism and discipleship techniques to airmen and families stationed at the base and beyond. The participants were dressed up in their "Sunday best," and confidently reciting the many principles and best practices which they had learned during many weeks of study. It was humbling to see how committed these young believers were, throwing their whole heart into their own spiritual growth and training to instill the same in others. It was doubly humbling to see the austere conditions in which they trained, in the back of a simple concrete chapel, in a dimly lit room without air conditioning and with only bars on the windows.

At the end of their presentation, they asked me to say a few words of encouragement to the students. As I was sharing what was on my heart that day, I noticed a rickety blackboard that was cracked and marred beyond use. I commented to the chaplain after the session that Mrs. Dees and I would like to invest in a new whiteboard for their chapel.

Then I became the student.

"Oh no, Sir," replied the Kenyan Chaplain. "Thank you so much, but we need to buy it with our own money—then we will fully appreciate it. We have all decided to fast one meal a week for the next month, and we should be able to buy it then."

That sums it up. Bookends representing the Pursuit of Happiness—a young African-American woman in America in the 1950s and a Chaplain in Kenya in 2007 in a country with a pittance of the wealth of America. Yet, they both demonstrated a true spirit of noble self-sufficiency:

- A sense of responsibility to work hard, sacrifice, and capture opportunities to provide for self and others

- A passionate commitment to do justice, to love kindness, and to walk humbly with their God

Would we get the same response in Detroit, Chicago, Atlanta, Houston, or Los Angeles today?

May it be so.

Now we have completed our survey of the unalienable rights set forth in the Declaration of Independence and imbedded in Constitutional principles. Chart 11, *Unalienable Rights*, on the next page, reminds us of these unalienable rights, the prevailing culture which currently exists in each category, and the top three issues within each unalienable right which we have highlighted in Chapters 5-7.

Chart 11

Unalienable Rights

LIFE	LIBERTY	PURSUIT OF HAPPINESS
Culture of Violence & Death	Culture of Appeasement	Culture of Dependency
"Respect For"	"Freedom From/To"	"Pursuit of"
1. Unborn	1. Threats	1. Education
2. Elderly	2. Government Intrusion	2. Prosperity & Work
3. Traditional Marriage	3. Religion	3. Health

After discussing urgent mandates for "We the People," "We the Church," and "We the Statesmen" in Chapter 8, we will provide a final call to action in Chapter 9.

Resilient Nations Takeaways

RN 7A – On the individual level, a "culture of dependency" takes the form of overdependence on the government to provide life support in the form of food stamps, long term unemployment benefits, and even healthy school lunches. America has just passed a dependency tipping point where less than half of our citizens actually pay taxes.

RN 7B – At the national level, a "culture of dependency" is at play within every sector where the government seeks to assume undue responsibility for that which individuals or local communities should be rightly responsible. A "bail out" mentality has become pervasive, creating deeper dependency on government.

RN 7C – America's culture of financial dependency is serious, mirroring a culture of dependency in every sector of society where government has reached into people's lives to provide "help" which quickly turns into addiction, dependency, and demotivation.

RN 7D – Related to the Spiritual Infrastructure subcomponent "Adherence to Constitutional Foundations," the Constitution makes no mention of public education. The Tenth Amendment to the Constitution reserved to the States everything not delegated to the federal government and not specifically prohibited to the States. <u>Hence, the function of public education is a STATE role</u>.

RN 7E – Centralized Federal public education which is controlled by special interests <u>cuts parents and local communities out of the process</u>.

RN 7F – The intent of Common Core may be noble, but <u>the implementing regulations written by liberal special interests require objectionable curriculum topics</u> including pornography, gender identity training, revisionist history, and overly complicated and directive methods for basic math procedures, among others.

RN 7G – American education has not truly discarded religion; it has just embraced counterfeit religions such as humanism, secular progressivism, and hypocritical toleration of deviancy, poor substitutes for the deep religious roots upon which American education was built.

RN 7H – By any measure, comparative performance by American students is declining. We are not providing our nation's children with sufficient moral or academic training to allow them to succeed as workers or responsible citizens.

RN 7I – Proverbs 1 is a treasure trove of wisdom regarding the value of education.

RN 7J – As a result of Joseph's fiscal prudence, including austerity measures which built reserves for coming hardships, the nation of Egypt was spared and provided for surrounding nations and peoples, including Joseph's very own family.

RN 7K – Actions and Policies Pursuing a Better Future through Education include: return control of public education to the States, revise or replace *Common Core*, reverse ongoing efforts to excise religion from public education, and reward excellence in the classroom by teachers and students.

RN 7L – Rampant deficit spending and the burgeoning national debt are clearly ticking time bombs that may explode in our generation, but will most definitely wreak havoc on our children and grandchildren.

RN 7M – Left unconstrained and without a moral governor, basic human tendencies toward greed become the very pit which swallows up the noblest of intentions—yet one more reason why a strong Spiritual Infrastructure is so critical to the America which God and our Founders put in place.

RN 7N – Regrettably, the American "work ethic" has increasingly gravitated from industriousness to sloth, from "going the extra mile" to complying with lowest common union standards, from an "honest wage for an honest day's work" to gaming welfare systems to work the least amount possible.

RN 7O – Essential traits for American workers include the sanctity of work, the principle of sowing and reaping, preparation and diligence, and stewardship. It is equally important for parents to model and inculcate these principles in their children.

RN 7P – Actions and policies for pursuing a prosperous future include: support for a Balanced Budget amendment, press for entitlement reform, and promote pro-growth revenue and taxation policies.

RN 7Q – Each of us has been given a body, mind, and soul which need to be nurtured and trained. Related to the culture of dependency, far too many Americans seek to have the medical system "fix" them, rather than placing greater upstream effort on health promotion and comprehensive personal fitness™ which was introduced in *Resilient Warriors*.

RN 7R – Overall, Obamacare has not worked, it has broken more than it has fixed and headed us in the wrong direction with the wrong motives, means, and methodology.

RN 7S – The broader implication of the Department of Veterans Affairs (VA) health care scandal is a picture of the U.S. health care system under Obamacare a decade from now: bureaucratic government control and gross inefficiencies, ever increasing consumption of taxpayer dollars, lack of competition leading to unsatisfactory delivery of care, institutional corruption, and gross lack of patient confidence in the compassion or competence afforded to them.

RN 7T – Cultural trends and politically expedient policy positions also have very tangible health consequences. An example is widespread legalization of marijuana.

RN 7U – Actions and Policies for Pursuing a Healthier Future include: repeal the Affordable Care Act, focus health care reform efforts on what is truly broken, and promote Biblically-based health promotion.

For Further Consideration

1. Consider your personal "Theology of Work." What are the central tenets? How does a sense of "calling" reinforce your work ethic? How does this impact your approach to vocation, avocation, and life maintenance tasks?
2. Craft a phased health care reform strategy to reform American health care. Leverage the useful information from SaveOurHealthcare (Dr. Ben Carson) and other conservative advocacy groups.

Additional References

1. Johnson, Jim. *Fracture Zone 2015*. Charleston, SC: Fire Source Media, 2013.
2. Tolstoy, Leo. *How Much Land Does A Man Need?* McLean, VA: Trinity Forum, 2011.
3. Eberstadt, Nicholas. A Nation of Takers. West Conshohocken, PA: Templeton Press, 2012.
4. Carson, Dr. Benjamin. www.SaveOurHealthcare.org.

8

Mandates

"If the foundations are destroyed,
what can the righteous do?"
(Psalm 11:3)

As I was recently driving away from our nation's Capital, I passed the White House, then the National Mall with the Capitol of Congress on one end, the Washington Monument in the middle, and Abraham Lincoln surveying the other end from inside the Lincoln Memorial. A little further ahead I passed the Jefferson Memorial, over the Potomac River, and then observed the Pentagon with Arlington Cemetery in the background. I could see the flag of the Iwo Jima Monument waving in the distance, standing proud. The grandeur was almost over-whelming. Such architecture, such traditions. For some reason my mind's eye also went to Beijing and Moscow. Those Capitals also have grandeur, but they mask dark chapters of tyranny, oppressive state control, religious persecution, political imprisonment for decades, and murder of millions of their own citizens. I suddenly realized that the American distinctive is not in the stately architecture; rather, the great Patriots behind the monuments and the ideas upon which they are founded. America truly is an exceptional nation with a heart and soul into which God Himself breathed life.

To this point in *Resilient Nations*, we have discussed "the foundations" of the United States of America. While there are always bright lights and noble acts, our American foundations are crumbling, even close to total destruction. We used Spiritual Infrastructure as our primary conceptual vehicle, supported by numerous trends and anecdotes across the annals of history and the arenas of Life, Liberty, and Pursuit of Happiness, as well as the Seven Mountains of Culture.

As brief reminder of these categories:

Spiritual Infrastructure

1. Adherence to Constitutional Foundations
2. Respect for the Rule of Law
3. Retention of National History and Traditions
4. Basic Morality in Respect of God and Man
5. Healthy, Traditional Families as the Primary Building Blocks of Society
6. Free Exercise and Relevance of Religion in Public and Private Venues
7. Unity, Diversity, and Civility
8. Moral and Practical Education of our Youth

9. Industrious, Resilient, and Engaged Citizenry
10. Spirit of Philanthropy and Volunteerism

Unalienable Rights

LIFE: In contrast to a prevailing Culture of Violence and Death: Respect for the Unborn, Respect for the Elderly, Respect for the Traditional Family, and others. Recommended Actions and Policies. (Chapter 5)

LIBERTY: In contrast to a prevailing Culture of Appeasement: Freedom from External and Internal Threats, Freedom from Government, and Freedom of Religion. Recommended Actions and Policies. (Chapter 6)

PURSUIT OF HAPPINESS: In contrast to a prevailing Culture of Dependency: Pursuing a Better Future (Education), Pursuing a Prosperous Future (Economy), and Pursuing a Healthy Future (Health Care). Recommended Actions and Policies. (Chapter 7)

Seven Mountains of Culture (Chapter 3 and beyond)

Arts and Entertainment
Business
Education
Family
Government
Media
Religion

What Can the Righteous Do?

We now shift to the latter portion of Psalm 11:3, "What can the righteous do?"

> *It is reported that Abraham Lincoln often slipped out of the White House on Wednesday evenings to listen to the sermons of Dr. Finnes Gurley at New York Avenue Presbyterian Church. He generally preferred to come and go unnoticed. So when Dr. Gurley knew the president was coming, he left his study door open. On one of those occasions, reportedly in 1863 during the dark days before Gettysburg, the President slipped through a side door in the church and took a seat in the minister's study, located just to the side of the sanctuary. There he propped the door open, just wide enough to hear Dr. Gurley.*

> *During the walk home, an aide asked Mr. Lincoln his appraisal of the sermon. The President thoughtfully replied, "The content was excellent; he delivered with elegance; he obviously put work into the message."*

> *"Then you thought it was an excellent sermon?" questioned the aide.*

> *"No," Lincoln answered.*

"But you said that the content was excellent. It was delivered with eloquence, and it showed how hard he worked," the aide pressed.

"That's true," Lincoln said. "But Dr. Gurley forgot the most important ingredient.

"He forgot to ask us to do something great."

Let us not make the same error. May we challenge one another toward the noble calling we have as citizens, as people of God, and as leaders in every living room, every board room and factory floor, every pulpit, and every elected position across this land. We now step through three mandates for greatness, directed at "We the People," "We the Church," and "We the Statesmen."

America truly is an exceptional nation with a heart and soul into which God Himself breathed life.

Mandate for "We the People"

Personal Spiritual Renewal. In his book, The *De-Valuing of America*, William Bennett states,

> "Cultural matters are not simply an add-on or an afterthought to the quality of life of a country; they determine the character and essence of the country itself. Private belief is a condition of public

spirit; personal responsibility is a condition of public well-being."

In short, private belief and personal responsibility result in public spirit and public well-being. Conversely, the lack of a personal belief system and lack of personal responsibility result in public chaos, the type that haunts every major city in America night after night.

As Americans consider solutions to national ills, we must first take personal spiritual inventory. What do we believe? How do those beliefs affect our lives and the lives of others? Do these beliefs lead to moral character, inner fortitude, and lasting relationship with God and others? The famous mathematician and philosopher Pascal maintained that, "within every human heart is a God-shaped vacuum." Humans often attempt to fill this vacuum with things other than God, with differing value systems, such as secular humanism, which worships man as a poor substitute. Another popular value system even professes to be "value free," a religion of pseudo-objectivity. These "religions" which do not recognize God's authority over men and nations produce spiritual bankruptcy and ultimate despair. The people and the leaders of numerous formerly atheistic, humanistic, and totally secular nations daily attest to this fact, and many are turning to God for solutions. America and Americans must do the same, returning to our God-based constitutional foundations. This begins with personal spiritual renewal—an individual decision and a critical first step. I refer the reader to *Resilient Warriors* to dive deeper into personal spiritual renewal and resilience.

Strong Traditional Families. While it is not our focus to highlight any merits or demerits of same-sex marriage, it certainly is our intent to reinforce the criticality of strong traditional families to America's Spiritual Infrastructure. <u>This must begin in our own homes</u>. President Ronald Reagan highlighted the importance of families when he stated:

> "The family has always been the cornerstone of American society. Our families nurture, preserve and pass on to each succeeding generation the values we share and cherish, values that are the foundation for our freedoms... the strength of our families is vital to the strength of our nation."

Chapter 5 spent considerable time laying out the merits of the traditional family as God's primary building block of society. Every day new statistics and anecdotal stories illustrate the benefits of a traditional family structure. With an abundance of Biblical and empirical justification, the only thing that remains is for "We the People" to make it happen in our own homes first, and then in our society.

As you may well know, this is easier said than done, particularly in our increasingly secular and humanistic culture. The recent apprehension and handcuffing of a father who objected to a pornographic reading requirement in his teenage girl's class illustrates how difficult it is becoming to stand up for basic decency on behalf of your children. We must nevertheless FIGHT for our children (and grandchildren); they need us more than ever before. This will increasingly pit us against secular authorities who do not acknowledge parents as the primary trainers and educators of our nation's children. May we align with Joshua when he said, "As for me and my house, we will serve the Lord."

Proverbs 22:6 contains the promise to "<u>Train up a child in the way he should go</u>, even when he is old, he will not depart from it." (underline added) In this context, training is a deliberate, progressive action which develops tangible and intangible life skills. We must ask, "<u>How intentional are we in our children's training</u>, and in the life skills training for those who are charges of the state or welfare organizations?" The reality is that "everyone does *not* get a trophy." We all need to know how to deal with the challenges, opportunities, and personal and civic responsibilities that God presents to each of us. Many of these responsibilities involve being good citizens, something which must be modeled and taught early and often, beginning in the home. Our earlier work in *Resilient Warriors* and *Resilient Leaders* addressed many of these life skills under the umbrella of resilience. Stand by for *Resilient Children* (to be published) in which we will discuss age-relevant resilience object lessons and skills training for children and teens.

… training is a deliberate, progressive action which develops tangible and intangible life skills.

The reality is that
"everyone does *not* get a trophy."

May we also align with other Biblical injunctions, particularly Ephesians 5:22-33 regarding husband-wife relationships and Ephesians 6:1-4 regarding children and parenting. There are many outstanding Christian marriage and family resources available today. Perhaps the best strategy is to obediently and resolutely apply one of these many resources, rather than gaining surface familiarity with many.

Civic Responsibility. Earlier we mentioned Supreme Court Justice Antonio Scalia's lament regarding the decline of civic responsibility in America. As well, we have highlighted consistently low voter turnout by "We the People." The civic responsibility mandate for "We the People" extends beyond consistently voting in local, state, and federal elections to being an "informed" voter (versus the newly minted term "low information voters"). We should align with like-minded citizens and organizations in this regard. For example, the Salt & Light Council (based in San Diego, www.saltandlightcouncil.org) does an excellent job offering citizenship training to those seeking to be informed and responsible voters. Many organizations such as Wallbuilders (www.wallbuilders.com) and others highlighted earlier in *Resilient Nations* also offer useful national election guides and civic education tools.

In addition to civic responsibility exercised through participation in the political process, engaged citizens embrace a spirit of philanthropy and volunteerism. None of us can solve ALL the problems of our local community, nation, or our world, but we can ALL DO SOMETHING to help others with the time, talents, and treasure that God has placed in our hands. My experience suggests that it is better to come alongside <u>a small number of worthy causes</u> which align with your passions and gifts in life, rather than be a wandering gadfly which does not truly commit to any particular cause.

> ... we can ALL DO SOMETHING to help others with the time, talents, and treasure that God has placed in our hands.

Cultural Change Agents. I often use the expression "If not now, then when? If not me (us), then who?" as an exhortation to action. This is certainly true as each of us see the accelerating trends of cultural decline in our nation. You were exposed to the "Seven Mountains of Culture" in Chapter 3 and beyond. It may be that your "point of passion" to win back culture <u>aligns with your vocation</u>. If you are a media executive, how do you act as "salt and light" in your media marketplace, serving to positively influence those around you and then entire media industry? Or maybe God has placed you vocationally in arts and entertainment, or business, or education, or family care, or government (including the military), or religion.

- What is *your* field and opportunity of service based on your vocation?

In addition to vocational access to a certain mountain of culture, you may also be personally aligned with a particular cause. For example, you may be a mother or father alarmed by the impacts of historical revisionism, or gender mis-education in our schools, or abysmally low math and English proficiency of our students, or bullying and violence in our nation's schools. You may be the parent who gives courage to other equally concerned parents. Remember, you are not alone. I encourage you to become informed, align with other like-minded individuals and organizations, and then stand up to be counted, to do the right thing. You may save your children in the process.

- What is *your* passion and cause as a concerned parent or grandparent?

Perhaps you want to reverse the tacit persecution of religion, particular Christians in our culture today. What would God have you to do? Perhaps your heart breaks for those held captive in prostitution and human trafficking. If not you, then who? Perhaps you have a prophetic personality that is righteously exorcised by a lack of integrity and transparency in government. If not now, then when?

- What is *your* passion and cause as a concerned citizen?

Without restating earlier discussion points regarding culture change, I can say with confidence that there are informed, professional, and passionate organizations with which you can align in your quest. If you need a jump start, begin with those I have referred in this book and expand outward.

Prayer Warriors and Merchants of Hope. When we close this chapter, we will "Gain Altitude" with a discussion of PRAYER, the common necessity across "We the People," "We the Church," and "We the Statesmen." For now, a reminder regarding our sacred duty to pray for those in authority:

"[1]First of all, I urge that entreaties and prayers, petitions and thanksgiving, be made on behalf of all men, [2]for kings and all who are in authority, so that we may lead a tranquil and quiet life in all godliness and dignity." (2 Timothy 2:1, 2, underline added)

In *Resilient Warriors*, Chapter 10, and *Resilient Leaders*, Chapter 7, we discussed HOPE at length. My mind first thinks of the Hope Diamond in the Smithsonian Museum—45.52 carats, worth hundreds of millions of dollars, an amazing gem. Yet the Hope Diamond has brought out the worst in many: greed, anger, violence. The other "Hope Diamond" is what we illustrated in *Resilient Warriors*, used with permission from *3:16: The Numbers of Hope* by Max Lucado. "'For God so loved the world, that He gave His only begotten Son, that whoever believes in Him shall not perish, but have eternal life.' (John 3:16)." This is the true "Hope Diamond" which brings out the very best in people: faith, peace, reconciliation with God and man, and hope.

In the Book of Romans, the Apostle Paul addresses such hope:

"... we exult in **hope of the glory of God** (an eternal expectation),

And not only this, but we also **exult in our tribulations** (a temporal expectation),

knowing that tribulation brings about perseverance; and perseverance, proven character; and proven character, **hope**; and **hope does not disappoint**, because the love of

God has been poured out within our hearts through the Holy Spirit who was given to us." (Romans 5:3-5, underlines and bold font added)

To be a merchant of hope, we must first have hope, both an eternal expectation and a temporal (here and now) expectation that gives us courage and strength. This hope, found in Jesus Christ, "does not disappoint."

Having such hope, we are equipped to be "Merchants of Hope." Without restating *Resilient Leaders* Chapter 7 ("Being a Merchant of Hope"), let me challenge you to simply observe the ethic and enthusiasm of successful merchants about you. They believe in their product. They understand their customer. They know how to navigate the culture. How much more should this be so with "Merchants of Hope" who bring the help, hope, and the healing of Jesus into an increasingly dark American culture and the world beyond!

If not you, then who? If not now, then when?

Mandate for "We the Church"

Over the centuries volumes have been written regarding revival through the church. Rather than dive into these many excellent works, I will approach this in a simple, binary way: what is God's caution to the church? In other words, what should the church not do? Secondly, what is God's promise to the church? What should the church do?

What the Church Should Not Do

<u>What the church should not do</u> is perhaps best highlighted in the Book of Revelation. The reality is that all churches are different, and the seven churches which are addressed in Revelation 2 and 3 are representative of a broad range of churches (Ephesus, Smyrna, Pergamum, Thyatira, Sardis, Philadelphia, and Laodicea) with strengths and weaknesses which are highlighted by the Lord, Himself. For instance in the case of Ephesus, after citing commendable traits and actions, the Lord continues, "But I have this against you, that you have <u>left your first love</u>." (Revelation 2:4) Similarly Pergamum is commended, but then confronted because they have <u>embraced several forms of false teaching and religious practice</u>. The same pattern applies to Thyatira, ending with the Lord's disdain that some continue to follow the false prophetess, Jezebel, who leads people astray with <u>immorality and idol worship</u>. Sardis is similarly condemned by the Lord: "Wake up, and strengthen the things that remain, which were about to die; for <u>I have not found your deeds completed</u> in the sight of My God. (Revelation 3:2, underline added) The church at Laodicea receives one of the sternest warnings:

> [16] So because you are lukewarm, and neither hot nor cold, I will spit you out of My mouth. [17] Because you say, "I am rich, and have become wealthy, and have need of nothing," and you do not know that you are wretched and miserable and poor and blind and naked, [18] I advise you to buy from Me gold refined by fire so that you may become rich, and white garments so that you may clothe

yourself, and *that* the shame of your nakedness will
not be revealed; and eye salve to anoint your eyes
so that you may see.   (Revelation 3:16-18,
underlines added)

To complete the record regarding the seven churches of
Revelation, Smyrna and Philadelphia received nothing but
commendation from our Lord. I urge a more detailed reading of
Revelation 2 and 3, with the Lord's commentary on each church
providing unique insight into the strengths and weaknesses which
afflict churches in America today.

To get personal for a moment, what about your church?
Maybe you are a member, or maybe you are a pastor or church
leader. Has your church lost its first love? Has it been derailed by
false teaching which contradicts Biblical truth? Has it condoned
immorality among its leaders or its members, or allowed a focus
on American idols such as wealth, fame, influence, or secular
popularity? Or maybe your church has started a number of
programs which remain incomplete and impotent? Has your
church simply grown lukewarm and complacent because of
material wealth and dependence upon self? Very likely, your
church mirrors some of the positives and many of the negatives of
the churches of Revelation. These are important cautionary tales
indicating what the church should not be and do, revealing the
mind of Christ in assessing His church.

What the Church Should Do

What the church should do is equally clear, stated in scripture in 2 Chronicles 7:14. There are a multitude of books, sermons, conferences, and even ministries crafted around this powerfully applicable verse. It is a simple conditional promise from God:

(IF, implied from earlier verses)
My People who are called by My Name
HUMBLE themselves and PRAY and SEEK My face
and
TURN from their wicked ways,
THEN
I will HEAR from Heaven, will FORGIVE their sin and
will HEAL their land.
(Caps and parentheses inserted)

We know that God is totally trustworthy and faithful. He will fulfill His part of the bargain. So what is the problem? "We The Church" have not been equally faithful. We have not met the conditions. While not many would disagree with the benefits of cashing in on this promise from God, our human tendency is to expect the person to our right or left in the church pew, or the pastor in a pulpit down the street to be the ones to begin such an obedient turn back to the living God. The reality is that church renewal, spiritual rearmament, and national revival begin with each of us who are part of "My People" referred to in 2 Chronicles 7:14. Each of us must HUMBLE, PRAY, SEEK, and TURN. THEN God will HEAR, FORGIVE, AND HEAL.

Perhaps, just perhaps, your reading of *Resilient Nations* will convince you and me as God's People that it begins with each of us. Perhaps the lamentable status of our nation's spiritual infrastructure will help you appreciate the depths to which we have fallen, the dire consequences which we are soon to reap. Perhaps as you look into your children's or grandchildren's eyes you will gather the moral courage to let it start with you. That is certainly my prayer for you and for me as "We the Church."

Gratefully, there are a number of organizations which seek to help church members, pastors, and churches meet this mandate. In particular, I highlight the American Renewal Project headed by David Lane, as well as Bob Vander Plaats' new book, *IF 7:14*. (See additional resources for both.)

Mandate for "We the Statesmen"

The great reformer, John Calvin, once wrote: "Civil authority is a calling, not only holy and lawful before God, but also the most sacred and by far the most honorable of all callings in the whole life of mortal men."

How do those serving in civil leadership exercise this high calling? Here we highlight three key mandates: Selfless Public Servants, Guardians of Truth, and Principled Collaborators for Change.

Selfless Public Servants. While the term "politician" is not inherently pejorative, it has taken on a jaundiced interpretation as one who seeks only their own self-interests, as one who is quick to compromise principles to make a political buck, as one who is simply a weather vane turning to align with the latest polls and special interest pressures.

The problem of self-seeking public officials is not new. Consider the Prophet Ezekiel's castigation of selfish political leadership ("the shepherds of Israel") during the time of the Babylonian Captivity. He did not mince words:

> "Then the word of the LORD came to me saying,
> ² "Son of man, <u>prophesy against the shepherds of Israel</u>. Prophesy and say to those shepherds, 'Thus says the Lord GOD, <u>"Woe, shepherds of Israel who have been feeding themselves</u>! Should not the shepherds feed the flock? ³ <u>You eat the fat and clothe yourselves with the wool, you slaughter the fat *sheep* without feeding the flock.</u> ⁴ Those who are sickly <u>you have not strengthened</u>, the diseased <u>you have not healed</u>, the broken <u>you have not bound up</u>, the scattered <u>you have not brought back</u>, <u>nor have you sought for the lost</u>; but <u>with force and with severity you have dominated them.</u> ⁵ They were scattered for lack of a shepherd, and they became food for every beast of the field and were scattered. ⁶ My flock wandered through all the mountains and on every high hill; My flock was scattered over all the surface of the earth, and <u>there was no one to search or seek *for them*."</u>" (Ezekiel 34:1-6, underlines added)

Regrettably we can identify many political "shepherds" in America in 2014 who are likewise feeding themselves to the detriment of "We the People." Through Ezekiel, the Sovereign God spoke condemnation to such self-serving shepherds:

> "[10] 'Thus says the Lord GOD, "Behold, I am against the shepherds, and <u>I will demand My sheep from them and make them cease from feeding sheep</u>. So the shepherds will not feed themselves anymore, but I will deliver My flock from their mouth, so that they will not be food for them."'" (Ezekiel 34: 10, underline added)

Our modern day analogy is that "We the People" as the "Sovereign" of the United States of America should also demand that these political wolves in shepherd's clothing should likewise be cast aside, voted out of office!

To continue the shepherding analogy, consider Jesus' words in the Book of John: "I am the good shepherd; the good shepherd lays down His life for the sheep. " (John 10:11) "We the People" must seek out and support political shepherds who are truly selfless servants. Many times such shepherds will come from the ranks of "We the People"—moms, businessmen, lawyers, doctors, educators—people who understand the plight of the sheep, and who only seek to lead out of love for their country, and a heart of compassion for others. We have used the term "Statesmen" to distinguish from the negative connotation of professional politicians who have forgotten who and why they serve, and to signal the need to return to the principled political leadership we have long revered in our Founding Fathers.

In *Resilient Leaders* we defined Leadership (and equally applicable to Statesmanship) as "selfless service over time from a platform of character and competence," and further high-lighted selflessness as one of three essential character traits (selflessness, integrity, courage) for leaders. Jesus certainly modeled such selfless service in His life and His teachings. We gratefully see similar role models in contemporary politics (albeit too few): servant leaders who possess the right motives and who pursue the right methods on behalf of others. These men and women deserve the title "Statesmen." May their tribe increase!

Guardians of Truth. The Greek tragic dramatist, Aeschylus (525 BC - 456 BC) is thought to have originated the saying, "In war, truth is the first casualty." This has always been the case in actual war, as well as in political and cultural wars over America's history, perhaps no more true than in 2014. Just as the dissembling and lying that occurred as Watergate shattered the aura of the Nixon Administration and the Monica Lewinsky scandal brought impeachment charges against President Bill Clinton, today we observe the familiar smoke signals of impending scandal in the Obama Administration. We are once again seeing the blatant denials, the inconsistent and changing narratives to fit inconvenient truths, the partisan recriminations against those who seek to shed light on the darkness, and soon the "smoking guns" which crack the final veneer of invincibility. Then the momentum changes: previous partisans and mainstream liberal media recognize they can no longer support the party line, backing away from indefensible lies. Suddenly it gets very lonely at the top.

At time of *Resilient Nations'* publication, scandals around the Benghazi Tragedy and Cover-up, the IRS Scandal and Cover-up, the Veterans Affairs Scandal which grows by the day, and the Obamacare Grand Lie and Cover-up are all reaching a boiling point. While one can never confidently predict the outcome of what appears to be a succession of "slam dunk" scandals (witness Bill Clinton's political recovery from blatant immorality and dishonesty in the White House), much less four major scandals at once, the truth eventually bubbles to the top, over the course of days or decades. Buddha said, "Three things cannot be long hidden: the sun, the moon, and the truth."

Another arena where truth is a casualty is in the main stream media. "Investigative reporting" seems to be a lost art. A recent survey indicates that seven percent of the media are Republican. The "main stream media" is decidedly liberal and biased, interpreting the news through a secular progressive lens and omitting news (truth) which does not support their liberal agenda. As a recent example, mainstream media networks (ABC, CBS, NBC, MSNBC, et al) did not report Lois Lerner's contempt of Congress vote, a key event in the ongoing IRS Scandal investigation. They simply skipped over a major news event of the day because it reflected poorly on the Obama Administration. Similarly, mainstream media reporting about Benghazi and adverse Obamacare statistics has been miniscule and often disingenuous. The reality of ongoing scandals in the Obama Administration will likely move some of the "mainstream media" toward greater objectivity, but the radical liberal media will no doubt continue to twist truth to further their liberal agendas.

Most of our nation's oldest universities (particularly the Ivy League) have also become liberal bastions of spin. We addressed this at length in Chapter 7 within "Pursuit of a Better Future (Education)," highlighting the May 2014 controversy regarding having Secretary Rice speak at Rutgers' graduation. Representative of the religious underpinnings of our first institutions of higher learning, Yale University's motto is "Light and <u>Truth</u>" (underline added) from biblical origins (Hebrew), and founded originally as a Christian University (Puritan) over 300 years ago. Regrettably, truth has become a casualty and religion a distant memory in most American institutions of higher education today, certainly antithetical to the original intent and practical designs of our Founders.

Napoleon used the term "2 a.m. Courage" to describe the sentry who could be counted upon to defend his post, even when no one was watching. These are the type of Statesmen that America needs in 2014 and beyond: men and women who guard truth at all costs, who do the right thing when no one is watching, or when a hostile press and constituents are watching.

The West Point Cadet Prayer (shown below) is a fitting exhortation to "We the Statesmen" to be guardians of truth: (note in particular the underlines)

> *O God, our Father, Thou Searcher of human hearts,*
> *help us to draw near to Thee in sincerity <u>and truth</u>.*
> *May our religion be filled with gladness and may*
> *our worship of Thee be natural.*

Strengthen and increase our admiration for <u>honest dealing</u> and clean thinking, and suffer not our <u>hatred of hypocrisy and pretense</u> ever to diminish. Encourage us in our endeavor to live above the common level of life. Make us to <u>choose the harder right instead of the easier wrong,</u> and <u>never to be content with a half-truth when the whole can be won</u>. Endow us with courage that is born of loyalty to all that is noble and worthy, that <u>scorns to compromise with vice and injustice</u> and <u>knows no fear when truth and right are in jeopardy</u>. Guard us against flippancy and irreverence in the sacred things of life. Grant us new ties of friendship and new opportunities of service. Kindle our hearts in fellowship with those of a cheerful countenance, and soften our hearts with sympathy for those who sorrow and suffer. Help us to <u>maintain the honor</u> of the Corps <u>untarnished and unsullied</u> and to show forth in our lives the ideals of West Point in doing our duty to Thee and to our Country. All of which we ask in the name of the Great Friend and Master of all. Amen.

"We the Statesmen" must be leaders who "know no fear when truth and right are in jeopardy," who are guardians of truth.

Principled Collaborators for Change. Democrats and Republicans are more polarized now than in my lifetime, perhaps in history. Congressman Randy Forbes, a Statesman of distinction, likens the current gridlock to a boxing match where there is a jubilant victor and a bloody loser. He describes the problem and the solution well:

> "There is no question Congress is divided. A recent report by the Brookings Institute showed that the 113th Congress is among the most polarized in a century...
>
> In the midst of it all, a majority of Americans are asking in chorus: *why can't you just work together?*
>
> It's a fair question, demonstrating just how deeply the battle lines have been drawn. With clearly defined maneuvers, the key players have taken their corners, Republicans on one side and Democrats on the other.
>
> We need to answer the question. I think everyone can agree that we have to work together if we want to see progress. However, I believe we won't unless we see a mind shift in strategy...
>
> So how do we begin this mind shift?
>
> It starts with relationships... For these relationships to work, we make time to listen to each other, to build friendships, and to grow partnerships. Instead of looking at the lines that separate us, we look for the issues where we find unity. And we make progress, because we

come to the negotiation table with respect for each other, an open mind to ideas, and an understanding of each other's unwavering principles. Respectful relationships birth a desire for common ground."

Congressman Forbes described what I have in mind with the term "Principled Collaborators for Change," and he is demonstrating what this looks like. Being a true Statesman instead of a mere politician involves art and science. The art finds common ground, crafts strategic partnership on both sides of the aisle, and collaborates with differing perspectives to make progress toward a common goal on behalf of "We the People." Certainly there will be times when a Statesman must "go to the mat" on behalf of principle, but generally real progress comes at the hands of Principled Collaborators for Change.

In Chapter 6 we discussed the strategy of isolating radicals and engaging moderates of a particular partisan group. This applies in every possible sector, including in the halls of Congress. The challenge is that since 2009, the Obama Administration and Democratic leadership in the House and Senate (Pelosi and Reid, respectively) have proven radical. They have demonstrated radical ideas to move America away from Constitutional intent and towards totalitarian socialism. Regrettably, on a broad range of issues they have not shown any inclination to seek or accept compromise. While Republican Congressmen, such as Randy Forbes, forge mutually beneficial alliances with moderate Democrats, the reality is that the 2014 and 2016 elections must be a referendum to vote radical politicians out of office and replace them with Statesmen on both sides of the aisle. Regardless of who holds the majority in both Houses, and even who wins the White House, progress will not occur without Statesmen who possess the courage, confidence, and tactical patience to be Principled Collaborators for Change.

A final note for "We the Statesmen" relates to PRAYER. If we are to be selfless public servants, guardians of truth, and principled collaborators for change, we have to recognize that prayer is a transformational first step. In accord with God's Sovereignty and timing, prayer changes us and prayer changes the situation about us. This is incredibly relevant when it comes to work "across the aisle" to collaborate for change with those who might have a different political persuasion.

> In accord with God's Sovereignty and timing,
> prayer changes us and
> prayer changes the situation about us.

United States Congressman Randy J. Forbes from Virginia is an example of a Statesman who appreciates the power of prayer and has demonstrated the moral courage to stand for righteousness in the halls of Congress first, and then extending across America. Knowing the power of prayer as a committed Christian believer, he founded the non-partisan Congressional Prayer Caucus which now extends to a membership of over 100 bipartisan U.S. Congressional Members and Prayer Caucus movements in 14 Statehouses (at the time of *Resilient Nations'* publication), all aimed at protecting religious liberty and recognizing our nation's rich, spiritual history. While it is certainly important (and commanded in scripture: I Timothy 2:1-4) that "We the People" pray for our elected representatives, it is equally important that legislators themselves are on their knees before the God who founded America.

If you are a Statesman seeking America's recovery from a crumbling Spiritual Infrastructure, you can do no better than start with prayer, individually and with like-minded colleagues. From there you can move forward with wisdom, strength, and direction to govern as God leads.

Chart 12, *Mandates,* on the next page summarizes the Mandates, indicating the fundamental importance of prayer for "We the People," "We the Church," and "We the Statesmen."

Chart 12

Mandates
People, Statesmen, Church

"We the People"

- Personal Spiritual Renewal
- Strong Traditional Families
- Civic Responsibility
- Cultural Change Agents
  - Seven Mountains of Culture
- Prayer Warriors &
  Merchants of Hope

"We the Statesmen"

- Selfless Public Servants
- Guardians of Truth
- Principled Collaborators
  for Change

"We the Church"

- Humble   GOD WILL:
- Pray   • HEAR
- Seek   • FORGIVE
- Turn   • HEAL

RFD LLC ©2014

PRAYER: KEEP UP THE FIRE!

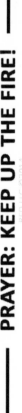

Gaining Altitude: KEEP UP THE FIRE, AMERICA!

Prayer is a common denominator across "We the People," "We the Church," and "We the Statesmen." American leaders over the course of history have spoken to the critical importance of prayer:

- *"I have been driven many times upon my knees by the overwhelming conviction that I had nowhere else to go. My own wisdom, and that of all about me, seemed insufficient for that day."* ~ **Abraham Lincoln**

- *"Knowing that intercessory prayer is our mightiest weapon and the supreme call for all Christians today, I pleadingly urge our people everywhere to pray. Believing that prayer is the greatest contribution that our people can make in this critical hour, I humbly urge that we take time to pray—to really pray."* ~ **Robert E. Lee**

- *"Almighty God: our sons, pride of our Nation, this day have set upon a mighty endeavor, a struggle to preserve our Republic, our religion, and our civilization, and to set free a suffering humanity. Lead them straight and true; give strength to their arms, stoutness to their hearts, steadfastness in their faith."*
  ~ **President Franklin D. Roosevelt**
  Praying for our troops on June 6, 1944, D-Day

- *"We've been a free people living under the law, with faith in our Maker and in our future. I've said before that the most sublime picture in American history is of George Washington on his knees in the snow at Valley Forge. That image personifies a people who know that it's not enough to depend on our own courage and goodness; we must also seek help from God, our Father and Preserver."*
  ~ President Ronald Wilson Reagan
  Remarks at a White House Ceremony in Observance of National Day of Prayer,
  6 May 1982

Threat clears a man's (and woman's) head. When we or those we love are in harm's way, we become very clear headed and we cry out to God. When we have no control over the outcome, we cry out to God.   We know that God is the only one who can truly help us in our day of trouble—"God is our refuge and strength, a very present help in trouble." (Psalm 46:1) In Romans, just before Paul instructs us about citizenship, he describes valuable guidelines for personal and corporate behavior, to include "rejoicing in hope, persevering in tribulation, <u>devoted to prayer</u>." (Romans 12:12, underline added) Jesus modeled prayer at the height of travail before his Crucifixion, lifting up prayer to His Father on behalf of His disciples. (John 17)

Have you ever had a child or a grandchild in pain or urgent need? What do we do?   We Pray Like Crazy! Or a spouse with cancer?   We Pray Like Crazy!   Or a painful betrayal?   We Pray

Like Crazy! Or a loved one on the battlefront? We Pray Like Crazy! Or the very fear of death? We Pray Like Crazy!

We have well established that the foundations of our beloved nation are crumbling. We have cried out "What can the righteous do?" So why are we not praying like crazy, why are we not passionately and persistently devoted to prayer? Perhaps we lack urgency because we don't full appreciate the reality that the very foundations of this great land are threatened. In fact, they are being destroyed. The God-honoring conscience of our nation has been muted to a bare whisper and generations of our children and grandchildren will pay the price if we do not quickly come to their defense.

Throughout *Resilient Nations* we have discussed the existential threats to the United States of America—both external and internal. We should have very clear heads, America. We can no longer claim ignorance. We can and should be "praying like crazy" whether we are a citizen, a church member, or an elected official.

When commanding the U.S. Army's Second Infantry Division in Korea, two of our mechanized infantry battalions were from the historic 9th Infantry "Manchu" Regiment. As reflected in their Regimental history:

> "In 1900, the Regiment deployed to China as the Boxer Rebellion threatened American lives and interests. Within a month of its arrival, the 9th Infantry Regiment found itself in combat in Manchuria. As a result of the actions in China, the

9th Infantry Regiment acquired its nickname as the "Manchu Regiment," earned its motto, "Keep Up The Fire"... Shortly after the 9th Infantry landed in China with the American Relief Expedition to China in 1900, the Regiment engaged in the relief of Tientsin. While assaulting the fortress walls, the regimental commander, Colonel Emerson H. Liscum was mortally wounded while in possession of the regiment's colors. While falling, Colonel Liscum passed the colors to another soldier and directed his regiment to: "KEEP UP THE FIRE!" on the seemingly impregnable walls."

History further records that the impregnable walls of Tientsin did fall, to the great gratitude of the Chinese government.

To draw the analogy, "Keep Up the Fire" is also an apt battle cry for prayer warriors across America. Just like the Manchus of old, we today face seemingly impregnable walls—not battlements of just flesh and blood; rather, of secular humanism, deeply rooted entitlement dependencies which are so difficult to reverse, an increasingly perverse culture that seeks to snatch our children and grandchildren from our very homes and the schools to which we entrust their education, an unabated appetite for that which we cannot afford, and an apathy or even defiance toward the very God who has so richly blessed this nation. Prayer is our spiritual firepower, the artillery that will set the conditions for national spiritual rearmament at this critical time in our nation's history.

Continuing the analogy, we know that our Founders and the great Patriots who followed were men and women of prayer who fought against seemingly insurmountable odds at many times in the annals of American history. Their fervent, heartfelt prayers were joined by so many others across this nation – school children, families, entire congregations, men and women of humble means as well as those of great influence. Many of them also fell at the walls, just like the Manchu Commander Colonel Liscum, not seeing the victory which was about to be won. Many of them "died in faith, without receiving the promises" (Hebrews 11:13). Yet they were faithful in prayer. I can hear them now, whispering and then shouting to us across the pages of history: Keep up the fire! KEEP UP THE FIRE!

> Prayer is our spiritual firepower, the artillery that will set
> the conditions for national spiritual rearmament
> at this critical time in our nation's history.

KEEP UP THE FIRE, AMERICA!

Resilient Nations Takeaways

RN 8A – America truly is an exceptional nation with a heart and soul into which God Himself breathed life.

RN 8B – Mandate for "We the People" includes personal spiritual renewal, strong traditional families, civic responsibility, cultural change agents, and prayer warriors and merchants of hope.

RN 8C – Private belief and personal responsibility result in public spirit and public well-being. Conversely, the lack of a personal belief system and lack of personal responsibility result in public chaos, the type that haunts every major city in America night after night.

RN 8D – We must FIGHT for our children (and grandchildren); they need us more than ever before. This will increasingly pit us against secular authorities who do not acknowledge parents as the primary trainers and educators of our nation's children.

RN 8E – Regarding a spirit of philanthropy and volunteerism, we can ALL DO SOMETHING to help others with the time, talents, and treasure that God has placed in our hands.

RN 8F – To be a merchant of hope, we must first have hope, both an eternal expectation and a temporal (here and now) expectation that gives us courage and strength. This hope, found in Jesus Christ, "does not disappoint."

RN 8G – Mandate for "We the Church" includes the admonitions for churches within Revelation and the promise of 2 Chronicles 7:14 that GOD will hear, forgive, and heal IF "We the Church" will humble, pray, seek, and turn.

RN 8H – Mandate for "We the Statesmen" includes being selfless public servants, guardians of truth, and principled collaborators for change.

RN 8I – Prayer is the common denominator across all mandates. Why are we not praying like crazy, why are we not passionately, and persistently devoted to prayer? Perhaps we lack urgency because we don't full appreciate the reality that the very foundations of this great land are threatened. In fact, they are being destroyed.

For Further Consideration

1. For "We the People," consider <u>your</u> personal spiritual renewal, <u>your</u> own traditional family as a primary building block, <u>your</u> civic responsibilities, <u>your</u> role as a cultural change agent, and <u>your</u> role as a prayer warrior and merchant of hope. Become intentional. Align with like-minded citizens. Reach out to others. Continue to cultivate your own hope and be a merchant of hope to others.

2. For "We the Church," look at <u>your</u> personal role in beginning a cycle of repentance (Humble-Pray-Seek-Turn) in your home and in your church. Encourage your pastor and church leaders to lead by example to model individual and collective renewal, and to align with like-minded organizations that can assist.

3. For "We the Statesmen," consider <u>what it means for you</u> to be a Selfless Public Servant. What are your objectives as a Guardian of Truth? (What specific causes do you sense God has equipped and positioned you to be a champion for truth and justice in the public square and the legislative process?) How will you exercise your role as a Principled Collaborator for Change? (Who will you choose to collaborate with? What positions are you willing to compromise while maintaining core principles?)

Additional References

1. Pinnacle Forum. www.PinnacleForum.com.
2. Seven Mountains of Culture Overview: PF 2014 National Conference Panel with Os Hillman, Joe Mattera, and Lance Wallnau. http://vimeo.com/90140830
3. Vander Plaats, Bob. *If 7:14*. Davenport, Iowa: The Family Leader, 2012.
4. Congressional Prayer Caucus Foundation (CPCF). www.cpcfoundation.com.

9

Uncle Sam Needs YOU!

"God is a righteous judge,
And a God who has indignation every day."
Psalm 7:11 (underline added)

We summarized our *Resilient Nations'* thesis early in Chapter 1:

- Our nation possesses a <u>spiritual infrastructure</u> which, like other types of national infrastructure, <u>is an essential element of national power</u>.
- The bedrock tenets of our nation's spiritual infrastructure, embodied in our founding documents, are <u>reverence for God and respect for man</u>.
- Responsible citizenship and statesmanship mandate a <u>critical assessment of spiritual infrastructure</u> at this pivotal time in our country's history.

- A critical assessment reveals that <u>America's Spiritual Infrastructure is nearing bankruptcy</u>. This constitutes <u>a national security crisis</u>.
- There is <u>hope for America IF</u> "We the People" and "We the Church" wake up now, and "We the Statesmen" lead us with character and competence.
- <u>National Spiritual Rearmament</u> is essential and must include:
  - <u>Personal and Family Renewal</u> by "We the People"
  - <u>Marketplace relevance</u> by "We the People" across every Mountain of Culture
  - <u>Obedience by "We the Church"</u> to humble ourselves, pray, seek God's face, and turn from our wicked ways; followed by compassionate outreach
  - <u>Moral and Wise Leadership</u> by "We the Statesmen" (Public and Private Servant Leaders)
  - <u>Reform of Politics and Policy</u> in accord with Founding Principles to restore Life, Liberty, and the Pursuit of Happiness

We determined in Chapter 4 that we were at a national inflection point, a crossroads in American history that requires concerted action to avoid a downward spiral into undesirable end states quite different from what God or our nation's Founders intended. Chart 13 on the next page, *The Road Not Taken*, reminds us graphically of the critical juncture at which we find ourselves.

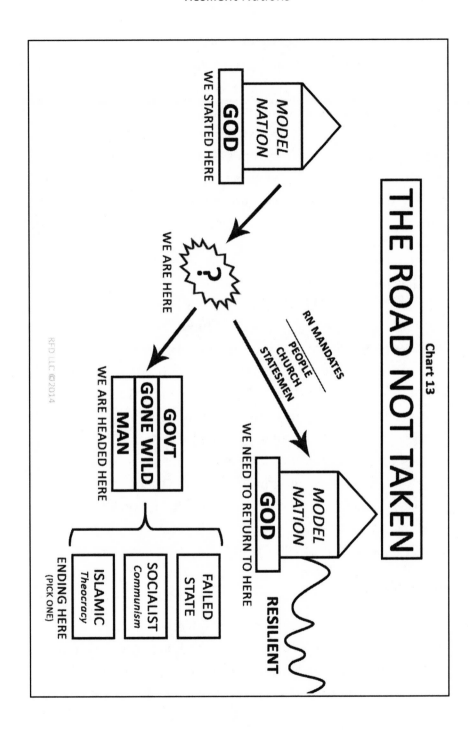

THE ROAD NOT TAKEN

Chart 13

MODEL NATION
GOD
WE STARTED HERE

?
WE ARE HERE

RN MANDATES
PEOPLE
CHURCH
STATESMEN

GOVT GONE WILD
MAN
WE ARE HEADED HERE

MODEL NATION
GOD
WE NEED TO RETURN TO HERE
RESILIENT

FAILED STATE

SOCIALIST
Communism

ISLAMIC
Theocracy
ENDING HERE
(PICK ONE)

RFD LLC ©2014

After working through *Resilient Nations* to this point, you are probably experiencing a number of different emotions. I know I am. You may be discouraged by the daunting statistics and the difficult challenges that our children and grandchildren will certainly face. Or you may feel helpless, wondering how you, or even "We the People," can possibly make a difference. One morning as I was preparing to labor over the *Resilient Nations'* text, I was questioning my prevailing sentiment and having difficulty identifying just the right description. Angry? Sad? Hopeless? Resigned? Apathetic?

That morning, however, God gave me important perspective through the words of Psalm 7:11: "God is a righteous judge, And a God who has <u>indignation</u> every day." (underline added) That's it – INDIGNATION. Suddenly I was reminded that this is not about me, and not about you, but about what God thinks and feels about America in the Year 2014 and beyond. God created this world and founded this nation. The scripture says He is "indignant," meaning "feeling or expressing strong displeasure at something considered unjust, offensive, insulting, or base." As a righteous God, He is truly indignant regarding the unjust, offensive, insulting, and base idolatry and immorality which we condone and even pursue in America today. I realized that is exactly how I feel also. INDIGNANT!

Indignation

God was rightly indignant and driven to action when His chosen people, Israel, turned to idolatry, building a golden idol at the very time He was providing for their every need. Christ was rightly indignant and driven to action when He turned over the tables of the moneychangers in the Temple. William Wilberforce was rightly indignant and driven to action by the slave trade and lack of civility in British culture. Dietrich Bonhoffer became increasingly indignant and driven to action as he observed the German church fail to speak out and even support Adolf Hitler. Martin Luther King was rightly indignant and moved to action as he confronted the racial prejudices of America in the 20th Century.

The young warrior, David, was rightly indignant and driven to action as he marched out to confront the Philistine giant, Goliath: "For who is this uncircumcised Philistine, that he should taunt the armies of the living God?" I am hopeful that you feel this same way, indicating that you and I are truly sensing the "heart of God" as we respond indignantly to the dire status of our spiritual infrastructure which is so critical to the future of our nation.

May we also be driven to action by our indignation. To paraphrase David, "Who are these forces, these special interest groups, these human philosophies, these theories of government that seek to separate us from the very God, the very spiritual strengths, which made the United States a nation after God's own heart and the envy of the entire world? How dare they continue to tear down the very Constitutional foundations on which this great nation resides? How dare they taunt the living God?

Fear

A second emotion I often felt in the Re*silient Nations* project was FEAR. This fear was often magnified when I looked in the eyes of my young grandchildren. Psalm 18:4 (underline added) says, "The cords of death encompassed me, and <u>the torrents of ungodliness terrified me</u>." This fear is understandable when we look at the "torrents of ungodliness" in our nation today and predictably for the future. We are surrounded.

While understandably fearful for our own lives, fearful for future generations, and fearful to get out of our own bunkers to fight the forces which threaten our future as a people and as a nation, "WE" ("We the People," "We the Church," and "We the Statesmen") can be "strong and courageous" (as Moses commanded Joshua) because David in Psalm 18 identifies other equally important truths:

- <u>God hears our cry</u> for help. (v. 6)
- <u>God delivers us</u> from our strong enemies. He is our stay. (v. 17, 18)
- <u>God rescues us</u> because He delights in us. He brings us to a "broad place." (v. 19)
- <u>By God</u>, we can run upon a troop; we can leap over a wall. He makes our feet like hinds feet, and sets us on high places. (v. 33)
- <u>God enlarges our steps</u> under us, and keeps our feet from slipping. (v. 36)

As we embrace these realities of God's Sufficiency for all of our fears and needs, we can move from fear to COURAGE and ACTION. In *Resilient Leaders*, we said:

"Fear + FAITH = COURAGE"

Now is the time for "WE" ("We the People," We the Church," and "We the Statesmen") to dip deeply into our personal and collective wells of faith and courage for "such a time as this" in our nation's history. Just as with Esther at a decisive moment in the life of her nation, God is truly calling you and me to action.

> God is truly calling you and me to action.

Call to Action

If WE do not RESIST the EVIL sweeping OUR land, then WHO will?

"Such a TIME as this" is NOW.

If WE do not act NOW, then WHEN?

None of us can do everything, but ALL OF US CAN DO SOMETHING.

> If WE do not RESIST the EVIL sweeping OUR land, then WHO will?
> "Such a TIME as this" is NOW.
> If WE do not NOW, then WHEN?
> None of us can do everything,
> but ALL OF US CAN DO SOMETHING.

It is so easy to turn a blind eye, to not act on the truth we know. There are plenty of "good" reasons: "We are so busy.

Nothing we can do will make a difference. I'm only one person. Speaking out might bring opposition."

Andy Andrews passes along a story, originally from Erin Lutzer, in *How to Kill 11 Million People?* which speaks of another time when people looked the other way. In this case it was the people in a German town, in a church, during the height of World War II:

> "We heard stories of what was happening to the Jews, but we tried to distance ourselves from it, because we felt, what could anyone do to stop it?
>
> "Each Sunday morning, we would hear the train whistle blowing in the distance, then the wheels coming over the tracks. We became disturbed when we heard cries coming from the train as it passed by. We realized that it was carrying Jews like cattle in the cars!
>
> "Week after week the whistle would blow. We dreaded to hear the sound of those wheels because we know that we would hear the cries of the Jews en route to a death camp. Their screams tormented us.
>
> "We knew the time the train was coming and when we heard the whistle blow we began singing hymns. By the time the train came past our church, we were singing at the top of our voices. If we

heard the screams, we sang more loudly and soon we heard them no more.

"Years have passed and not one talks about it now, but I still hear that train whistle in my sleep."

May we avoid a similar tragedy of forever knowing we could have done something, yet failed to act. This very moment we can do something to stop the suffering of our fellow citizens, to stop the suicide of our beloved nation, to bring the love, grace, and righteousness of God to every dark corner of this United States. None of us can do everything, but all of us can do something. We also have train whistles, alarm bells, ringing all across our America—in our homes, our schools, our churches, our board rooms, our halls of government, our judicial chambers, our media, our arts and entertainment, our public square. The train whistles are blowing—Will we simply sing louder, or will we act?

Speaking to those with similar choices, King Solomon instructs the wise to resist the torrents of godliness, to intervene when evil darkens the land, and to escape the sure wrath of a righteous God:

[11] Deliver those who are being taken away to death, And those who are staggering to slaughter, Oh hold *them* back. [12] If you say, "See, we did not know this," Does He not consider *it* who weighs the hearts? And does He not know *it* who keeps your soul? And will He not render to man according to his work? Proverbs 24:11, 12 (underlines added)

Thomas Jefferson expressed similar concern regarding God's judgment for our national waywardness, "Indeed, I tremble for my country when I reflect that God is just, and that His justice cannot sleep forever."

Other American Presidents urged America to return to God, considering the alternative to be unfathomable. Consider President Abraham Lincoln's *Proclamation for a National Day of Fasting, Humiliation and Prayer* on March 30, 1863, proclaimed the following:

> "We have been the recipients of the choicest bounties of heaven. We have been preserved these many years, in peace and prosperity. We have grown in numbers, wealth and power, as no other nation has ever grown. <u>But we have forgotten God</u>. We have forgotten the gracious hand which preserved us in peace, and multiplied and enriched and strengthened us; and we have vainly imagined, in the deceitfulness of our hearts, that all these blessings were produced by some superior wisdom and virtue of our own. <u>Intoxicated with unbroken success, we have become too self-sufficient to feel the necessity of redeeming and preserving grace, too proud to pray to the God that made us</u>! It behooves us, then to humble ourselves before the offended Power, to confess our national sins, and to pray for clemency and forgiveness." (underlines added)

Issuing this proclamation during the darkest days of the American Civil War, President Lincoln reminded himself and others that God was the "gracious hand" protecting and strengthening America. While America of the 1860s faced tremendous challenges, it also had a strong Spiritual Infrastructure which gave the country inner strength and direction to navigate trauma as a people and as a nation.

Today our predicament is even more challenging, however. Not only have we "forgotten God," but we as a nation and as a people are largely trying to sweep God out of our nation (and even out of our national history) completely. Consider the alternative to Lincoln's exhortation to remember God. What if the dismantling of an America established by God and our Founders continues unabated?

An America without God

Certainly man cannot kick the Almighty God out of any nation, but Americans and America can certainly forfeit their respect for and awareness of God to the extent that He is no longer a relevant aspect of their individual or collectives lives. As we have seen, the nation of Israel did this repetitively, and suffered the consequences.

Have you ever thought about an America without God? Just consider the nascent 21st Century alone: as the twin idols of commerce in New York City succumbed to the death blows of 9/11 terrorists, what if Americans' only recourse for consolation and hope was another manmade idol? What if business leaders and investors across America only had their bank accounts to trust in during the early days of the Great Recession in 2008? Or what if American military members in harm's way could not draw courage from a God to guide and protect them? Or what if the military chaplain were not present to provide God's comfort to the grieving parents or widow or children of a fallen soldier? What would the citizens of New Orleans, or the residents of New Jersey, have done as their homes and hopes were washed away by Hurricane Katrina and Superstorm Sandy? Who would they have prayed to? Where would they have received the compassionate care supplied by thousands of churches? Where would the parents of Sandy Hook school shooting victims have received solace?

Perhaps you have an even more relevant example in your own life. Where would you, and your family, and your future generations be without a merciful, compassionate, protective, and sovereign God in your lives, or in America? The alternative is grim and depressing. Less God, more government. Less compassion, more control. Less grace, more law. Less morality, more deviancy. Less peace, more violence. Less love, more hate.

Is this our alternative to trusting God?
Less God, more government. Less compassion, more control.
Less grace, more law. Less morality, more deviancy.
Less peace, more violence. Less love, more hate.

Do you really want this kind of a future for yourself and your loved ones?

Do we really want this kind of a future for America?

Yet there is HOPE.

Gaining Altitude: A Hopeful America with God

People can live without food for weeks and water for days, but they can only live without HOPE for seconds. So it is with nations. Nations can live a long time while tangible elements of power erode, but the loss of HOPE often results in catastrophic collapse. While there were tremendous economic and military pressures applied to the former Soviet Union, no one predicted the rapid fall of the Iron Curtain and the seemingly sudden demise of the U.S.S.R. Yet it happened almost instantaneously, largely the result of HOPE lost by a long oppressed peoples and HOPE gained by others thirsty for freedom. The moment was breathtaking. The Orange Revolution in the Ukraine and the Solidarity Movement under Lech Walesa in Poland were similar events fueled not by economics or military might, but by new found HOPE.

Collectively the ten elements of Spiritual Infrastructure are the means by which a nation cultivates, grows, and sustains HOPE. They are also the means by which a nation conveys HOPE to its own people and to others. Certainly economic deprivation is unpleasant, but it is bearable with HOPE. A "chicken in every pot" is a good thing (alluding to the phrase used by Herbert Hoover and numerous other politicians that promises prosperity to the people), but it does not compare to HOPE. I have seen very wealthy people who were miserable and even despairing of their own lives. Conversely, I have seen poverty-stricken people in the ghettos of America and beyond who possessed enviable joy, the obvious result of HOPE.

<u>God is the ultimate author and source of temporal and eternal HOPE</u>. Consider several reminders of this HOPE from the Scriptures:

- **Hope in God.** "[22] The Lord's lovingkindnesses indeed never cease, For His compassions never fail. [23] *They* are new every morning; Great is Your faithfulness. [24] "The Lord is my portion," says my soul, "<u>Therefore I have hope in Him</u>." (Lamentations 3:22-24, underline added)
- **Hope does not disappoint.** "… we exult in **hope of the glory of God**. (an eternal expectation) And not only this, but we also **exult in our tribulations** (a temporal expectation), knowing that <u>tribulation</u> brings about <u>perseverance</u>; and perseverance, proven <u>character</u>; and proven character, **hope**; and **hope does not disappoint**, because <u>the love of God has been poured out within our hearts</u> through the Holy Spirit who was given to us." (Romans 5:3-5, underlines, parentheticals, and bold added)
- **Hope through the Scriptures.** "For whatever was written in earlier times was written for our instruction, so that <u>through perseverance and the encouragement of the Scriptures we might have **hope**</u>." (Romans 15:4, underline and bolds added)

- **Hope as an Anchor for the Soul.** "... we who would have taken refuge would have <u>strong encouragement</u> to take hold of the **hope** set before us. This **hope** we have as <u>an anchor of the soul</u>, a **hope** both <u>sure and steadfast</u> ..." (Hebrews 6:18-20, underlines and bolds added)
- **Christ in you, the hope of glory**... "... the riches of the glory of this mystery among the Gentiles, which is **Christ in you, the hope of glory**." (Colossians 1:27, bold added)

God does provide temporal and eternal hope for all Americans, and for America. He has blessed this nation richly in the past. And He will do so again when America reestablishes her Spiritual Infrastructure and begins to rely upon Almighty God.

God Has Not Forgotten America

<u>God truly has demonstrated his love and provision for America in many ways over our history as a nation</u>. The American Revolution was truly miraculous; fueled on HOPE, certainly not on ample musketry or shoes for our patriots at Valley Forge. The Great Awakenings were a resurgence of HOPE in God and HOPE in America, both preceding existential national trials (American Revolution and Civil War). The Civil War became a springboard for HOPE, that enslaved people might become free, that true respect for God and for all men and women might become reality. During the 20th Century, there was the Great Depression, the Dust Bowl, the World Wars, and the tumultuous 60s which would have knocked out a less hopeful people, or a nation with an insufficient Spiritual Infrastructure. Great leaders and public influencers that

immediately come to mind—British Prime Ministers Churchill and Thatcher, Presidents Roosevelt and Reagan, modern day prophets Billy Graham, Martin Luther King, Jr., Nelson Mandela, and Sarah Palin—these were all Merchants of HOPE to rally the soul and spirit of downtrodden and fearful people time and again.

Jesus, the earthly and visible manifestation of the Triune God, was and is the ultimate Merchant of HOPE. This is why we need Him more than ever before. The secular humanist and progressive philosophies of our day would have us believe that we can hope and trust in ourselves. Rhetorically, how is that working for you, America? Solomon reminded us that, "The horse is prepared for the day of battle, but victory belongs to the LORD." (Proverbs 21:31). There are a lot of things that "We" must do in America, but we must not forget that ultimately we are "one nation under God." It is God who brings the victory, and who brings HOPE. A similar verse of Scripture, echoed by Benjamin Franklin at the Constitutional Convention, is, "Unless the Lord builds the house, They labor in vain who build it; Unless the Lord guards the city, The watchman keeps awake in vain." (Psalm 127:1, underlines added)

You Are Not Alone

It is no accident that the Army puts more than one soldier in a foxhole. When facing mortal danger, being alone is a fearful thing. Solomon, the world's wisest man, reminds us of the same principle:

> "[11] Furthermore, if two lie down together they keep warm, but how can one be warm *alone*? [12] And if

<u>one can overpower him who is alone, two can resist him</u>. A cord of three *strands* is not quickly torn apart." (Ecclesiastes 4:11, 12, underlines added)

Being alone also leads to despair. Sharing a life experience (no matter how difficult) with fellow travelers, or remembrance of past examples, often brings and sustains HOPE and courage. In this vein, it is good to remember that we are not alone as we "fight the good fight" in an increasingly hostile, divisive, and self-destructive culture—a time when good is becoming evil and evil is becoming good.

Prayerfully, God will give our nation the ability to rediscover our values, be convicted of flawed policy and practice, accept the direction of God-honoring resilient leaders, and respond nationally with reversal, renewal, and spiritual rearmament. Or we as a nation may have to "weather a storm" of unprecedented severity, one from which we may never recover.

Yet, we are not alone. As young "millennials" of their day, Shadrach, Meshach, and Abednego made an astounding declaration as they stood at the doors of the fiery furnace of persecution:

> "[17] If it be *so*, our God whom we serve is able to deliver us from the furnace of blazing fire; and He will deliver us out of your hand, O king. [18] But *even* if *He does* not, let it be known to you, O king, that we are not going to serve your gods or

worship the golden image that you have set up." (Daniel 3:17, 18)

They were strong and courageous, confident, committed. As you and I HOPE and pray and work for the best in America, will we make the same declaration in the face of similar persecution? We have their example. **WE** must follow it. God will be our constant companion. We are not alone.

For fathers and mothers: As fathers and mothers who are charged with the nurture of young children, will we have the persistence and HOPE to keep training our children in the way they should go? Will we be able to resist the culture of an increasingly Godless educational system and the equally detrimental impacts of a pervasively secular culture? Joshua challenged, "If it is disagreeable in your sight to serve the Lord, choose for yourselves today whom you will serve... but as for me and my house, we will serve the Lord." (Joshua 24:15) Joshua did it. So can we.

> Joshua did it. So can we.

For business leaders: A successful business woman named Lydia, living in Thyatira, responded to Paul's gospel message on one of his missionary journeys. (Acts 16:14, 15) She and her whole household were saved and baptized, after which they openly served the Lord. She took the professional risk to integrate her faith, family, and profession into a God-honoring life message. Are we willing to do the same, to be salt and light in our chosen marketplace? Lydia did it. So can we.

For besieged culture warriors: As the king of Aram surrounded Elisha with horses and chariots at Dothan, Elisha's servant cried out in fear, "Alas, my master! What shall we do?" (2 Kings 6:15b). Elisha, seeing with spiritual eyes, answered, "Do not fear, for those who are with us are more than those who are with them." (2 Kings 6:16) The life lesson continues, demonstrating once again that "we are not alone:"

> "Then Elisha prayed and said, 'O LORD, I pray, open his eyes that he may see.' And the LORD opened the servant's eyes and he saw; and behold, the mountain was full of horses and chariots of fire all around Elisha." (2 Kings 6:17)

Perhaps you feel outnumbered by the forces of evil and secular humanism around you. You can take heart that God also surrounds you with a great cloud of witnesses and chariots of fire to win the day. If Elisha maintained a confident spiritual perspective when all those around him were losing theirs, then so can we. Elisha did it, so can we.

For the Elderly: For the person who is waning in vigor or doubting their future significance, remember Caleb. He remained engaged, he fought the good fight. Caleb did it. So can we.

For the Pastor: Ezra was a prophet and priest in very difficult times. He spoke truth to power. He fortified the leaders around him. Are you a pastor willing to speak truth today? Does your impact on society extend beyond the pews? Ezra did it. So can we.

For the outnumbered: As Gideon was preparing for battle, God kept reducing his numbers, from thousands to three hundred. He remained strong and courageous, knowing that God was able. The brave 300, fully committed to God, became the instrument of God's deliverance. Are you and I willing to join the ranks of the 300? Gideon did it. So can we.

From a national perspective: Israel has modeled resilience over its history. Likewise America demonstrated resilience over its first 180 years. If Israel and America did it in the past, so can America today. So can we.

You get the point. In I Corinthians 10:13, Paul challenges the Corinthians, and us:

> "No temptation has overtaken you but <u>such as is common to man</u>; and <u>God is faithful</u>, who <u>will not allow you to be tempted beyond what you are able</u>, but with the temptation <u>will provide the way of escape also, so that you will be able to endure it</u>." (underlines added)

This verse (and promise) certainly covers the temptation to doubt, to despair, to not stand up for what is just and right and true. The good news is that we never walk alone on this difficult journey. We have others, and we have God.

A New Birth of Freedom

Two hundred and twenty-five years ago our Founding Fathers had a vision, to form "a more perfect Union," based upon the sovereignty of God and the dignity of man. God richly blessed our new nation, America.

Eighty-seven years later, and one hundred and fifty years ago our "perfect Union" was being ravaged by the American Civil War. Abraham Lincoln rallied national aspirations with his vision "...that this nation under God shall have a new birth of freedom." (Gettysburg Address, November 19, 1863)

Today, as well, our people cry for vision, for direction, for renewal. May the revolution to rediscover our national roots begin *now*. May our nation's spiritual rearmament begin *now*. May Hope Abound. May God Arise. May His Enemies Be Scattered.

> ## America, you are too young to die.

Resilient Nations Takeaways

RN 9A – INDIGNATION is an understandable emotion resulting from a candid assessment of our nation's current Spiritual Infrastructure. May this indignation drive us to action as obedient servants of the God and future generations of Americans.

RN 9B – FEAR for our own lives, fear for future generations, and fear to get out of our own bunkers to fight the forces which threaten our future as a people and as a nation is understandable when we look at the "torrents of ungodliness" around us. Yet, God hears our cry, delivers us, and enlarges our steps as we allow faith to transform fear to courage and action.

RN 9C – If WE do not RESIST the EVIL sweeping OUR land, then WHO will? If not NOW, then WHEN? None of us can do everything, but ALL OF US CAN DO SOMETHING.

RN 9D – Certainly man cannot kick the Almighty God out of any nation, but Americans and America can certainly forfeit their respect for and awareness of God to the extent that He is no longer a relevant and welcome dimension of their individual or collectives lives. Where would you, and your family, and your future generations be without a merciful, compassionate, protective, and sovereign God in your lives, or in America? The alternative is grim and depressing. Less God, more government. Less compassion, more control. Less grace, more law. Less morality, more deviancy. Less peace, more violence. Less love, more hate.

RN 9E – God does provide temporal and eternal HOPE for all Americans, and for America. He has blessed this nation richly in the past. And He will do so again when America reestablishes her Spiritual Infrastructure and begins to rely upon Almighty God.

RN 9F – WE ARE NOT ALONE as we "fight the good fight" in an increasingly hostile, divisive, and self-destructive culture—a time when good is becoming evil and evil is becoming good. The good news is that we never walk alone on this difficult journey. We have others, and we have God.

RN 9G – Prayerfully, God will give our nation the ability to rediscover our values, be convicted of flawed policy and practice, accept the direction of God-honoring resilient leaders, and respond nationally with reversal, renewal, and spiritual rearmament. May the revolution to rediscover our national roots begin *now*. May Hope Abound. May God Arise. May His Enemies Be Scattered.

For Further Consideration

Review the mandates for "We the People," We the Church," and "We the Statesmen" in Chapter 8. Develop your own "personal action plan" to this *Resilient Nations'* "Call to Action." Your family, your church, your community, your nation need you now. What is your plan?

Additional References

1. Andrews, Andy. *How Do You Kill 11 MILLION PEOPLE?* Nashville, TN: Thomas Nelson, 2011.
2. *The Rebirth of America*. Philadelphia: Arthur S. DeMoss Foundation, 1986.
3. *Salt & Light Council*. www.SaltandLightCouncil.org.
4. Matt Redman, *"Never Once"*, in 10,000 Reasons, Kingsway Music, ©2011, Compact Disc.
5. Carson, Ben and Candy. *One Nation*. New York, NY: Sentinel, 2014.

Appendix 1
Listing of Charts

Chart 1: *A Resilient Beginning 1740-1960*
Chapter 1, page 48

Chart 2: *Resilience Life Cycle* ©
Chapter 2, page 59

Chart 3: *Model Nation*
Chapter 3, page 103

Chart 4: *Decline Sets In 1960-2001*
Chapter 4, page 137

Chart 5: *Decline Accelerates 2001-2014*
Chapter 4, page 148

Chart 6: *Macro Trendlines 1740-2014*
Chapter 4, page 161

Chart 7: *Government "Gone Wild"*
Chapter 4, page 163

Chart 8: *The Road Not Taken*
Chapter 4, page 165

Chart 9: *Unalienable Rights*
Chapter 5, page 177

Chart 10: *Devolution of Religion in America*
Chapter 6, page 254

Chart 11: *Unalienable Rights*
Chapter 7, page 310

Chart 12: *Mandates*
Chapter 8, page 344

Chart 13: *The Road Not Taken*
Chapter 9, page 355

Appendix 2
Products and Services

FOR SUPPORTING RESILIENCE CONTENT

www.ResilienceTrilogy.com

FOR SPECIFIC BOOK INFORMATION AND ORDERING

RESILIENT WARRIORS
www.ResilientWarriorsBook.com
ISBN: 978-0-9838919-4-9

RESILIENT WARRIORS ADVANCED STUDY GUIDE
www.ResilientWarriorsBook.com
ISBN: 978-0-9838919-5-6

Bob Dees

RESILIENT LEADERS
www.ResilientLeadersBook.com
ISBN: 978-0-9855979-9-3

RESILIENT NATIONS
www.ResilientNationsBook.com
ISBN: 978-0-9897975-6-6

FOR COMMENTS, QUESTIONS, AND
QUANTITY DISCOUNTING

author@ResilienceTrilogy.com
customercare@ResilienceTrilogy.com

Acknowledgements

Dr. James Dobson has kindly provided permission to use one of his quotes which I hold most dear,

> "What really matters at the end of life is
> who we loved,
> who loved us, and
> what we did in the service of the Lord together."

As with our other books in *The Resilience Trilogy*, I am truly grateful for the many who traveled together in this labor of love on behalf of future generations, and ultimately our Lord.

When I started this *Spiritual Infrastructure as an Element of National Power* adventure in 1991 at the National Defense University, there were two men who became my mentors in cultural issues, Constitutional foundations, and the Biblical origins of western government: David Barton, Founder of Wallbuilders, and Neil Markva, a Northern Virginia attorney and Sunday school teacher. I am grateful for the jumpstart they provided, allowing me to sustain and complete this *Resilient Nations* journey.

My beloved wife, Kathleen, has been the perfect helpmate yet once again, consistently sacrificing time and energy to create a work of value for others while she concurrently "kept the home fires burning" for family and friends. As I reflected in *Resilient Warriors* and *Resilient Leaders*, still waters run deep, and Kathleen's wise insights along the way have been invaluable. As my bride for 40 years, she has been a wonderful life partner, mother, grandmother, and friend. As well, she has the true heart of an American patriot, particularly valuable on this *Resilient Nations* journey. Kathleen no doubt acquired this trait from her wonderful father and mother, Charlie and Bobbie Sue Robinson, who have modeled patriotism at every turn.

Another source of wisdom, encouragement, and tangible assistance on this *Resilient Nations* journey has been our dear circle of "9/11 friends" and family, role models and wise counselors such as: Drs. Andy and Gail Seidel, Bobby and Kandy Farino, Gene and Randi Frazier, Jim and Brenda Johnson, Ron and Cristy Varela, Sharni and Dorothy Rakhra, Jim Amos, Jeff and Karen Koob, Kathy Magnuson, Susan Burton, Dr. Colonel (Chaplain) Ron Huggler and Colonel Sue Huggler, U.S. Army, Retired, Dr. Eric and Donna Scalise, Rolfe and Lea Carawan, Dr. LuAnn Callaway, Paul and Betty Lou Martin, John and Beverly Grant, Bobbie Sue Robinson, Charles and Nancy Robinson, and our beloved children, Major Rob Dees and Allison Dees Barry, along with their respective families.

Our "Resilience God Style" Vine Life Class from Williamsburg Community Chapel provided wonderful friendship and feedback during the writing process. As well, I am grateful to the New

Canaan Society, the American Association of Christian Counselors, and Liberty University for the opportunities to present emerging *Resilient Nations* content in a variety of venues, affording valuable feedback and refinement of the material. As well from Liberty University, Vice Provost Ron Hawkins, Dean Mat Staver of the Liberty School of Law, Dean Shawn Akers of the Helms School of Government, and Dean Scott Hicks of the Liberty School of Business have been particularly encouraging and helpful. My equal appreciation goes to Franklin Graham, President and CEO of Samaritan's Purse for his stage setting FOREWORD, and to General Jerry Boykin, David Barton, Mat Staver, Shawn Akers, and Jeff Reeter for their supportive endorsements. Congressman Randy Forbes' constant example of statesmanship under the toughest of conditions provided needed courage and commitment to stay the course.

I am also appreciative for the assistance from many like-minded organizations, among them the Alliance Defending Freedom, the American Center for Law and Justice, the American Renewal Project, the Becket Fund, the Congressional Prayer Caucus Foundation, the Family Research Council, Family Talk, Focus on the Family, the International Association for Evangelical Chaplains, the Invictus Foundation, the Liberty Counsel, the Liberty Institute, Military Community Youth Ministries, Military Outreach of USA, Operation Military Family, the Pinnacle Forum, the Salt and Light Council, and Wallbuilders.

Glen Aubrey of Creative Team Publishing (CTP) (www.CreativeTeamPublishing.com) has been an outstanding editor, publisher, and friend. Justin Aubrey's artistic giftedness was indispensable to the cover designs. The CTP editing team masterfully prepared the final manuscript for publication.

Randy Beck of My Domain Tools (www.MyDomainTools.com) did a great job expanding the *Resilience Trilogy* website (www.ResilienceTrilogy.com), and provided marketing collateral for new content. As well, Beth Scherbing has been a wonderful Trilogy administrator, untiringly moving forward with research and securing permissions from many contributing organizations and individuals. She has become a valuable member of *The Resilience Trilogy* team.

Foundational to my appreciation and understanding of Spiritual Infrastructure have been the many statesmen and culture warriors I was privileged to serve with while in the military, business, and non-profit sectors. I am forever indebted to the many I have named in *Resilient Nations* whose specific input is further recognized in Permissions and Credits. I also provide a thank you in advance to the many who will embrace the material and seek to recover America's greatness through the information and motivation provided in *Resilient Nations*.

Most importantly, God truly is my Rock, Fortress, and Deliver ("RFD" from Psalm 18). Without the friendship of Jesus, the comfort of His Holy Spirit, the wisdom of His Word, and the Sovereign and Sufficient Hand of God the Father, my efforts would only be clanging cymbals and tinkling brass. To Him Be the Glory!

About the Author

ROBERT F. DEES

Major General, U.S. Army, Retired

Major General (Retired) Robert F. Dees was born in Amarillo, Texas on 2 February 1950. Graduating from the U.S. Military Academy in 1972, he was commissioned as a second lieutenant of Infantry and awarded a Bachelor of Science degree. He also holds a Masters Degree in Operations Research from the Naval Postgraduate School. His military education includes the Infantry Officer Basic and Advanced Courses, the U.S. Army Command and General Staff College, and the Industrial College of the Armed Forces. He was also a Research Fellow at the Royal College of Defence Studies in London and is a registered Professional Engineer in the State of Virginia.

General Dees served in a wide variety of command and staff positions culminating in his last three assignments as Assistant Division Commander for Operations, 101st Airborne Division (Air Assault); Commander, Second Infantry Division, United States Forces Korea; and as Deputy Commanding General, V (US/GE) Corps in Europe, concurrently serving as Commander, US-Israeli

Combined Task Force for Missile Defense. He commanded airborne, air assault, and mechanized infantry forces from platoon through division level; including two tours as company commander and regimental commander in the historic "Rakkasans," the 187th Regimental Combat Team. General Dees is a Distinguished Member of the Regiment, and now serves as Honorary Colonel of the Regiment for the Rakkasans.

General Dees' awards and decorations include the Defense Distinguished Service Medal, Distinguished Service Medal (2), Legion of Merit (2), Meritorious Service Medal (6), Joint Service Commendation Medal, Army Commendation Medal, and the Republic of Korea Chonsu Order of National Security. General Dees has also been awarded the Ranger Tab, Senior Parachutist and Air Assault Badges, the Expert Infantryman's Badge, the Army Staff Identification Badge, and the Joint Staff Identification Badge. General Dees was also awarded the 2003 Centurion Award by the National Association for Evangelicals for long term support to chaplains while in command positions.

Officially retiring from the Army on 1 January 2003, he worked as Director of Homeland Security for Electronic Warfare Associates, then as Executive Director, Defense Strategies, Microsoft Corporation for two years. In that role, General Dees formulated the strategy for Microsoft's U.S. Defense sector and engaged with leadership of Microsoft's major defense partners. In addition, he served as Microsoft lead for Reconstruction of Iraq, coordinating efforts with U.S. Government, foreign governments, and private sector partners in the U.S. and abroad. General Dees then served for five years (2005-2010) as Executive Director,

Military Ministry, providing spiritual nurture to troops and families around the world. He is now President of RFD, LLC, serving a variety of constituents in the arenas of business, defense, counterterrorism, and care for military troops and families. As well, General Dees now serves as Associate Vice President for Military Outreach for Liberty University (leading the Liberty University Institute for Military Resilience), Military Director for the American Association of Christian Counselors, and Senior Military Advisor for DNA Military. He also serves on a number of non-profit boards including Military Community Youth Ministries, Operation Military Family, Hope for the Home Front, and the Invictus Foundation.

General Dees frequently provides motivational talks at a variety of seminars, webinars, and conferences, as well as commentary on current military and combat trauma issues in venues such as FOX Huckabee, FOX Business, Focus on the Family, Christian Broadcasting Network, American Association of Christian Counselors, American Family Radio, New Canaan Society, Pinnacle Forum, Wallbuilders Live, Iron Sharpens Iron Men's Conferences, Wildfire Men's Conferences, and numerous churches and military bases. He was featured as one of thirty *"Master Leaders"* by George Barna.

General Dees is married to the former Kathleen Robinson of Houston, Texas. They have two married children and seven grandchildren, and currently live in Texas. General and Mrs. Dees are grateful for the privilege of continuing to serve our nation during these critical times.

Permissions and Credits

In Order of Appearance in *Resilient Nations*

Grateful acknowledgement is made to the following for permission to cite previously published material, quotes and concepts:

Foreword

Franklin Graham, President & CEO, Samaritan's Purse, Billy Graham Evangelistic Association.

Dedication

Castings Crowns for lyrics to "While You Were Sleeping", ©Mark Hall Publishing Designee, Lifesong Album, August 30, 2005. Publishing, Sony/ATV Music. Used with permission.

Introduction

Bulgarian President Georgi Parvanov for 2007 quote "the people don't have a will to work" in response to author's question regarding "What is your biggest problem?" on 07.04.07.

Joint Forces Staff College for excerpts from Elements of National Power taken from http://www.jfsc.ndu.edu/library/publications/bibliography/Elements_of_National_Power.pdf. Last update: unknown. Accessed 01.14.14.

By permission. From *Merriam-Webster's Collegiate® Dictionary, 11th Edition* ©2014 by Merriam-Webster, Inc. (www.Merriam-Webster.com) for definition of infra. Accessed 05.08.14.

Aristotle, Ancient Greek Philosopher, for the quotation "All who have meditated on the art of governing mankind have been convinced that the fate of empires depends on the education of youth." Held within public domain.

For school violence statistics:
http://www.msnbc.com/morning-joe/nearly-30-more-students-killed-newtown
Accessed 5/26/14

For STEM data accessed at http://www.fas.org/sgp/crs/misc/RL33434.pdf on 5.16.14. Held within the public domain.

Chapter 1

President Dwight D. Eisenhower for statement taken from a speech given at ICAF, Washington, 1960. Held within the public domain.

Bernard Baruch for the inscription on a plaque located on the wall of the Baruch Auditorium, Eisenhower Hall, Industrial College of the Armed Forces, Washington D.C.

Dr. John George for his saying, "a lesson learned is a project earned". Used with permission.

Major General Robert F. Dees for excerpts taken from his paper *Spiritual infrastructure as an Element of National Power* 1992.
President George Bush for the quotation, "America is still the freest, kindest, and strongest nation on earth" from The State of The Union Address given on January 28, 1992. Held within the public domain.

Napoleon Bonaparte for his quotation, "the moral is to the physical as three is to one". Held within the public domain.

President John F. Kennedy for his statement, "This country cannot afford to be materially rich and spiritually poor." http://www.jfklibrary.org/Research/Research-Aids/Ready-Reference/JFK-Quotations.aspx. Held within the public domain.

President Dwight Eisenhower for his statement, "The spirit of man is more important than mere physical strength, and the spiritual fiber of a nation than its wealth.", accessed at http://www.famous-quotes.com/author.php?page=1&aid=2262 on 05.16.14. Held within the public domain.

Alexis de Tocqueville for statement attributed to him from his writings in *Democracy in America*, "America is great because she is good, and if America ever ceases to be good, America will cease to be great." Held within the public domain.

Chapter 2

Edward Gibbon for excerpts taken from *The History of the Decline and Fall of the Roman Empire*, Volume 6, Chapter XXXVIII. © 1906. New York: Fred de Fau and Co. (found on "The Online Library of Liberty, a project of Liberty Fund, Inc.") Accessed from http://oll.libertyfund.org on 11.20.13. Held within the public domain.

George Santayana quote taken from *The Life of Reason or the Phases of Human Progress*, © 1917. Published by Charles Scribner's Sons in New York. Book is held within the public domain.

Alexander Fraser Tytler, Lord Houselee for quotations attributed to him taken from *Respectfully Quoted*, Library of Congress, Washington. 1989. Held within the public domain.

Edward Gibbon for an excerpt taken from *The History of the Decline and Fall of the Roman Empire*, Volume 6, Chapter XXXVIII (found on "The Online Library of Liberty, a project of Liberty Fund, Inc.") Accessed from http://oll.libertyfund.org on 11.20.13. Held within the public domain.

Random House, Inc. for excerpt from *Things That Matter* by Charles Krauthammer. Copyright © 2013. Used by permission of Random House, Inc., New York NY 10019. All rights reserved.

Zondervan Publishing for excerpt taken from Explore the Book by J. Sidlow Baxter, pages 18-21. Copyright © 1960 by Zondervan Publishing. Used with permission. http://www.zondervan.com.

Fandango.com Washington Q&A for the description of the film *The Book of Eli*. January 15, 2010. Tara Bennett, Fandango Film Commentator. Used with permission.

Edward Gibbon excerpt taken from The *History of the Decline and Fall of the Roman Empire*, Volume 12, Chapter LXXI (found on "The Online Library of Liberty, a project of Liberty Fund, Inc.") Accessed from http://oll.libertyfund.org on 11.20.13. Held within the public domain.

Edward Gibbon for excerpt taken from *The History of the Decline and Fall of the Roman Empire*, Volume 12, Chapter LXXI (found on "The Online Library of Liberty, a project of Liberty Fund, Inc.") Accessed from http://oll.libertyfund.org on 11.20.13. Held within the public domain.

Archibald Signorelli: "If we yield to evil persuasions, it is because we fall the way we lean." Quote taken from *Plan of Creation, or Sword of Truth* by Archibald Signorelli. Published by Charles H. Kerr & Company in Chicago. © 1916. Book is held within the public domain.

Chapter 3

Sir William Blackstone, excerpts taken from Commentaries of the Laws of England, 1753. Book is held within the public domain.

David Barton, excerpts taken from Original Intent, The Courts, The Constitution and Religion, page 5, 2013. Used with permission.

Thomas Paine for excerpts taken from Common Sense, 1776. Book is held within the public domain.

Neil F. Markva, excerpts taken from his paper *Our Christian Heritage*, 1, ©Neil F. Markva 1990. Used with permission.

Sir William Blackstone, excerpts taken from Commentaries of the Laws of England, Volume I, 2nd Section, 1753. Book is held within the public domain.

William Slomanson, Fundamental Perspectives on International Law. Boston, USA: Wadsworth, 2011.
http://en.wikipedia.org/wiki/International_law
Accessed 04.16.14. Used with permission.
Wikipedia contributors, "International Law", "Wikipedia, The Free Encyclopedia, http://en.wikipedia.org/wiki/International_law
Accessed 04.16.14.

Answers.com for a reference to the Kyoto protocol accessed at http://www.answers.com/mt/kyoto-protocol on 6.3.14

Preamble of the U.S. Constitution. Accessed at
http://www.usconstitution.net/xconst_preamble.html
on 05/16/14. Held within the public domain.

Neil F. Markva, excerpts taken from his paper *Our Christian Heritage*, 4, ©Neil F. Markva 1990. Used with permission.

Declaration of Independence "Declaration of Independence, "
http://www.archives.gov/exhibits/charters/declaration_transcript
.html. Accessed 04.16.14. Held within the public domain.

Neil F. Markva, excerpts taken from his paper *Our Christian Heritage*, 4, ©Neil F. Markva 1990. Used with permission.

Sir William Blackstone, excerpts taken from Commentaries of the Laws of England, Volume I, 2nd Section, 1753. Book is held within the public domain.

Major General Robert F. Dees, *Resilient Leaders*, Copyright ©2013 by Robert F. Dees.

Chapter 4

C. S. Lewis for excerpts taken from The Abolition of Man by C.S. Lewis ©Copyright C.S. Lewis Ptd. Ltd. 1943, 1946, 1978. Used with permission.

Anonymous Korean War Veteran for "One Minute Prayer for Our Country".

William Bennett for excerpts taken from "The De-valuing of America", New York, Simon & Schuster Publishing Group, Copyright ©1992 William J. Bennett. Used with permission.

William Bennett for *The Index Of Leading Cultural Indicators.* New York: Broadway Books, 1999.

U. S. Supreme Court. "Stone v. Graham, 449 U.S. 39 (1980)." *First Amendment Center.* November 17, 1980.
http://www.firstamendmentschools.org/freedoms/case.aspx?id=1422.
Accessed 04.18.14. Held within the public domain.

Establishment Clause excerpt accessed at
http://constitution.findlaw.com/amendment1/amendment.html
on 05.16.14. Held under the public domain.

Newt Gingrich, excerpt taken from To Save America: Stopping Obama's Secular-Socialist Machine, Copyright©2010. Published by Regnery Publishing, Inc. All rights reserved. Reprinted by special permission of Regnery Publishing, Washington. D.C.

Last stanza of "The Road Not Taken" from the book The Poetry of Robert Frost edited by Edward Connery Lathem. Copyright ©1969 by Henry Holt and Company. Reprinted arrangement of Henry Holt and Company, LLC. Used with permission.

Major General Robert F. Dees, *Resilient Leaders*, Copyright ©2013 by Robert F. Dees.

Chapter 5

Mother Teresa of Calcutta for quote from the National Prayer Breakfast, 1994.
http://www.priestsforlife.org/brochures/mtspeech.html.
Accessed on 4.14.14. Used with permission.

John Grant excerpts taken from, page 17, *This Is Life*, ©2013. Used with permission.

The New York City Department of Health & Mental Hygiene, Office of Vital Statistics for the Summary of Vital Statistics 2012 The City of New York, Pregnancy Outcomes.

CNSNews.com for "Black Pastor: Administration 'Is Promoting Murder' by Promoting Abortion" by Penny Starr, February 28, 2014. Used with permission from CNSNews.com.

John Grant excerpts taken from page 103, *This Is Life*, ©2013. Used with permission.

John Grant excerpts taken from page 90, *This Is Life*, ©2013. Used with permission.

Melissa Steffan excerpt taken from The Gleanings, "Abortion Restrictions hit Second-Highest Total Ever in 2012", dated 01.04.2014. Used with permission.
Kate Tracy excerpt taken from The Gleanings, "US Abortions Fall to Lowest Rate Since Roe vs. Wade", dated 02.03.2014. Used with permission.

Tom Strode excerpt taken from The Gleanings, "Abortion Clinics Closing at Record Rate," dated 09.13.2013. Used with permission.

Indian Journal of Medical Research, for reference to the December 2012; 136(6): 899-902 article. Found at http://www.ncbi.nlm.nih.gov/pmc/articles/PMC3612319/. Accessed 05.09.14.

Dr. Jim Eckman excerpt taken from Issues In Perspective article, The Growing Acceptance of Euthanasia, June 29, 2013. http://graceuniversity.edu/iip/2013/06/13-06-29-1/. Accessed 04.03.14. Used with permission.

Fox News for reference to "Cultural Problem Across the Board': Will Defends Paul Ryan Amid Race Controversy", March 24, 2014 on the O'Reilly Factor. http://foxnewsinsider.com/2014/03/24/%E2%80%98-cultural-problem-across-board%E2%80%99-george-will-defends-paul-ryans-poverty-remarks. Accessed 05.07.14. Used with permission.

Charles Krauthammer for his AEI Bradley Lecture, "Defining Deviancy Up", presented September 13, 1993. Used with permission.

Fox news for reference to, http://www.foxnews.com/on-air/oreilly/2014/03/25/paul-ryan-attacked-over-poverty-remark, accessed 04/18/14. Used with permission.

American Family Association for quote from the press release dated March 27, 2014. Accessed at http://www.afa.net/Media/PressRelease.aspx?id=2147544607 on 04/22/2014.

Vice President Dan Quayle for reference to his May 19, 1992 speech given to the Commonwealth Club of California.

James Kennedy and Jerry Newcombe, *What's Wrong with Same-Sex Marriage* (Wheaton, IL: Crossway, 2004), pp. 53-69. Used with permission.

Dr. Franklin Graham for statements during his interview on March 28, 2013 airing on CNN. Also found at http://piersmorgan.blogs.cnn.com/2013/03/28/franklin-graham-on-same-sex-marriage-god-is-the-one-who-defined-marriage-not-government-its-between-one-man-and-one-woman/. Accessed 05.09.14.

Mika Brzezinski, Morning Joe Show airing March 20, 2014, for reference to her statement regarding women and men.

American Foundation for Suicide Prevention for their educational information at http://www.afsp.org/. Accessed 05/19/14.

The A21 Campaign for comprehensive information regarding human trafficking at www.thea21campaign.org. Accessed 04.22.14.

Diane Langberg, PhD for additional resources regarding human trafficking at www.dianelangberg.com/work/resources.html. Accessed 05/19/14.

Oscar Wilde for his quote, "A red rose is not selfish because it wants to be a red rose. It would be horribly selfish if it wanted all the other flowers in the garden to be both red and roses." Accessed at
http://www.finestquotes.com/select_quote-category-Selfishness-page-0.htm on 05/19/14.

Alexander Solzhenitsyn for his quote, "It is not because the truth is too difficult to see that we make mistakes... we make mistakes because the easiest and most comfortable course for us is to seek insight where it accords with our emotions—especially selfish ones."
Accessed at http://www.brainyquote.com/quotes/
authors/a/aleksandr_solzhenitsyn.html on 05.10.14.

Chapter 6

Inscription "Freedom Is Not Free", located at the Korean War Veterans Memorial, 900 Ohio Drive SW, Washington, D.C. U.S. National Park Service.

Neville Chamberlain for his statement made September 30, 1938. Accessed at http://britannia.com/history/docs/peactime.html on 04.24.14.

President Teddy Roosevelt for his quote "walk softly and carry a big stick", during a speech given on September 2, 1901 at the Minnesota State Fair. Accessed 04.24.14 at
http://www.theodore-roosevelt.com/images/research/txtspeeches/678.pdf.
Held within the public domain.

President Ronald Reagan for his quote "peace through strength", during his address to the nation regarding Defense and National Security given on March 23, 1983. Accessed 04.24.14 at
http://reagan2020.us/speeches/Defense_and_Security.asp.
Held within the public domain.

President Ronald Reagan for his quote "None of the wars in my lifetime came about because we were too strong" in his remarks given on August 23, 1984 at the Republican National Convention in Dallas, TX. Accessed 04.24.14 at
http://reagan2020.us/speeches/nomination_acceptance_1984.asp. Held within the public domain.

President Ronald Reagan for his quote "Our military strength is a prerequisite to peace" during his address to the British Parliament on June 8, 1982. Accessed 04.24.14 at
http://millercenter.org/president/speeches/detail/3408.
Held within the public domain.

Military Officer Newsletter with Alan W. Dowd article excerpt, "Preserving a Strong Defense", dated April 2014, accessed at www.moaa.org on 04.24.14.

Congressman Randy Forbes for military budget projected data. Accessed 04.24.14 at
http://forbes.house.gov/uploadedfiles/defense_forecasts.pdf.

http://www.pbs.org/wgbh/pages/frontline/shows/sleeper/inside/profiles.html. Accessed 04.06.14.

The Huffington Post for article dated April 6, 2008, "Obama: No Surprise That Hard-Pressed Pennsylvanians Turn Bitter."
Accessed at
http://www.huffingtonpost.com/mayhill-fowler/obama_no_surprise_that_ha_b_96188.html on 05/08/14.

GOPUSA.com for quote from their article, "Detroit Prosecutor Files Ethnic Intimidation Charges Against One", dated April 11, 2014. Accessed at
http://www.usobserver.com/archive/june-11/apathy-in-america.html on 04.16.14.

Alexis Simendinger for quote from article, "Turnout in Mind, Obama Cites Voting Rights "Threat", dated April 12, 2014. Accessed on 05.07.14 at
http://www.realclearpolitics.com/articles/2014/04/12/turnout_in_mind_obama_cites_voting_rights_threat_122260.html

President Barack Obama, for quote from his April 10, 2014 speech.
http://www.whitehouse.gov/the-press-office/2014/04/10/remarks-president-lbj-presidential-library-civil-rights-summit
Accessed 05.06.14. Held within the public domain.

By permission. From *Merriam-Webster's Collegiate® Dictionary, 11th Edition* ©2014 by Merriam-Webster, Inc. (www.Merriam-Webster.com) for the definition of "civility".

Fox News for reference to their March 30, 2014 article, http://www.foxnews.com/us/2014/03/30/university-arizona-students-riot-after-ncaa-tournament-loss/. Accessed 05.07.14.

By permission. From *Merriam-Webster's Learner's Dictionary* ©2014 by Merriam-Webster, Inc. (www.LearnersDictionary.com) for the definition of "apathy".

Chuck Colson for quotes from his article, "Apathy in America", dated July 11, 2011. Accessed at http://www.colsoncenter.org/the-center/columns/colson-files/16754-apathy-in-america on 04/16/2014. Reprinted with permission of Prison Fellowship, P.O. Box 1550, Merrifield, VA 22116, www.pfm.org.

J. M. Appleton from quotes from his article, "Apathy in America" dated June 2011. Accessed at http://www.usobserver.com/archive/june-11/apathy-in-america.html on 04.16.14.

U.S. Constitution Article 1 Section 8 for the Powers of Congress. Accessed at http://www.usconstitution.net/xconst_A1Sec8.html and at http://en.wikipedia.org/wiki/Enumerated_powers on 05.07.14. Held within the public domain.

Fox News for their reporting of an interview with President Obama and Bill O'Reilly on February 3, 2014. Accessed at http://www.foxnews.com/politics/2014/02/03/not-even-smidgen-corruption-obama-downplays-irs-other-scandals/ on 05-07-2014. Used within the Fair Use guidelines.

Justice Rehnquist in his argument in the Wallace vs. Jaffree, 472 U.S. 38 case, argued December 4, 1984. Accessed at https://bulk.resource.org/courts.gov/c/US/472/472.US.38.83-929.83-812.html on 05.07.14 Held within the public domain.

David Barton from the back cover of Original Intent: The Courts, the Constitution, and Religion. Copyright ©1996, 2000, 2008,2001. 5th Edition, 5th Printing, February 2013. Used with permission.

Huffington Post for President Obama remarks accessed at www.huffingtonpost.com/mayhill-fowler/obama-no-surprise-that-ha_b_96188.html on 05/08/14.

Time Magazine article by Amy Sullivan, "Rise of the Nones", dated March 12, 2012. Accessed at http://content.time.com/magazine/article/0,9171,2108027,00.html on 05.08.14.

Randy Newman for his insights regarding Rise of the Nones found at http://www.randydavidnewman.com/2012/04/05/the-rise-of-the-nones/ Accessed 05.08.14.

Harold Koenig, for his brief presented at Liberty University. Survey based on a random-digit dialing survey of the U.S. on Sept 14-16, as reported in New England Journal of Medicine 2001; 345:1507-1512. Used with permission.

Chapter 7

Jim Johnson for excerpts from Fracture Zone 2015 page 287, Copyright ©2013. Used with permission.

President Franklin D. Roosevelt for quote taken from his State of the Union Address given on January 4, 1935. Accessed at http://www.presidency.ucsb.edu/ws/?pid=14890 on 05.13.14.

Jim Johnson for excerpts from Fracture Zone 2015 page 231, Copyright ©2013. Used with permission.
Jim Johnson for excerpts from Fracture Zone 2015 pages x, xi, Copyright ©2013. Used with permission.

Aristotle, Ancient Greek Philosopher, for the quotation "All who have meditated on the art of governing mankind have been convinced that the fate of empires depends on the education of youth." Held within public domain.

Allan C. Ornstein for content in The Changing Federal Role in Education, by Allan C. Ornstein, American Education, Vol. 20 No. 10, December 1984, pages 4-7.

The Stop Common Core for additional information for radical reform or replacement of Common Core. Accessed at www.stopcommoncore.com accessed 5/19/14.

Alliance Defending Freedom for information accessed in the March 2014 newsletter, pages 1-2.

GOPUSA for data obtained in the article http://www.gopusa.com/news/2014/05/08/public-schools-fail/ Accessed 05/20/14.

Jim Johnson for excerpts from Fracture Zone 2015 page 80, Copyright ©2013. Used with permission.

Jim Johnson for excerpts from Fracture Zone 2015 page 230, Copyright ©2013. Used with permission.

Patrick J. Buchanan for excerpt from Franklin D. Roosevelt Accessed at http://www.humanevents.com/2005/09/14/the-great-society-failure-of-an-idea-and-a-people/ on 05.13.14.

Jim Johnson for excerpts from Fracture Zone 2015 page 230, Copyright ©2013. Used with permission.

Dr. Ben Carson for comments from direct mail received as Chairman of "Save Our Healthcare," an initiative of the American Legacy PAC, www.SaveOurHealthcare.org, accessed January 29. 2014.

Congressman Earnest Istook for comments entitled "The blunt truth—White house drug czar contradicts Obama on marijuana," dated January 21, 2014.

Chapter 8

President Abraham Lincoln's story, as reiterated by Jesse Lyn Stoner at http://seapointcenter.com/dont-be-great-do-great/ accessed on 05.05.14. Used with permission.

William Bennett for excerpts taken from "The De-valuing of America", page 35, New York, Simon & Schuster Publishing Group, Copyright ©1992 William J. Bennett. Used with permission.

Pascal for his quote, "within every human heart is a God-shaped vacuum," accessed at
http://www.brainyquote.com/quotes/quotes/b/blaisepasc39550 8.html on 05/20/14.

President Ronald Reagan for quote from Proclamation 4999 – National Family Week, 1982 Accessed at http://www.reagan.utexas.edu/archives/speeches/1982/111282b .htm on 05.13.14.

Christian News Network for reference to an article accessed at http://christiannews.net/2014/05/08/father-arrested-while-objecting-to-porn-novel-on-schools-required-reading-list/ on 05.13.14.

Chuck Colson for quotes from his article, "Apathy in America", dated July 11, 2011. Accessed at http://www.colsoncenter.org/the-center/columns/colson-files/16754-apathy-in-america on 04.16.14.
Reprinted with permission of Prison Fellowship, P.O. Box 1550, Merrifield, VA 22116, www.pfm.org.

Aeschylus for quote attributed to him, "In war, truth is the first casualty." Accessed at http://classiclit.about.com/cs/profileswriters/p/aa_aeschylus.htm on 05.13.14.

Buddha quote, "Three things cannot be long hidden: the sun, the moon, and the truth. Accessed at http://www.brainyquote.com/quotes/quotes/b/buddha133884.h tml on 05.13.14.

Fox News for reference to a survey results of 7% of journalists are Republican Accessed at http://video.foxnews.com/v/3560929245001/just-7-percent-of-journalists-are-republicans-/#sp=show-clips on 05.13.14.

United States Military Academy West Point for quote from the "Cadet Prayer." United States Military Academy. http://www.usma.edu/chaplain/sitepages/cadet%20prayer.aspx. Accessed 05.13.14.

Arthur DeMoss Foundation for the Abraham Lincoln quote, "I have been drive many times upon my knees by the overwhelming conviction that I had nowhere else to go. My own wisdom, and that of all about me, seemed insufficient for that day." Taken from The Rebirth of America, page 182. Publisher: Arthur S. DeMoss Foundation, Philadelphia.

Arthur DeMoss Foundation for the Robert E. Lee quote "Knowing that intercessory prayer is our mightiest weapon and the supreme call for all Christians today, I pleadingly urge our people everywhere to pray. Believing that prayer is the greatest contribution that our people can make in this critical hour, I humbly urge that we take time to pray – to really pray." Taken from The Rebirth of America, page 183. Publisher: Arthur S. DeMoss Foundation, Philadelphia.

President Franklin D. Roosevelt for quote from the D-Day Prayer dated June 6, 1944. Accessed at http://www.wallbuilders.com/LIBprinterfriendly.asp?id=144635 on 05.13.14.

Global Security.org for excerpt taken from www.globalsecurity.org/military/agency/army/2-9inf.htm Accessed on 05/14/14.

Ben Carson article accessed at http://www.gopusa.com/commentary/2014/02/26/acting-like-a-founder/ Accessed on 05/19/14.

Chapter 9

Dictionary.com for their definition of "indignant", accessed at
http://dictionary.reference.com/browse/indignant?s=t
on 05/14/14.

Major General Robert F. Dees for excerpt from Resilient Leaders,
Copyright©2013. Used with permission.

Erwin W. Lutzer for excerpts from When A Nation Forgets God,
Copyright©2010 Erwin Lutzer. Used with permission.

President Thomas Jefferson for inscription on the Thomas
Jefferson Memorial Northeast Portico, "Indeed, I tremble for my
country when I reflect that God is just, and that His justice cannot
sleep forever." Accessed at
http://www.nps.gov/thje/photosmultimedia/quotations.htm
on 05.06.14.

President Abraham Lincoln for quote from his Proclamation 97 –
Appointing a Day of National Humiliation, Fasting and Prayer
given March 30, 1863. Accessed at
http://www.presidency.ucsb.edu/ws/?pid=69891 on 05.13.14.

Arthur DeMoss Foundation for the statement, "America You're
Too Young To Die!" taken from The Rebirth of America, Publisher:
Arthur S. DeMoss Foundation, Philadelphia.

Bibliography

A Call to Prayer for a Nation at War: Prayers of Blessing and Protection for Those Who Serve. Lakeland: White Stone Books, 2003.

Aeschylus. "Classic Literature." *About.com.* http://classiclit.about.com/cs/profileswriters/p/aa_aeschylus.htm (accessed May 13, 2014).

Alinsky, Saul D. *Rules for Radicals.* New York: Vintage Books, 1971.

Alliance Defending Freedom. "March 2014 Newsletter." *Allance Defending Freedom*, 2014: 1-2.

Amos Jr., James H. *Focus Or Failure.* 2nd Ed. Mechanicsburg: Executive Books, 2005.

Amos, Gary T. *Defending the Declaration.* Brentwood: Wolgemuth & Hyatt Publishers, Inc., 1989.

Appleton, J M. *USObserver.com.* June 2011.
http://www.usobserver.com/archive/june-11/apathy-in-america.html (accessed April 16, 2014).

Arthur S. DeMoss Foundation. *The Rebirth of America.* Philadelphia: Arthur S. DeMoss Foundation, 1986.

Ashcroft, John. *Never Again.* New York: Center Street, 2006.

Aziz, Roya and Monica Lam. "Profiles: The Lackawanna Cell." *PBS.* October 16, 2003.

http://www.pbs.org/wgbh/pages/frontline/shows/sleeper/inside/profiles.html (accessed April 6, 2014).

Bada Math, Suresh and Santosh K. Chaturvedi,. *Indian Journal of Medical Research.* December 2012.
http://www.ncbi.nlm.nih.gov/pmc/articles/PMC3612319/ (accessed May 9, 2014).

Barna, George. *Revolution.* Wheaton: Tyndale House Publishers, Inc., 2005.

—. *The Seven Faith Tribes.* Carol Stream: Tyndale House Publishers, Inc., 2009.

Bartholomew, Sam. *God's Rule In America.* Nashville: Eggman Publishing Company, 1996.

Barton, David. *America's Godly Heritage.* Aledo, TX: Wallbuilders, Inc., 1990.

—. *Original Intent.* Aledo, TX: WallBuilder Press, 2013.

—. *The Jefferson Lies.* Nashville, TN: Thomas Nelson, 2012.

Baruch, Bernard. "Plaque Inscription." Baruch Auditorium. *"The Armed Forces today have to be versed not alone in war, but in government, politics, the humanities - economics, social and spiritual.* Washington D.C., 2013.

Bauer, Dr. Gary L. *Questions And Answers On Homosexuality.* Talk Given At Harvard University, Washington: Family Research Council, 1998.

Bauer, Gary L. Newsletter, Washington: Family Research Council, 1998.

—. *Our Hopes Our Dreams.* Colorado Springs: Focus On The Family Publishing, 1996.

Baxter, J. Sidlow. *Explore The Book.* Grand Rapids: Zondervan Publishing House, 1960.

Beck, Glenn and Kevin Balfe. *Arguing With Idiots: How to Stop Small Minds And Big Government.* New York: Threshhold Editions, 2009.

Beck, Glenn. *Common Sense: The Case Against An Out-Of-Control Government.* New York: Mercury Radio Arts, Inc., 2009.

Beliles, Mark and Stephen McDowell. *Liberating The Nations: Biblical Principles of Government, Education, Economics & Politics.* Charlottesville: The Providence Foundation, 1995.

Bell, Dr. Donald. *Equipping Christian Warriors for End-Time Tribulation.* 2012.

Bennett, Tara. *Fandango Film Commentator.* Los Angeles, CA, January 15, 2010.

Bennett, William J. *Devaluing of America: The fight For Our Culture and Our Children.* New York: Simon & Schuster Publishing Group, 1992.

—. *Our Country's Founders.* New York: Simon & Schuster, 1998.

—. *The Book of Virtues.* New York: Simon & Schuster, 1996.

—. *The Death of Outrage: Bill Clinton And The Assault On American Ideals.* New York: The Free Press, 1998.

—. *The Index of Leading Cultural Indicators: American Society At The End Of The Twentieth Century.* Colorado Springs: Broadway Books/WaterBrook Press, 1999.

Blackman, Josh. *Liberty Fund's Library of Law and Liberty.* February 21, 2014.
http://www.libertylawsite.org/2014/02/21/justice-scalia-on-the-importance-of-the-republican-spirit-and-civic-education/.
(accessed April 24, 2014).

Blackstone, Sir William. *Commentaries of the Laws of England.* London: A. Straham, 1825.

Blanton, Stephen. *The Heart of Islam.* Bloomington: AuthorHouse, 2011.

Bonaparte, Napoleon. *Statement: The moral is to the physical as three to one.* 1769-1821. http://www.military-quotes.com/napoleon.htm (accessed May 6, 2014).

Bonhoeffer, Dietrich. *Ethics.* 1st Touchstone Ed. New York: Touchstone, 1995.

—. *Letters & Papers From Prison.* 1st Touchstone Ed. New York: Touchstone, 1997.

—. *The Cost Of Discipleship.* 1st Touchstone Ed. New York: Touchstone, 1995.

Boykin, William G. *Never Surrender: A Soldier's Journey To The Crossroads Of Faith And Freedom with Lynn Vincent.* New York: Faith Words, 2008.

Bonhoeffer. Directed by Martin Doblmeier. Performed by Voice of Klaus Maria Brandauer. 2003.

Bright, Brad. *God Is The Issue: Recapturing The Cultural Initiative.* Peachtree City: NewLife Publications, 2003.

Brown, Callum G. *The Death Of Christian Britain.* New York: Routledge, 2009.

Brownback, Sam. "A New Contract With America." *Policy Review,* 1996: 16-20.

Buchanan, Patrick J. *Suicide Of A Superpower: Will America Survive To 2025?* New York: Thomas Dunne Books, 2011.

Buckley Jr., William F. *God & Man At Yale.* Washington: Regnery Publishing, 1951.

Buddha. *Brainy Quotes.* http://www.brainyquote.com/quotes/quotes/b/buddha133884.html (accessed May 13, 2014).

Bush, George. *America 2000: An Education Strategy.* Washington: U.S. Department of Education, 1991.

Bush, President George H. W. *The American Presidency Project.* January 28, 1992. http://www.presidency.ucsb.edu/ws/?pid=20544 (accessed May 6, 2014).

Calcutta, Mother Teresa of. "www.priestsforlife.org." *Priests for Life.* February 3, 1994. http://www.priestsforlife.org/brochures/mtspeech.html (accessed April 14, 2014).

Carson, Ben M.D., with Candy Carson. *America The Beautiful.* Grand Rapids: Zondervan, 2012.

Carson, Ben. "www.gopusa.com." *GOPUSA.* 02 26, 2014. http://www.gopusa.com/commentary/2014/02/26/acting-like-a-founder/ (accessed May 19, 2014).

Casting Crowns. *While You Were Sleeping.* Comp. Mark Hall Publishing Designee. 2005.

Cathy, S. Truett. *Eat Mor Chikin: Inspire More People In Collaboration With Dick Parker.* Decatur: Looking Glass Books, 2002.

Center For The Study of Political Islam. *Sharia Law for Non-Muslims.* United States: CSPI, LLC, 2010.

Chamberlain, Neville. *Britannia.com.* September 30, 1938. http://www.britannia.com/history/docs/peacetime.html (accessed April 24, 2014).

Clark, Heather. *Christian News Network.* May 8, 2014. http://christiannews.net/2014/05/08/father-arrested-while-objecting-to-porn-novel-on-schools-required-reading-list/ (accessed May 13, 2014).

Colson, Charles and Jack Eckert. *Why America Doesn't Work.* Dallas: Word Publishing, 1991.

Colson, Charles. *Kingdoms In Conflict: An Insider's Challenging View Of Politics, Power, and the Pulpit.* United States: Zondervan Publishing House, 1989.

Colson, Chuck. *Colsoncenter.org.* July 11, 2011. http://www.colsoncenter.org/the-center/columns/colson-files/16754-apathy-in-america (accessed April 16, 2014).

Congressional Research Service. *Respectfully Quoted.* Washington: Government Printing Office, 1989.

Cord, Robert L. *Separation of Church and State, Historical Fact and Current Fiction.* Grand Rapids: Baker Book House, 1988.

David Aikman, Ph.D. *Hope The Heart's Great Quest.* Ann Arbor, MI: Servant Publications, 1995.

Dees, Major General Robert F. *Resilient Leaders.* San Diego: Creative Team Publishing, 2013.

—. *Resilient Warriors.* San Diego: Creative Team Publishing, 2011.

Dees, Major General Robert F. *Spiritual Infrastructure as an Element of National Power.* Report, Washington, D.C.: Robert F. Dees, 1992.

Diamond, Jared. *Guns, Germs, and Steel.* New York: W. W. Norton & Company, Inc., 1997.

Dobson, Dr. James. *Family News from Dr. James Dobson.* Newsletter, Colorado Springs: Focus on The Family, 1998.

Dowd, Alan W. "Preserving a Strong Defense." *Military Officers*, April 2014: 50-53, 82.

Eberstadt, Mary. *How The West Really Lost God.* West Conshohocken: Templeton Press, 2013.

Eberstadt, Nicholas. *A Nation of Takers, America's Entitlement Epidemic.* West Shohocken, PA: Templeton Press, 2012.

Eckman, Dr. Jim. *www.graceuniversity.edu/iip.* June 29, 2013. http://graceuniversity.edu/iip/2013/06/13-06-29-1/ (accessed April 3, 2014).

Eisenhower, President Dwight. *The American Presidency Project.* September 6, 1960. http://www.presidency.ucsb.edu/ws/?pid=11932 (accessed May 6, 2014).

Ellis, Joseph J. *Founding Brothers: The Revolutionary Generation.* New York: Alfred A. Knopf, 2000.

EQ Excellent Quotes. http://excellentquotations.com/quote-by-id?qid=1872 (accessed May 6, 2014).

Evans, Michael D. *Showdown.* Unpublished Confidential Draft, 2006.

—. *The American Prophecies: Ancient Scriptures Reveal Our Nation's Future.* New York: Warner Faith, 2004.

Family Research Council. *Let Freedom Ring 2nd Edition.* Washington.

Federer, William J. *America's God And Country: Encyclopedia of Quotations.* St. Louis: AmeriSearch, Inc., 2000.

Flood, Robert. *The Rebirth of America.* United States: The Arthur S. DeMoss Foundation, 1986.

Forbes, Congressman Randy. *http://forbes.house.gov/.* http://forbes.house.gov/uploadedfiles/defense_forecasts.pdf (accessed April 24, 2014).

Forbes, J. Randy Forbes and Rolfe Carawan. *Run to the Roar.* Garden City, NY: Morgan James Publishing, 2010.

Forbes, J. Randy. *randy.forbes@mail.house.gov.* January 28th, 2014. (accessed January 28th, 2014).

—. *Run to the Roar.* Garden City: Morgan James, 2010.

Fox News. *Fox News.* March 30, 2014.

http://www.foxnews.com/us/2014/03/30/university-arizona-students-riot-after-ncaa-tournament-loss/ (accessed May 7, 2014).

—. *Fox News.* February 3, 2014. http://www.foxnews.com/politics/2014/02/03/not-even-smidgen-corruption-obama-downplays-irs-other-scandals/ (accessed May 7, 2014).

—. *Fox News.* May 12, 2014. http://video.foxnews.com/v/3560929245001/just-7-percent-of-journalists-are-republicans-/#sp=show-clips (accessed May 13, 2014).

Franklin Graham. *www.cnn.com.* March 28, 2013. http://piersmorgan.blogs.cnn.com/2013/03/28/franklin-graham-on-same-sex-marriage-god-is-the-one-who-defined-marriage-not-government-its-between-one-man-and-one-woman/ (accessed April 22, 2014).

Fredericks, Bob. "68K undocumented immirgrants with driminal records released in 2013:repot." *New York Post.* March 31, 2014. http://nypost.com/2014/03/31/68k-undocumented-immigrants-with-criminal-records-released-in-2013-report (accessed April 6, 2014).

Friedman, Thomas L. *The World Is Flat.* New York: Farrar, Strauss and Giroux, 2006.

Frost, Michael and Alan Hirsch. *The Shaping of Things to Come: Innovation And Mission For The 21st Century Church.* Peabody: Hendrickson Publlishers, 2003.

Frost, Robert. *The Poetry of Robert Frost.* New York: Copyright Henry Holt & Company, Edited by Edward Connery Lathem, 1969.

Gabriel, Brigette. *Because They Hate: A Survivor of Islamic Terror Warns America.* New York: St. Martin's Press, 2006.

Gibbon, Edward. *The History of the Decline and Fall of the Roman Empire.* New York: Fred de Fau and Co. (http://oll.libertyfund.org), 1906.

Gilbert, James B. *Another Chance.* Philadelphia: Temple University Press, 1981.

Gilbert, Martin. *Israel, A History.* New York: HarperCollins Publishers, 1998, 2008.

Gingrich, Newt. *Lessons Learned The Hard Way.* New York: HarperCollins Publishers, Inc., 1998.

—. *Rediscovering God In America.* Franklin: Integrity Publishers, 2006.

—. *To Renew America.* New York: Harper Collins Publishers, 1995.

—. *To Save America: Stopping Obama's Securlar-Socialist Machine With Joe DeSantis.* Washington: Regnery Publishing, Inc., 2010.

Global Security. "2nd Battalion, 9th Infantry Regiment (Mechanized)." *www.globalsecurity.org.* http://www.globalsecurity.org/military/agency/army/2-9inf.htm (accessed May 10, 2014).

GOPUSA. "GOPUSA." *GOPUSA.com.* 04 11, 2014. http://www.gopusa.com/news/2014/04/11/detroit-prosecutor-files-ethnic-intimidation-charges-against-one/ (accessed 05 08, 2014).

—. *GOPUSA.com.* April 11, 2014. http://www.usobserver.com/archive/june-11/apathy-in-america.html (accessed April 16, 2014).

Grant, John. *The Issue Is Life.* Atlanta, GA: Steven Lester, dba MindShift Publications, 2013.

Hamilton, Deborah. "World Vision Reverses Decision to Hire Employees in "Same-Sex" Marriages." *American Family Association.* March 27, 2014. http://www.afa.net/Media/PressRelease.aspx?id=2147544607 (accessed April 22, 2014).

Harold G. Koenig, M.D. *Faith & Mental Health Religious Resources for Healing.* Weset Conshohocken: Templeton Foundation Press, 2005.

—. *In The Wake Of Disaster.* West Conshohocken: Templeton Foundation Press, 2006.

—. *The Healing Power of Faith.* New York: Touchstone, 1999 Touchstone Edition 2001.

Henry, Patrick. *Patrick Henry Center.* March 23, 1775. http://www.patrickhenrycenter.com/Speeches.aspx (accessed March 31, 2014).

Hill, Alexander. *Just Business.* Downers Grove: InverVarsity Press, 2008.

Hillman, O.S. *Change Agent: Engaging Your Passion to Be the One Who Makes a Difference.* Lake Mary, FL: Charisma House, 2011.

Himmelfarb, Gertrude. *The De-moralization Of Society.* New York: Alfred A. Knopf, Inc., 1995.

History, Primary Documents of America. *Declaration of Independence.* Philadelphia: Virtual Programs and Services, Library of Congress, 1776.

Huckabee, Mike. *Do The Right Thing: Inside The Movement That's Bringing Common Sense Back To American.* Reprint Ed. New York: Sentinel, 2009 First Published By Sentinel., 2008.

The Book of Eli. Directed by Albert and Allen Hughes Hughes. 2010.

Hughes, Robert. "Time ." *The Fraying Of America*, February 3, 1992: 44-49.

Hygiene, New York City Department of Health and Mental. *Summary of Vital Statistics 2012, The City of New York, Pregnancy Outcomes.* Summary of Vital Statistics, New York: Bureau of Vital Statistics, 2012.

Inspirio. *God Bless America Prayers & Reflections For Our Country.* Grand Rapids: Zondervan, 1999.

Jackson Jr., Harry R. and Perkins, Tony. *Personal Faith Public Policy.* Lake Mary: FrontLine, 2008.

Jefferson, Thomas. *U.S. National Park Service.* 1784. http://www.nps.gov/thje/photosmultimedia/quotations.htm (accessed May 6, 2014).

Johnson, Jim. *Fracture Zone 2015.* Charleston: Fire Source Media, 2013.

Joint Forces Staff College. *Elements of National Power.* http://www.jfsc.ndu.edu/library/publications/bibliography/Elements_of_National_Power.pdf (accessed April 30, 2014).

Kennedy, President John F. "This Country Cannot Afford To Be Materially Rich And Spiritually Poor." *State of The Union Message.* Washington, January 14, 1963.

Keyes, Alan. *Our Character, Our Future: Reclaiming America's Moral Destiny.* Grand Rapids: Zondervan Publishing House, 1996.

Kinnaman, David. *Unchristian: What A New Generation Really Thinks About Christianity...And Why It Matters.* Grand Rapids: Baker Books, 2007.

Knight, Robert H. *The Age of Consent: The Rise Of Relativism And The Corruption Of Popular Culture.* Dallas: Spence Publishing Company, 1998.

Kottmeyer, William. *Our Constitution and What It Means.* St. Louis: The Webster Publishing Company, 1949, 1961.

Krauthammer, Charles. "Defining Deviancy Up." *AEI Bradley Lecture.* Washington: AEI, 1993.

—. *Things That Matter.* New York: Crown Publishing Group, a division of Random House, LLC. a Penguin Random House Company, 2013.

The Biblical Call: A Christian Response to Human Trafficking & Sexual Abuse. Directed by GS2 Films. Performed by Dr. Diane, Bethany Hoang, Bob Morrison and Pearl Kim Langberg. 2011.

Lee, Dr. Richard G., General Editor. *The American Patriot's Bible.* Nashville: Thomas Nelson, Inc., 2009.

Lerner, Max. *America as a Civilization, The Basic Frame Vol. 1.* New York: Simon and Schuster, 1957.

Levin, Mark R. *Ameritopia: The Unmaking Of America.* New York: Threshold Editions, 2012.

—. *The Liberty Amendments.* New York: Threshold Editions, 2013.

Lewis, C. S. *The Abolition of Man.* New York: HarperCollins, 1974.

Lincoln, President Abraham. "Jesse Lyn Stoner's Blog." *Seapoint Center for Collaborative Leadership.* February 27, 2011. http://seapointcenter.com/dont-be-great-do-great/ (accessed May 6, 2014).

Louis Nelson, Frank Gaylor. "Korean War Veterans Memorial." U.S. National Park Service. *The Korean War Veterans Memorial.* Washington, D.C., 1995.

Lutzer, Erwin W. *When A Nation Forgets God.* Chicago: Moody Publishers, 2010.

MacArthur, John. *Can God Bless America? The Biblical Pathway To Blessing.* Nashville: Thomas Nelson Publishers, 2002.

Mansfield, Stephen. *The Faith of Barack Obama.* Nashville, TN: Thomas Nelson, Inc., 2008.

—. *The Faith Of The American Soldier.* New York: Penguin Group, 2005.

Manuel, David and Peter Marshall. *The Light and The Glory.* Old Tappan: Fleming H. Revell, 1977.

Markva, Neil. *Our Christian Heritage.* Copyrighted Notes, 1990.

Matthews, William. "Soul Searching." *Air Force Times*, 1997: 12-16.

McDowell, Josh. *The Last Christian Generation.* Holiday: Green Key Books, 2006.

Medved, Michael. "Has Hollywood Gone Too Far." *USA Weekend*, 1992: 4-6.

Merriam Webster, Inc. *Merriam-Webster's Collegiate Dictionary, 11th Edition.* 2014. http://www.merriam-webster.com/ (accessed April 23, 2014).

Merriam-Webster, Inc. *Merriam-Webster's Learner's Dictionary.* 2014.
http://www.learnersdictionary.com/definition/apathy (accessed May 7, 2014).

Metaxas, Eric. *No Pressure, Mr. President!* Nashville: Thomas Nelson, 2012.

Millard, Catherine. *The Rewriting Of America's History.* Camp Hill: Horizon House Publishers, 1991.

Miller, Ron. *Sellout, Musings From uncle Tom's Porch.* Breinigsville, PA : Xulon Press, 2010.

Naisbitt, John and Patricia Aburdene. *Megatrends 2000.* New York: William Morrow and Company Inc., 1990.

Newman, Randy. "randydavidnewman.com." *The Rise of the Nones.* April 5, 2012.
http://www.randydavidnewman.com/2012/04/05/the-rise-of-the-nones/ (accessed May 8, 2014).

Noebel, David A. *Understanding The Times.* Manitou Springs: Harvest House Publishers, 1991.

North, Oliver. *American Heroes: In The Fight Against Radical Islam.* Nashville: B&H, 2008.

Novak, Michael. *Awakening From Nihilism.* West Sussex: Goron Pro-Print Co., Ltd, 1995.

—. *Morality, Capitalism And Democracy.* West Sussex: Goron Pro-Print Co., Ltd, 1990.

Nuttle, Mark. *Moment of Truth.* Lake Mary, FL: FrontLine, 2008.

Obama, President Barack. *WhiteHouse.gov.* April 10, 2014.
http://www.whitehouse.gov/the-press-office/2014/04/10/remarks-president-lbj-presidential-library-civil-rights-summit (accessed May 6, 2014).

O'Reilly, Bill. *Culture Warrior.* New York: Broadway Books, 2006.

Ornstein, Allan C. "The Changing Federal Role in Education." *American Education*, 1984: 4-7.

Oster, Merrill J. *You Can Change The World.* Scottsdale: Pinnacle Forum Institute, 2012.

Paine, Thomas. *Commense Sense.* Philadelphia printed: Sold by W. & T. Bradford, 1776.

Pascal. "http://www.brainyquote.com/quotes/." *Brainy Quotes.* http://www.brainyquote.com/quotes/quotes/b/blaisepasc39550 8.html (accessed 05 20, 2014).

Piper, John. *Amazing Grace In the Life Of Willim Wilberforce.* Wheaton: Crossway Books, 2006.

Platt, David. *Radical: Taking Back Your Faith From The American Dream.* Colorado Springs: Multnomah Books, 2010.

Quayle, Vice President Dan. *www.vicepresidentdanquayle.com.* May 19, 1992. http://www.vicepresidentdanquayle.com/copyright.html (accessed April 22, 2014).

Reagan, President Ronald. *http://millercenter.org.* June 8, 1982. http://millercenter.org/president/speeches/detail/3408 (accessed April 24, 2014).

—. *Miller Center, University of Virginia.* June 2, 1982. http://millercenter.org/president/speeches/detail/3408 (accessed April 24, 2014).

—. "Proclamation 4999 --National Family Week, 1982." *www.reagan.utexas.edu.* November 12, 1982. http://www.reagan.utexas.edu/archives/speeches/1982/111282b .htm (accessed May 13, 2014).

—. *Reagan 2020*US.* August 23, 1984. http://reagan2020.us/speeches/Defense_and_Security.asp (accessed April 24, 2014).

—. *Reagan 2020*US.* March 23, 1983. http://reagan2020.us/speeches/Defense_and_Security.asp (accessed April 24, 2014).

Robertson, Pat. *The New World Order.* Dallas: Thomas Nelson, Inc., 1991.

Robison, James and Jay W. Richards. *Indivisible: Restoring Faith, Family, And Freedom Before It's Too Late.* New York: FaithWords, 2012.

Roosevelt, President Franklin D. *Wallbuilders.* June 6, 1944. http://www.wallbuilders.com/LIBprinterfriendly.asp?id=144635 (accessed May 13, 2014).

Roosevelt, President Teddy. *http://www.theodore-roosevelt.com.* September 2, 1901. http://www.theodore-roosevelt.com/images/research/txtspeeches/678.pdf (accessed April 24, 2014).

—. *Theodore Roosevelt.* September 2, 1901. http://www.theodore-roosevelt.com/images/research/txtspeeches/678.pdf (accessed April 24, 2014).

Rutland, Mark. *Hanging On By A Thread.* Lake Mary: Creation House, 1991.

Santayana, George. *The Life of Reason or the Phases of Human Progress.* New York: Charles Scribner's Sons, 1917.

Schaeffer, Francis A. *The God Who is There.* Downer's Grove: InterVarsity Press, 1968.

Schaeffer, Franky. *A Time For Anger, The Myth of Neutrality.* Westchester: Crossway Books, 1982.

Schlafly, Phyllis. *No High Power.* Washington: Regnery Publishing, Inc., 2012.

Sears, Alan and Craig Osten. *The ACLU vs America.* Nashville: Bradman & Holman Publishers, 2005.

Sears, Alan. *In Justice.* Enumclaw: WinePress Publishing, 2009.

Selfless Service Is Our Nation's Strength. Reagan Quotes: Daily Quotes From The Statesman. October 26, 2007. http://www.usma.edu/chaplain/SitePages/Cadet%20Prayers.aspx (accessed September 2012).

Signorelli, Archibald. *Plan of Creation* . Chicago: Charles H. Kerr & Company, 1916.

Simendinger, Alexis. "Turnout in Mind, Obama Cites Voting Rights "Threat"." *Real Clear Politics.* April 12, 2014. http://www.realclearpolitics.com/articles/2014/04/12/turnout_in_mind_obama_cites_voting_rights_threat_122260.html (accessed May 7, 2014).

Slomanson, William. *http://en.wikipedia.org/wiki/International_law.* April 11, 2014. www.wikipedia.org (accessed April 16, 2014).

Starr, Kenneth. *A Legal View of Business Ethics.* Compact Disc , Dallas: Lecture Given At The Leader Board II Conference at Dallas Theological Seminary, 2004.

Starr, Kenneth. *Legal/Constitutional Issues In The Years Ahead.* Compact Disc Recording, Dallas: Lecture given at The Leader Board II Conference, Dallas Theological Seminary, 2004.

Starr, Penny. "Black Pastor: Administration 'Is Promoting Murder' by Promoting Abortion." *www.CNSNews.com.* February 28, 2014. http://cnsnews.com/news/article/penny-starr/black-pastor-administration-promoting-murder-promoting-abortion (accessed March 31, 2014).

Steffan, Melissa. *www.christianitytoday.com.* January 4, 2013. http://www.christianitytoday.com/gleanings/2013/january/abortion-restrictions-hit-second-highest-total-ever-in-2012.html (accessed March 20, 2014).

Expelled No Intelligence Allowed. Directed by Nathan Frankowski. Performed by Ben Stein. 2008.

Stetson, Chuck. *Creating The Better Hour.* Macon: Stroud & Hall, 2007.

Stice, Ralph W. *From 9/11 to 666.* Ozark: ACW Press, 2005.

Stoner, Jesse Lyn. *Seapoint Center.* February 27, 2011. http://seapointcenter.com/dont-be-great-do-great/ (accessed May 6, 2014).

Strode, Tom. *www.christianitytoday.com.* September 13, 2013. http://www.christianitytoday.com/gleanings/2013/september/abortion-clinics-closing-planned-parenthood-abby-johnson.html (accessed March 20, 2014).

Sullivan, Amy. "Rise of the Nones." *Time Magazine.* 12 2012, March. http://content.time.com/magazine/article/0,9171,2108027,00.html (accessed May 8, 2014).

The A21 Campaign. http://www.thea21campaign.org/ (accessed April 22, 2014).

America You're Too Young To Die! Performed by The Arthur S. DeMoss Foundation. 1986.

The Huffington Post. "Obama: No Surprise That Hard-Pressed Pennsylvanians Turn Bitter." *The Huffington Post.* April 6, 2008. http://www.huffingtonpost.com/mayhill-fowler/obama-no-surprise-that-ha_b_96188.html (accessed May 8, 2014).

Thomas, Clarence. *My Grandfather's Son.* New York: HarperCollins Publishers, 2007.

Thompson, Kenneth W. and Hans Morgenthau. *Politics Among Nations.* New York: Alfred A. Knopf, 1985.

Time . "What Ever Happened to Ethics." Month 25, 1987: 14-29.

Tocqueville, Alexis de. *Democracy in America.* New York: George Dearborn & Co., Adlard and Saunders, Henry Reeve Translation revised & corrected 1899, 1838.

Tolstoy, Leo. *How Much Land Does A Man Need?* McLean, VA: The Trinity Forum, 2011.

Tracy, Kate. *www.christianitytoday.com.* February 3, 2014. http://www.christianitytoday.com/gleanings/2014/february/us-abortions-fall-to-lowest-rate-since-roe-v-wade.html (accessed March 20, 2014).

The Better Hour Gatherings. Directed by Essentials In Education. Performed by Geoff, Corkie Haan, Chuck Stetson, Hosted by Sheila Weber Tunnicliffe. 2008.

U. S. Supreme Court. "Stone v. Graham, 449 U.S. 39 (1980)." *First Amendment Center.* November 17, 1980. http://www.firstamendmentschools.org/freedoms/case.aspx?id= 1422 (accessed April 18, 2014).

U.S. Supreme Court. "Wallace v. Jaffree 472 U.S. 38." *bulkresource.org.* December 4, 1984. https://bulk.resource.org/courts.gov/c/US/472/472.US.38.83-929.83-812.html (accessed May 6, 2014).

U.S. Supreme Court, Justice Rehnquist. *bulk.resource.org.* December 4, 1984. https://bulk.resource.org/courts.gov/c/US/472/472.US.38.83-929.83-812.html (accessed May 6, 2014).

United States Consitution. *usconstitution.net.* http://en.wikipedia.org/wiki/Enumerated_powers and http://www.usconstitution.net/xconst_A1Sec8.html (accessed May 6, 2014).

United States Continental Congress. *The Declaration of Independence.* July 4, 1776. http://www.archives.gov/exhibits/charters/declaration.html (accessed May 6, 2014).

United States Military Academy. *USMA.edu.* http://www.usma.edu/chaplain/sitepages/cadet%20prayer.aspx (accessed May 13, 2014).

United States of America. "United States Constitution." *archives.gov.* September 17, 1787. http://www.archives.gov/exhibits/charters/constitution.html (accessed May 13, 2014).

Walker, John. *Costly Grace: A Contemporary View of Bonhoeffer's "The Cost Of Discipleship".* Abilene: Leafwood Publishers, 2010.

Wallerstein, Judith S., Julia M. Lewis, Sandra Blakeslee. *The Unexpected Legacy of Divorce.* New York: Hyperion, 2000.

Welch, Bob. *American Nightingale: The Story of Frances Slanger, Forgotten Heroine Of Normandy.* New York: Atria Books, 2004.

Wheeler, Joe. *Abraham Lincoln A Man of Faith And Courage.* New York: Howard Books, 2008.

Whitehead, Barbara Darfoe. "The Family And Public Policy." *The Atlantic*, 1993: 70-71.

Whitehead, John W. *The Stealing of America.* Westchester: Crossway Books, 1983.

Wilson, Jim. *Principles of War.* 8th Printing 1994 Colombia: Community Christian Ministries, 1991.

Winter, Ralph D., and Steven C. Hawthorne. *Perspectives On The World Christian Movement.* Pasadena: Paternoster, 2002.

yourdictionary.com. Copyright 2014. http://www.yourdictionary.com/pursuit-of-happiness (accessed March 31, 2014).

Zacharias, Ravi. *Light In The Shadow Of Jihad.* Orlando: Multnomah Publishers, Inc., 2002.

Index

1960s	46, 82,136,199,237,255,283,304
1970s	139,142,143,171
1980s	143,145,286
1990s	145,198,261, 302,308
2 a.m. Courage	338
Abortion	14, 94,142,180,181,183, 184,187,188,211,287
Abraham	81
Adoption	184,185,197,218
Alliance Defending Freedom (ADF)	203,260,287,326
Alinsky, Saul	152
American Center for Law and Justice (ACLJ)	260
American Civil Liberties Union (ACLU)	260
American Dream	206,282
American Entitlement Society	280
American Experiment	49, 58, 68,124,170
American Family Association (AFA)	201,221
American Foundation for Suicide Prevention (AFSP)	212,221
American Humanist Association (AHA)	260
American Psychological Association (APA)	203
American Renewal Project	256,333
American Worker	294,295,298,313
Apathy	50,62,71,88,124,225,233, 242,244,296,348

Appleton, J. M. 244
Aquinas, Saint Thomas 111
Aristotle 31,282
Association of Community Organizing for
    Reform Now (ACORN) 152,156,226,259
Atheists/ism 114,122,155,180,265,322
Americans United for Separation of
    Church and State (AU) 260
Augustine, Saint 111
Bail Out Mentality 281,311
Barton, David 2, 38, 93, 257, 286
Baxter, J. Sidlow 73
Becket Fund for Religious Liberty 260,383
Bennett, Tara 82
Bennett, William 123,126,138-142,173,321
Bin Laden, Usama 146,158,178
Black Panthers 226
Blackstone, Sir William 93,104,107-113,125-132
Book of Eli 82, 83,166
British government/empire 60, 63,104,111,123,
    224,357,368

Buddhism 190
Bush, President George H. W. 145
Bush, President George W. 39,147,149,150,172,259,283
Cadet Prayer 338
Council for American Islamic Relations (CAIR) 267
Capitalism 282,293,294
Carter, President Jimmy 142-145,171
Chamberlain, Neville 224
Christian (90 references) 63, 64,100,105,111,115,119,155,
    188,194,201,203,211,219
Christianity 155,188,201,255,260,263,286
Churchill, Sir Winston 231,368
Civic responsibility 223,243,325,349

Civil rights   140,153,199,236,239
Civility   28,45,55,69,135,142,212,305
Climate change   111,156,157, 214
Clinton, Hillary   228,302
Clinton, President Bill   145,336,337
Cold War   119,140,145,146
Colson, Chuck   242,272
Common Core (CCSSI)   32,283-285,291
Confucianism   190
Constitution, U. S.   43, 44, 54, 94, 95,101,113, 115-118,
                                  132-136,144,164,182,188,213,
                                  246-253,253,257,266,
                                  283,309,357
CPCF (Congressional Prayer
      Caucus Foundation)   260,273,342,383
Cultural Change Agents   126,326,349
Cultural warfare   32,138,255
Culture of appeasement   223-227,279,319
Culture of Dependency   237,279,281,301,311,
                                             314,319
Culture of Violence/ Death   87,140,178-180,215,241,319
David, King   75, 97,357,358
D-Day   53,345
Declaration of Independence   80, 95,101, 105,106, 119,132,
                                  175,180,257,266,309
Defining Deviancy Down   198-203,312,364
Depression, economic   30,47,84,91,367
Devolution of Religion   156,255,272
Disability   280
Diversity   45, 55,135,318
Defense of Marriage Act (DOMA)   210,255
Don't Ask Don't Tell (DADT)   255
Dowd, Alan W.   230
Eckman, Dr. Jim   191

Education 28, 31, 45,124,126,142,250
Employment Non-Discrimination Act (ENDA) 256
Entitlements 152,184,225,239,277,280-282
Enumerated powers 115,246,250, 252,258,302
Environment 98,105,110,156,207,214,258,267
Establishment clause 115,144,253
Esther, Queen 75, 89,359
Euthanasia 179,188,190-195,211,219
Ezra 76-79,371
Faith-based and Neighborhood Partnerships (FBNP) 259
Feminist/Women's Rights 199,204-211,219,267
Forbes, Randy 231,268,339,341,383
Fracture Zone 2015 55,153,173,280,293,303
Francois, Doris 275-279,282,304
Family Research Council (FRC) 200,211,221,260,383
Free Enterprise 282
Free exercise clause 115,253,257,272
Free Exercise of Religion 115,258,291
Freedom of religion 44,119,145,252,258,266,319
Frost, Robert 164,166,397
George, Dr. John 37
Gibbon, Edward 57, 58, 68,69,84,85,392
Gideon 73,256,372
Gilbert, Martin 90
Gingrich, Newt 173
Global war on terror 143,157,158,229,440
Government Gone Wild 162,166,226,285
Graham, Billy 238,368
Graham, Franklin 23, 24,203,268,383
Grant, John 221
Great Awakening 47, 83,217,263,367
Great Society 70,109,141,239,277,283
Greatest nation on earth 31, 49,134,286
Guardians of Truth 333,336,338,339,342

Hassan, Major 226,235
Healing Power of Faith 195,221
Healthcare 121,154,281,301,303,315
Henry, Patrick 118,395
Heterogeneous accommodation 265
Hitler, Adolf 51,224,357
Holder, Eric 156,236
Homosexual Agenda 203,210,221
Homosexuality 200,203,204,211,220
Hope (450 total references) 41, 60, 83,152,264,328
Human trafficking 64,180,212,232,327
Humanism 47,288,322,348,371
Industrial College of the Armed Forces (ICAF) 36, 37
Immigration 232,233,246,266,270
International law/"Law of Nations" 109-111
Iron Curtain 63,119,140,365
Internal Revenue Service (IRS) Scandal 250,251,337
Islam/Muslims 155,157,226,234,255,267
Israel 191,206,227,263,334,356,372
Issue is Life (by John Grant) 183,189,221
Ivy League Schools 338
Jackson, Rev. Jesse 236
Jasser, Dr. Zhudi 267,272
Jesus (120 total references) 30,60,98,100,195,204,329
Johnson, Jim 153,280,293,303
Johnson, President Lyndon 141,268
Joseph 89,292,312
Joshua 72,210,256,324,358,370
Just War theory 111
Kennedy, D. James 200
Kennedy, President John F. 42,139
King, Dr. Martin Luther, Jr. 126,140,238,357,368
Koenig, Dr. Harold 195,221,264,306
Krauthammer, Charles 70, 71,198

Kyoto Protocol 110,111,394
Lackawanna Seven 234,235
Lane, David 256,333
Langberg, Dr. Diane 213,221
Law of war 109-111
Lee, Robert E. 345
Lewis, C. S. 133,261,396
Liberty Institute (LI) 260,288,383
Liberty Counsel 260,272,383
Lincoln, President Abraham 86,173,317,320,345,362,373
Manchu Regiment 347,348
Mandates 63,160,311,317,321,333,
343,350
Markva, Neil 38,105,114,116,122,381
Martin, Trayvon 154
Media 337,361,368
Merchants of Hope 327,329,349,368
Military Officer's Association of America 401
Model Nation 102,104 (Chart 3), 126,
135, 166, 377
Molech 206
Moral Education of Children 45, 55,286,318
Morgan, Piers 203
Moses 72, 78, 92,108,175,358
Mother Teresa 180,397
Moynihan, Daniel Patrick 198
Military Religious Freedom Foundation (MRFF) 260
Napoleon 42,338
National Action Network 236
National debt 150,154,170,233,268,
281,294,300
NATO (North Atlantic Treaty Organization 229
Natural law 43,105,109,110,111,112,129
Nazi regime 64,126,180

NEA (National Education Association) 203
Nehemiah 76, 77, 266
Newcombe, Jerry 200,221
Newman, Randy 404
Nixon, President Richard 142,242
Obama, President Barack 152,153,158,184,225,236,
239,250,253,256,259,303
Obamacare/Affordable Care Act 84,188,250,268,283,285,
302,303,304,314,337
Original Intent 93, 95,132,257, 272, 286,338
Orwell, George 180
Osten, Craig 203,221
Paine, Thomas 101,102,246,247,269
Palin, Sarah 368
Parvanov, Georgi 27
Patriot Act, The 151
Paul, Apostle 99,216,295,328
Pelosi, Nancy 158,159,268
Planned Parenthood 181,183,189
PMESII (Elements of National Power) 28,31,36,78,113,228
Prayer 65, 97,133,150,194,255,260,
272,278,286,342
Prayer- Removal from Schools 141
Public Schools 143,144,286
Pursuit of a Healthier Future 121,301
Pursuit of a Prosperous Future 17,121
Pursuit of Happiness 12, 30, 42,105,116,119,120,
136,164,170,318,319
Putin, Vladimir 158,225
Quayle, Dan 199
Rahab 256
Reagan, President Ronald 143,171,225,268,323,368
Rehnquist, Hon. William 144,257
Reid, Harry 158,268,341

Religion (127 references)	38,44,54,94,115,119, 145
	155,260,263,266
Resilience Life Cycle©	30,58,76,92,135
Rise of the Nones	261,262
Roe v. Wade	140,142,179,188,189
Roman Empire	57, 66, 85, 244
Roosevelt, President Franklin D.	145,280,302,345,368
Roosevelt, President Theodore	225
Rosen, James	155
Ryan, Paul	199,398
Salt and Light Council	325,383
Same-Sex Marriage	180,200,221,323
Santayana, George	61,392
Scalia, Honorable Antonin	124,325,395
Sears, Alan	126,203,221
Secular Coalition for America (SCA)	260
Secular Progressive/Secular	39, 47,141,164,258,291,337
Selfishness	216,217
Selflessness	30,216,336
Self-Sufficiency	307,308
Separation of Church and State	44, 98,252,257,260
September 11, 2001 (or 9/11)	39, 54, 60, 84,145,169,
	230,264,363
Seven Mountains of Culture	126,164,255,318,352,326
Sexual abuse	180,221
Sexual revolution	140,182,203
Sharpton, Rev. Al	236
Signorelli, Archbishop	87,393
Sinema, Kyrsten	261
Sexual Orientation Change Efforts (SOCE)	210,211
Social Security	184,280,300
Socialism	341,355 (Chart 13)
Solomon, King	97,290,361,368
Solzhenitsyn, Alexander	216

Soviet Union/empire	27, 63, 140,180,365
Spiritual Infrastructure	28, 31, 39, 42, 46, 81,115,127, 134,160, 213,280,294,373
Statesmen	97,169,246,342
Staver, Mat	126,257,272,383
Stearns, Richard	201
Stephens, Christopher	251
Stewardship	40,157,180,214,297,313
Suicide	32,142,179,191,212,361
TEA Party (Taxed Enough Already)	250
Ten Commandments	44,129,143,186,189,255,286
Terrorism/ists	146,157,225,230,233,363
Theology of Work	315
Tobias, Carol	187
Tocqueville, Alexis de	50,391
Tolerance	216,220,224,267,271
Traditional/Natural family	180,197,202,206,211,323,351
Truth	75, 95,116,122, 204, 331, 336
Tytler, Alexander	61, 71, 72
Unalienable Rights	96,117,164,175,266,309
Unemployment	143,154,171,226,237,279,311
United Nations	109,111
Utash, Steve	235
Voting Rights Act of 1965	140,236,238
Wallbuilders	38, 55, 260, 272, 325
War on poverty	70,141
Washington, President George	173,346
We the Church	34, 41, 51,176,239,266, 272,329,333,340,354
We the People	34,39,63,96,105,115,122,153, 164,223,246,266,325
We the Statesmen	34,41,51,96,101,160,166, 189,223,239, 354

West Point (United States Military Academy)   66,166,205,338
Wilberforce, William   126,212,239,357
Wilde, Oscar   215
Will, George   197
World Vision   201,202,422
World War II   231,360
Worldview   29,194,197,272,287,304
Wright, Rev. Jeremiah   152
Zero Dark Thirty   178

www.ResilienceTrilogy.com